HANDS-ON GUIDE SERIES®

Hands-On Guide to

Video Blogging
and Podcasting

Focal Press Hands-On Guide Series

The Hands-On Guide series serves as the ultimate resource in streaming and digital media-based subjects for industry professionals. The books cover solutions for enterprise, media and entertainment, and educational institutions. A compendium of everything you need to know for streaming and digital media subjects, this series is known in the industry as a must-have tool of the trade.

Books in the series cover streaming media-based technologies, applications and solutions as well as how they are applied to specific industry verticals. Because these books are not part of a vendor-based press they offer objective insight into the technology weaknesses and strengths, as well as solutions to problems you face in the real-world.

Competitive books in this category have sometimes been criticized for being either technically overwhelming or too general an overview to actually impart information. The Hands-On Guide series combats these problems by ensuring both ease-of-use and specific focus on streaming and digital media-based topics broken into separate books.

Developed in collaboration with the series editor, Dan Rayburn, these books are written by authorities in their field, those who have actually been in the trenches and done the work first-hand.

All Hands-On Guide books share the following qualities:

- Easy-to-follow practical application information
- Step-by-step instructions that readers can use in real-world situations
- Unique author tips from "in-the-trenches" experience
- Compact at 250–300 pages in length

The Hands-On Guides series is the essential reference for Streaming and Digital Media professionals!

Series Editor: Dan Rayburn (www.danrayburn.com)

Executive Vice President for StreamingMedia.com, a diversified news media company with a mission to serve and educate the streaming media industry and corporations adopting Internet based audio and video technology. Recognized as the "voice for the streaming media industry" and as one of the Internet industry's foremost authorities, speakers, teachers, and writers on Streaming and Digital Media Technologies.

Titles in the series:

- *Hands-On Guide to Webcasting*
- *Hands-On Guide to Windows Media*
- *Hands-On Guide to Video Blogging and Podcasting*
- *Hands-On Guide to Flash Communication Server*

HANDS-ON GUIDE SERIES®

Hands-On Guide to

Video Blogging and Podcasting

LIONEL FELIX

DAMIEN STOLARZ

Illustrations by Jennifer Jurick

ELSEVIER

AMSTERDAM • BOSTON • HEIDLEBERG • LONDON
NEW YORK • OXFORD PARIS • SAN DIEGO
SAN FRANCISCO • SINGAPORE • SYDNEY • TOKYO
Focal Press is an imprint of Elsevier

Focal Press

Acquisitions Editor: Angelina Ward
Project Manager: Paul Gottehrer
Assistant Editor: Rachel Epstein
Marketing Manager: Christine Degon Veroulis
Series Editor: Dan Rayburn
Cover and Interior Design Coordinator: Cate Barr
Cover and Interior Designer: Maycreate (www.maycreate.com)
Book Production: Borrego Publishing (www.borregopublishing.com)

Focal Press is an imprint of Elsevier
30 Corporate Drive, Suite 400, Burlington, MA 01803, USA
Linacre House, Jordan Hill, Oxford OX2 8DP, UK

 Recognizing the importance of preserving what has been written, Elsevier prints its books on acid-free paper whenever possible.

Library of Congress Cataloging-in-Publication Data

(Application submitted)

British Library Cataloguing-in-Publication Data
A catalogue record for this book is available from the British Library.

ISBN-13: 978-0-240-80831-4
ISBN-10: 0-240-80831-2

For information on all Focal Press publications
visit our website at www.books.elsevier.com.

06 07 08 09 10   10 9 8 7 6 5 4 3 2 1

Printed in the United States of America

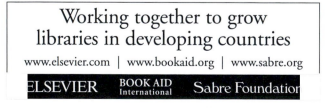

Working together to grow
libraries in developing countries

www.elsevier.com | www.bookaid.org | www.sabre.org

ELSEVIER   BOOK AID International   Sabre Foundation

This book is dedicated to

Andrew Michael Baron

and

Amanda Congdon,

creators of Rocketboom.

Table of Contents

Acknowledgments...xi
About the Authors xiii
Introduction xv

Chapter 1: Quick Start

Record Some Video... 2
Edit Your Video 5
Conclusion 14

Chapter 2: Podcasting and Video Blogging Basics

Anatomy of a Blog 16
A Brief History of Blogs...............................19
Conclusion 25

Chapter 3: Podcasting and Video Blogging Uses

Getting Familiar with Rich-Media Blogging...........28
Personal and Special Interest Uses 31
Mainstream Media Uses... 33
Corporate Uses 36
Conclusion 41

Chapter 4: Tuning In to Multimedia Blogs

Multimedia Blogs: Feeds and Enclosures..............44
Web-Based Aggregators...48
Local Clients 51

Linux and Friends 57

Mobile Clients 60

Conclusion 64

Chapter 5: Monetizing New Content Delivery Models

Mainstream Media Invasion 65

Success Criteria 66

Mainstream Media Advertising 68

Business Models for Podcasts and Video Blogs ... 72

Ancillary Business Models 85

Conclusion 90

Chapter 6: New Skills for a New Technology

Blog Basics 92

Enter the Blogosphere 101

Conclusion 120

Chapter 7: Mobile Video Blogging and Podcasting

Quick Start Moblogging 122

Other Moblogging Options 128

Laptop "Moblog" 129

Posting From PDAs 135

Conclusion 137

Chapter 8: In the Studio and On-the-Go

Spaces and Acoustics 140

Spaces and Video 144

Virtual Spaces 150

Audio and Video On-the-Go 153

Conclusion 155

Chapter 9: Essential Tools

A Powerful Computer............................. 158
A/V Editing Software 161
A/V Hardware... 171
Conclusion 175

Chapter 10: Audio Production and Post-Production

Microphones and Mixers........................177
Production Preparation and Voice Talent 184
Recording... 186
Editing and Mixing 190
Mixdown and Compressing for Podcasting.......... 195
Conclusion 196

Chapter 11: Video Production and Post-Production

Think Post-Production While in Pre-Production ..197
Encoding Video 204
Editing 209
Conclusion 220

Chapter 12: Hosting and Bandwidth

Bandwidth Pricing.................................. 222
Content Hosting 225
Basic Web Hosts.....................................227
Web Hosts with Blogging Services..................... 229
Feed Converters......................................232
Torrents and Alternative Content Delivery 232

Free Video Blog and Podcast Hosts......................233
Podcast Specific Services...236
High Volume Hosting Services 238
In-House and Co-Located Hosting 240
Negotiating Large Hosting Deals 241
Conclusion 244

Chapter 13: Assembling Blog Entries

Blogging Applications...245
FeedBurner..252
Hosted Media Services 257
Conclusion 261

Chapter 14: Licensing and Copyrights

Copyrights and Other Rights.................................. 264
Podsafe Source Material..273
Conclusion 281

Chapter 15: Case Studies

EricRice.com 283
RyanEdit.com 289
Rocketboom.com 294

Appendix: Administration

Conclusion 314

Glossary 315

Index 325

Acknowledgments

We've worked hard to produce a book that, in MBA-speak "adds tremendous value" for the reader. In slacker-speak, we've tried extremely hard not to suck.

Some of the people that particularly helped us not suck are Kevin Marks, Eric Rice, Dave Glassco, Jay Dedman, Ryanne Hodson, and Andrew Baron.

We'd like to thank Dan Rayburn for conceiving the Hands-On Guide series and getting it established, and also Joe Follansbee and Steve Mack for trailblazing the format.

We would also like to acknowledge the Focal Press production staff who worked very hard to get this to press under seemingly impossible deadlines, which we continued to stretch beyond comfort. In particular, we'd like to thank Angelina Ward, Paul Gottehrer, as well as Kelly Johnson and Becky Fulker. We'd also like to thank Jennifer Jurick for her lovely and timely illustrations.

Lionel Felix

I would like to extend warm thanks to Greg Swaney, Steve Banfield, Dave Chaimson, Eli Weisman, and Mike Watts for their help.

Working on a book is a major undertaking and shares some similarities to substance abuse or depression; long hours spent in isolation, lack of sleep, avoiding friends and family, talking to yourself, dark circles under the eyes, not being able to account for periods of time. Fortunately, after the book is finished, no one has to go to rehab. A nice dinner out and re-discovering television perhaps, but a 12-step program isn't needed.

That said, some people were affected and some people were supported and the two aren't mutually exclusive. I want to thank my wife Gillian for bringing me food and drink during my late-night keyboard beatings, my mother who is new to the Internet and did a wonderful job of pretending to be interested in the topic, my wonderful dogs who knew when it was work time and when it was play time, and my father, Martin, who may be gone but still inspires me in all of my writing.

Damien Stolarz
First off, I would like to offer a long delayed "thank you" to my first co-author, Richard Koman. Your invaluable help in translating *Mastering Internet Video* from my native tongue into American English was invaluable and helped me get where I am today...doing the same thing for another.

I would also like to thank Michael Robinette, Rafael Sagula, Jason Tokunaga and Ben Stragnell, and more recently, Vlad Zarney, James Rossfeld, Stephen Brown, Justin Hirsch, and Dan Brent for their help with all of my peer-to-peer video endeavors.

I would also like to thank Bill McCall, Peter Sheedy, Lynne Elander and my good friend Raffi Krikorian, who helped me quickly learn so very much about the television industry.

Oh, and Angelina has been a dream editor to work with.

I would like to tell my wife that this is my third and final book. Alas, I'm already working on another one. Nonetheless, it's great to be able to hold my head up again without the looming specter of an incomplete manuscript darkening my every waking hour.

About the Authors

Lionel Felix

Lionel Felix has spent the better part of the last 12 years working in video post production, live TV production and enterprise technology management, giving him a unique perspective into the challenges and opportunities around the marriage of media production and Internet technologies.

As a writer, Lionel has contributed numerous articles to Gizmodo, CNET and Telematics Journal, as well as serving as Editor in Chief for Car Hacks (*http://www.carhacks.org*), a blog covering the convergence of consumer electronics, navigation, wireless Internet and the common car.

Previously at Sony Pictures Digital Entertainment, Lionel served as Director of Technology where he oversaw the management of over 1,400 Sony Pictures and Sony Corporation Internet properties including Sony.com and Sonypictures.com.

Before his career at Sony Pictures, Lionel wore a few hats for a few companies including Director of Technology for Firstlook, Systems Consultant for Dell, IBM and Motorola and Associate Producer/Video Editor for numerous Los Angeles area post production houses. He's even listed in IMDB as Music Coordinator for Cyborg 3.

Damien Stolarz

Damien is an inventor, writer, and entrepreneur who has spent over half his life making different kinds of computers talk to each other.

He is currently the Chief Technology Officer of StreetDeck (*http://www.streetdeck.com*), an in-car computing company that delivers digital media entertainment and information into the vehicle. Damien is also the owner of Robotarmy Corp. (*http://www.robotarmy.com*), a software/R&D consultancy specializing in digital media distribution.

Damien has written several books on digital media convergence including *Mastering Internet Video* (Wiley 2004) and *Car PC Hacks* (O'Reilly 2005). Damien holds a B.S. in Computer Science/Engineering from UCLA.

Damien's blog can be found at *http://www.damienstolarz.com*.

Introduction

This is a book about a new phenomena, called *audio* and *video blogging*. If you're already familiar with blogs, then you know how significantly they've changed the face of online communication. What you may not know is how the mere addition of audio and video attachments to blogs has started another media revolution.

Streaming media, online audio and video consumption, is as old as the net itself. But while Internet radio has made some strong inroads, online video has never seriously challenged television—until now.

The Internet vs. TV

The Internet has spent years trying to be more like TV. Video compressors were optimized in a vain attempt to get streaming video to look as good as a VHS tape. Various hardware devices have been built to make streaming audio accessible in the living room instead of the PC. But all these streaming efforts could never overcome this basic reality: Most always-on "broadband" Internet connections are simply too small to give users a traditional television experience.

Recently, however, some interesting things happened. Gadgets like TiVo® have come out and the entire television experience has started changing. Sure, there are still channel surfers, but a large segment of the population has stopped worrying about when anything is on. The fact that television shows actually come on at a set time has become sort of quaint. Sure, you might hear spoilers at work if you neglect to watch the much-anticipated finale; nonetheless, the traditional timed programming was becoming only one of several ways to consume TV.

How does the blogosphere fit into this? Well, blogs have grown far faster than most fast-growing Internet trends. Arguably, the second coming of personal websites, blogging tools are as easy to use as web-based email. The age-old diary format of blogs made them an instantly familiar medium, and remarkably, the medium has taken off for the stars. Blogs have had incredible staying power, thousands of blogs are created daily, and they have become a much-studied phenomenon all unto themselves.

When blogs weren't busy campaigning for elections, whistleblowing, fact checking mainstream media, and creating a revolution in social networking, they found some time to dabble in the media arts.

New Media

Audio and video blogging have several characteristics of traditional media. They are episodic: each blog post has a specific date and time, and they are thematic: each blog has its own voice and style, so an appropriate audience tends to form around the blog.

But blogs differ in some key ways. Most blogs are permanent. If you miss an episode or are completely new to the blog, you can go back to the archives and catch up. Blogs are also more of a conversation than a lecture: the audience can usually comment on any post and interact. Blogs are trackable: bloggers can see exactly how many people viewed a post or downloaded a show, and blogs are subscribable: viewers can run programs that automatically fetch all new posts so they're always ready to view.

Inside the Industry

What's in a Name?

In this book, a variety of names are used to describe video blogs and audio blogs. In fact, we agonized over the title of the book and tried to be both "buzzword compliant" and recognizable at the same time.

Podcast is probably the most popular term for audio blogging, but it implies iPod® (even though it doesn't require it all) and thus Microsoft can't bring itself to call it that. The term *audio blogging* sounds clumsy, and carries with it the implication that it's a blog, whereas the format of the audio program may be a lecture, song or a radio show, and not in a blog format at all.

The same problem applies to the term *video blogging*. Many of the most avid video bloggers whose video closely follows the personal diary blog format prefer the term *vlogging*. Apple calls it *video podcasting*, for obvious reasons, but this is a mouthful when vlogging is concise and less partisan. Other video-over-RSS-feed efforts have tried to popularize the term *VODcasting*, because VOD stands for video on demand, and it rhymes with podcasting. Other hopefuls have been *vidcasting*, monotheistic religious broadcasts and sermons in a podcast or video blog format have been appropriately dubbed *Godcasting*.

Webcasting has its roots in nonblog technologies and it's not a great moniker; however, many existing rich-media websites are simply being updated to a blog format.

There does not seem to be a perfect one-size-fits-all name for the new technology. The benefit of podcasting is that it has the most recognition for the audio format, in no small part due to Apple's strong promotion of the name and the market dominance of the iPod. The benefit of video blogging is that it is somewhat self-descriptive; assuming people know what a blog is, they can put it together. Thus, we mostly use those two names in this book: *podcasting* and *video blogging*.

We've also used the term *multimedia blog* on occasion. Although multimedia sounds oh-so-1990s, the term is somewhat future-proof and will describe whatever exciting form of content people will be sticking in RSS feeds in the near future.

New Media Standards

Podcasts and video blogs are the new standards for Internet TV and radio. They are quickly permeating most existing streaming installations. Companies small and large are formulating blogging and podcasting strategies.

Podcasts and video blogs jump from the Internet straight onto portable media devices, completely eliminating the television middleman.

The Internet tried for years to emulate television through streaming media, but it could never effectively emulate a one-way broadcast to hundreds of millions of passive viewers. Now it is television that is emulating the Internet, with on-demand video and interactive features.

It cannot be overstated how much of a democratizing medium the Internet has become. It is now possible for anyone to produce audio content and put it up for millions to hear, at virtually no cost. Not thousands of dollars, not hundreds of dollars, but as easily as they can get a hold of a telephone and leave a voice mail. And video content is almost as cheap—a borrowed video camera or webcam and an Internet connection is all it takes.

Internet delivery of audiovisual media is finally reaching its long-awaited potential! And blogs are the platform to achieve this.

Who Should Read This Book

You should.

This book is about the new standards for Internet-based TV and radio. It is now possible for anyone to put up a radio show or a TV show on the Internet and reach an audience of millions. Remarkably, is also possible to do this for free.

All of the simple tools necessary to blog with audio and video exist. Many of the tools are already on your computer. If you don't have the tools, there are dozens of websites that will provide them for free. Web hosting, a costly problem for traditional streaming media endeavors, has been solved. It costs next to nothing, often nothing, to put up audio and video on the Internet.

Traditional streaming media required specialized servers and specialized skills. Audio and video blogging requires little of that. Creating and uploading a website takes a certain amount of effort, yet blogging takes far less.

This book is targeted at anyone who has ever uploaded audio or video content on the Internet. It is also for anyone who has ever wanted to do this. Finally, it is a useful and educational read for people who think they could never communicate using audio or video on the Internet, but simply want more information about where this technology is going.

How to Use This Book

This book is designed to be a very practical, balanced presentation of the technical aspects of video blogging and podcasting, along with information on how it can be used in a business environment and the financial ramifications involved. The majority of the chapters cover tools, production techniques and new technologies, while several chapters cover the context of blogs in Internet technology, their uses, monetization, and licensing issues.

Organization

Chapter 1 begins with a Quick Start, which describes how quickly you can get an audio or video blog set up. If you already have a blog set up, the task will be even quicker.

Chapters 2 and 3 cover some of the basics of multimedia blogging, including its roots and development, how it differs from other online media forms. Chapter 3 enumerates the many ways in which the new technologies can be put to use.

Chapter 4 illustrates the full scope of devices and platforms that can receive podcasts or video blogs and the applications that enable this.

Chapter 5 thoroughly examines how commercial and noncommercial podcasts and video blogs can be funded, as well as the profitable ecosystem that surrounds these new media forms.

Chapter 6 is Blogging 101, covering the key blog technological literacy needed to effectively exploit its multimedia forms.

Chapters 7 and 8 covers the audio video capture environment, both on the road and in the studio.

Chapter 9 goes over some of the important tools for creating podcasts and video blogs.

Chapters 10 and 11 details the production pipeline for audio podcasts and video blogs.

Chapter 12 explores the economics of hosting **rich-media b**logs, which are different than streaming media and web hosting in several key ways.

Chapter 13 shows how to assemble and post a podcast or video blog.

Chapter 14 presents a roadmap of the issues of licensing and copyrights. Podcasting and video blogging must often navigate around old media rules.

Chapter 15 completes the book with case studies, analyzing the objectives, methods, and successes of three kinds of multimedia bloggers.

The appendix outlines some routine administrative tasks relevant to podcasting and video blogging.

Sidebars

There are three types of sidebars used in this book: "Author Tip," "Inside the Industry," and "Alert." Each is separated from the text and gives you quick, helpful information that is easy to find.

 Author Tip: Gives tips that are directly from the author's experience in the field.

 Inside the Industry: Relays information about companies, behind the scenes happenings, quotes from people in the industry, a bit from a case study, statistics, market research, anything to do with the topic's industry that doesn't necessarily come from the author's experience.

 Alert: Spells out important information such as technical considerations, troubleshooting, warning of potential pitfalls, and anything else that needs special attention.

CHAPTER 1

Quick Start

In this chapter we're going to upload a video blog or a podcast, your call. The steps to do it are quite straightforward, and if you have any experience with posting web pages or blog entries, or serving MP3s from a website, you know enough to quickly get a podcast up.

All video blogs or podcasts are, in reality, blogs with links to multimedia. If you create a blog and link it to video, then you have technically created a "video blog." However, to make such a blog into a compatible multimedia feed that can be subscribed to and automatically downloaded by programs such as iTunes, you're going to need to learn a few more details.

This chapter will briefly cover the steps of creating your first podcast, including:

1. Recording audio or video
2. Editing
3. Converting and compressing
4. Uploading to a web page
5. Creating a blog
6. Adding an enclosure to your RSS feed
7. Subscribing to your podcast

Podcasting and video blogging in its current state is divided into a few specific tasks, all of which are required for them to work properly. Even as more flexible tools are developed to combine these tasks, there will always be a manual way to create and post content.

While the term *podcast* initially implied only audio content, that may change over time now that iPods can handle video as well. *Video blogging*, as a term, is very specific. We're going to use the royal sense of podcasting to include both audio and video blog posting. In this chapter, we'll focus on a simple video blog posting; however, the steps are virtually identical for an audio blog.

Record Some Video

The first part of making a podcast is simply to record something to attach to your blog. To do this, you're going to need to get audio or video recorded and imported into the computer. A digital video (DV) camera works well with computers. Its strength is in its native digital recording and remote control capabilities when plugged into a computer's FireWire® port. If you're wondering which DV cam to buy, it's important to keep its purpose, quality, features and costs in mind. If you'll be capturing video where there is not too much motion and plenty of light, a low-end JVC or Samsung should do the trick for about $300 (see **Figure 1-1**).

Figure 1-1
Samsung SC-D103 DV camera

The more expensive cameras get you higher quality, many more manual settings like white balance and three CCD chips that separates recording into RGB signals. The split of red, green and blue offer a much higher quality master recording. Features may include the ability to edit on the camera, make use of transparency functions such as a Greenscreen, and more advanced remote options.

Whichever one you choose, make sure it has a FireWire port (also called *iLink*® or *IEEE1394*). With that port, your software editing program can control the tape system, allowing you better DV-to-hard drive transfers. Having that control over the DV cam, it can go through editing software such as Sony's Vegas product, which offers far more flexibility in what video you pull from the tape, saving space and making the editing process simpler. That's not to say you can't use other types of video cameras. If you already have a High8, VHS-C or SVHS camera floating around, it can be used with good results. The picture quality will not be as high as a DV cam, but you'll be able to get a decent picture to work with.

The non-DV cams necessitate using a video capture device. There are so many to choose from, that the sheer number of them can cause confusion for the buyers. There are a few things to keep in mind when trying to decide on a capture device and the first is budget. Fortunately, there are many boards available in the $100 range that will provide a high level of capture quality.

USB-based devices, while easy to use, still have some bugs that prevent optimal video transfer. For the purpose of video blogging, the Dazzle devices from Pinnacle (*http://www.pinaclesys.com*) may do the job but you run the risk of over-dedicating your USB chain. This issue comes from the ability of USB devices to stay fully engaged to their task without dropping important data. In the case of a USB video capture device, the failure can result in dropped frames. Many USB devices are happy to sit and wait a few milliseconds to get their data through; video on the other hand is very needy and when the chain is too busy, it shows up in the dub.

The best route for capturing non-DVs is with the good old-fashioned add-on card. There are two varieties of capture cards. ATI's All-In-Wonder cards are everything cards. They are graphics engines, TV tuners, video output cards, input cards and come with a massive suite of software tools. ATI has been at it for a long time and their cards are well supported, but you may end up paying for features you don't care for and the cards usually prefer to be the primary graphics device. If you're interested in a full multimedia upgrade, this might work for you.

Figure 1-2
ATI All-In-Wonder

The second type of card is the audio/video capture board. It's a dedicated video and audio input device. It does not have any outputs and lives only to ingest audio and video. Some of the boards are video only and can help reduce any confusion and redundancy with other on-board audio devices or prosumer audio capture boards. These boards are often geared specifically for processing audio and video and nothing else. That nonsharing attitude allows the board to focus on the one task, high-resolution ingest and no dropped frames.

Dedicated capture cards are a rare breed and can be more difficult to find. Most big box retailers have slim offerings in the video capture area, and what they do carry will be USB connected devices don't offer up the best transfers. What's more, these devices often cost about the same as a high quality PCI capture card that can handle as much as four times the data throughput. The Winnov card (*http://www.winnov.com*) is one of those video capture card manufacturers that is not expensive, provides high quality products that do exactly what you need them to do. Their Videum 1000 VO (VO means Video Only) has a street price of about $150 and supports a 640 × 480 capture at 30 frames per second, uncompressed (see **Figure 1-4**). It works with all major editing packages such as Windows Movie Maker, Adobe Premiere and Vegas Video. Spending the little bit of extra money on a part you don't have to worry about can reduce any unnecessary suffering at the hands of a fickle video capture. KWorld and Turtle Beach also manufacture quality video capture boards that offer high quality video transfers. On the professional side of analog video capture cards, however, the Osprey is the best and most supported champion. If your encoding and streaming software supports any cards, it will support an Osprey. These cards range from the $150 range to many hundreds of dollars depending on how many different audio and video inputs they have, but they are the industry standard.

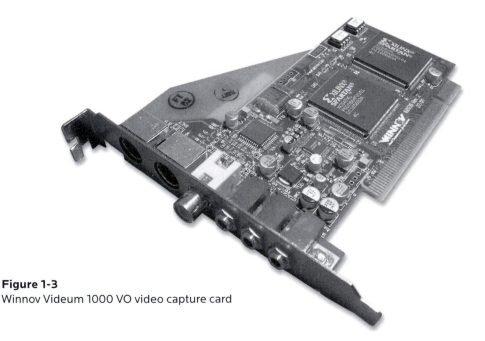

Figure 1-3
Winnov Videum 1000 VO video capture card

A webcam can be used for video recording and capturing in as much as any low-end video device for the task. It will take video and make a file out of it. The quality of that file will only be as good as the camera, and most webcams simply don't have the frame rate to offer decent video. Webcams are best suited for chatting applications where low frame rate is tolerated. Even the higher-end webcams just don't offer what an old High8 or inexpensive DV cam does. That being said, it will work, just not well and not like something you would want to show other people. If the video is supposed to look like an informal webcam, then there is no problem, but you'll still probably want to record the audio using a lavalier (clip-on) microphone or other setup to ensure the resulting production looks faux-amateur and not, well, amateur.

Edit Your Video

Once the video has been transferred to your computer, it's time to edit it, if only to snip off the ragged ends. Most video editing packages offer a try before you buy setup with various limitations, be it time or the ability to render a final product. Before settling on any one product, try a few out. Some may be more feature-rich than you need, some may not have the interface that works for you, and others may be too expensive. The first one to try is the one that comes with your computer. While often a bare-bones approach, it might just render what you need it to.

If not, there are professional editing programs, which includes some that are not cheap. Vegas Video Pro 6 (**Figure 1-4**) runs about $500, and Adobe Premiere weighs in at close to $700, but fortunately, there is a happy middle ground. Sony Media Software has a pared-down editor called *Vegas Movie Studio + DVD* for only $90. Adobe also has the $100 Premiere Elements, which gives you the power to edit video without breaking the bank. I mention the more expensive programs first because of their professional pedigrees. The less expensive programs are chips off the big ticket block that look and feel more like expensive editing programs. Your local big-box retailer may have an extensive collection of video editing applications, but you run the risk of buying a GUI wizard type editor that ends up being

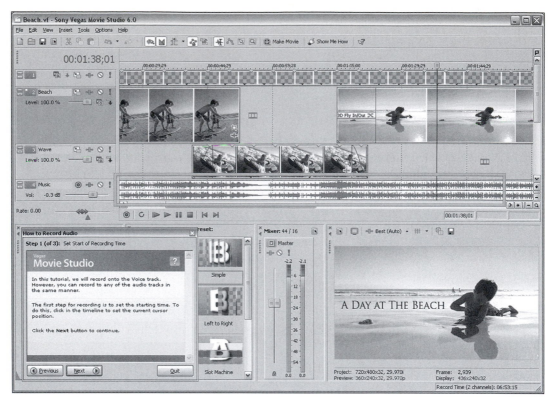

Figure 1-4
Sony Media Software—Vegas Movie Studio 6 video editing application

Mac users are familiar with the Adobe applications, but they also have access to a few other very powerful video editing tools: iMovie and Final Cut Pro. As with the PC editing options, there is a Pro (expensive) version and the lighter one (far less expensive) and your needs will dictate which one to buy, although in this case iMovie is free so starting there makes sense.

The best video clips to test in your prospective editing program will be the video you just shot and captured. Snip out the ragged ends, add in a few stills, even go in and smooth out some "ums" and "uhs" from the audio track (for more information on audio editing, see Chapter 10, Audio Production and Post-Production. Most programs should let you render the new clip. It will take the edit decision list (EDL) that you created and work that magic on the video, providing you with a new clip. The rendering may take a little time and will likely be large if you specified uncompressed video. Having an uncompressed master is good because then you can play with different compression schemes. With the final edit created, the original capture can be discarded. The new master is going to be used as the reference for the next step.

Converting and Compressing

Video blogs should look good as it's a more personal medium. The production quality should show through. In the same way a video editing program does its best work editing, a compression program does its best work compressing. Most editors will come with some compression tools to help you render the master into the final format. Formats for vlogging include MOV, AVI, M4V, and MPEG types of video. The formats may be the same but no compression programs are created equal. Some compression programs are very efficient at making the conversion happen quickly, some are good at making the video file small, some are good at neither. Apple's QuickTime Pro (**Figure 1-5**) does a superb job at making nearly any kind of file into small footprint MOV and M4V files. In fact, its newest release has a setting just for video blogs and it makes the file sizes very small. At $30, it's a tool you should not be without. Canopus ProCoder Express at $59 also offers a host of conversion options and the company has a long history of making quality video conversion tools. If money is no object and you are looking to convert a wide variety of encoded video, Canopus ProCoder 2 can stitch together multiple formats into a single file, re-encoded to any format under the sun for a cool $500. It's a great tool if exporting to a wide variety of platforms is important to you.

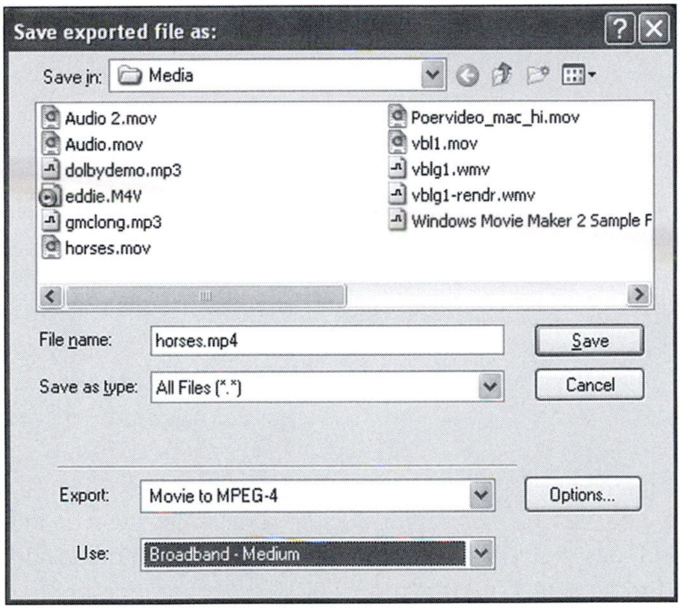

Figure 1-5
Apple QuickTime Pro export dialog

The QuickTime format is currently the most popular file type in the video blogging world for a number of reasons. There are a lot of Mac video bloggers that make QuickTime the default; iTunes is a very popular Vlog aggregator and iTunes likes QuickTime files, the codec is loaded on most computers and the recent MOV format looks great even when highly compressed. That combination makes it a good first place to start. There are plenty of other file formats, but it's important to look at what people are going to be able to view without having to dig up and install a new codec. The viewer drop-off rate skyrockets when people have to install something in order to play a file.

Using QuickTime Pro, the process is simple: open the file, go to the menu, select export, pick the file export type and start. A few minutes later a little version is born. It's good to try many different variations to see which final rendering fits your size and quality requirements. Small file sizes may be good on the bandwidth bill, but small videos may be too tiny on the screen and drive people away. A recommended size that offers a decent size picture while not gobbling up too much disk space and bandwidth is 320 × 240.

Upload the Content

Once the video has been converted and compressed into its final state, it should be uploaded to a publicly accessible server and tested. A publicly accessible server would be someplace on the Internet that can be accessed by the use of a URL, such as a web page you already have access to. You don't need a streaming server or anything like that; you're uploading the video file just as if it was a JPG or other graphics file. If you upload a video file called "vlogpost01.mov" to a directory named "vlog" in the space allocated to you by your ISP, it might show up as *http://vlogbook.isp.net/vlog/vlogpost01.mov* and anyone on the Internet who knew that URL could enter it in directly and the file could be downloaded.

ALERT You can avoid unnecessary head scratching by testing the file link before posting it in the vlog. If it doesn't work as a plain URL, it won't work as a podcast.

Setting Up A Simple Blog

Blogger.com and typepad.com are two of the larger blog communities that play host to a large number of bloggers. Blogger is a free service that offers very straightforward log hosting (see **Figure 1-6**). While it has many features, it does not currently support the proper enclosure tags that allow podcasting client applications to see the audio and video content. TypePad on the other hand does support enclosures natively, but they charge a nominal fee of $5 per month for service.

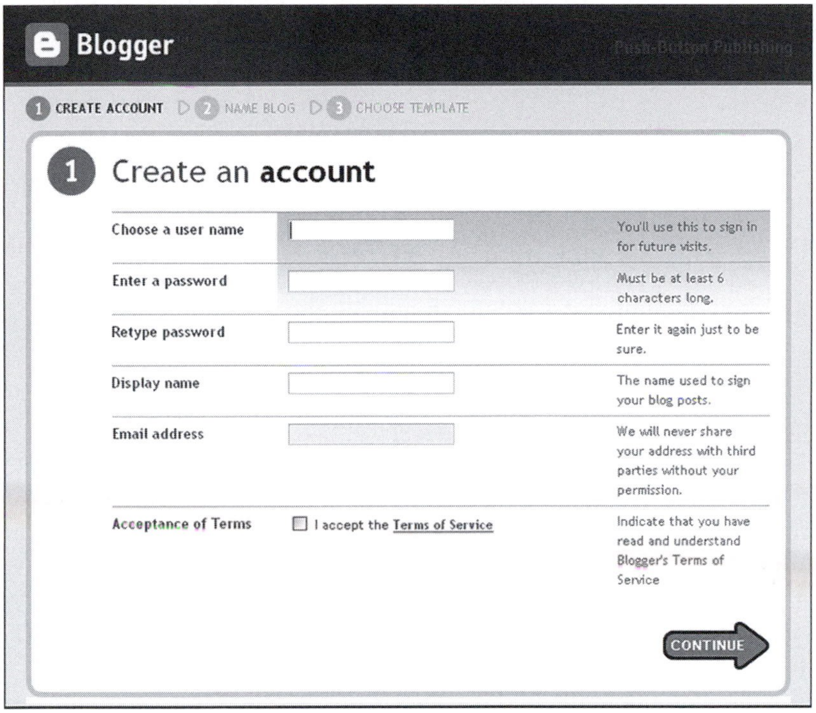

Figure 1-6
Blogger.com new account page

Setting up a free blog account on Blogger.com is so simple you'll be able to do it before you read the next sentence. Once you've created your Blogger account, make a simple text post, perhaps one simply saying "Hello World." The purpose of the test post is to demonstrate that the blog is publishing properly and that what you put in is what comes out. Blogger has two options when entering text for a post: a text editor mode and an HTML mode. When adding an outside bit of code like the tag for a video file, switch over to HTML mode. The media file URL you created earlier comes into play now. Enter some descriptive text then the link to the video file:

```
<a href="http://vlogbook.isp.net/vlog/vlogpost01.mov">Vlog Post</a>
```

The `<a>` tag should be familiar to anyone who has written any HTML. If not, the tag tells a browser that the text in the quotes is the target and the text in between the >< characters is the description. When that's done, post the entry and in another window bring up the blog and see if the link works. If it did work and the video downloads, then in a sense you've just posted a video blog. The post you're looking at in your web browser is the web-based post. The blog was also published as an XML file. The XML file feed for your blog will be: *http://yourfeed.blogspot.com/atom.xml* (where yourfeed is the name you gave the blog). The atom XML file does not contain the kind of tags the podcasting aggregators need to see in order for them to pull the video enclosure, (namely, enclosure tags). If your blogging software generates an "RSS 2.0 feed with enclosures" (check your documentation) then your job is almost done. This RSS feed will be something like *feed://yourfeed.blogspot.com/index.xml*. However, any blog feed can be instantly turned into a podcast. That's where FeedBurner comes in to save the day and make life easier for you.

FeedBurner takes a feed that is in need of enclosure tag help and re-publishes it in a far friendlier format that all aggregators can use. FeedBurner is a free service that is very useful for any blogger who has a blogging host that does not publish the correct enclosure tags. Signing up for FeedBurner is a very straightforward process that, at the end of the setup, will offer you a feed link that looks similar to *http://feeds.feedburner.com/yoursitename*. That link will be what you post on your page as the one to use for iTunes, FireAnt or any other feed aggregators (see Chapter 4, Tuning in to Multimedia Blogs).

You can also put that URL into a browser window and get the FeedBurner version of your site to ensure the posts are up to date and the feed looks good. The next step is to enter that FeedBurner URL into your feed reading program. iTunes, FireAnt, MyYahoo!, Technorati, they should all recognize the feed, see the enclosure and offer up the podcast. It's likely that if it works in iTunes and FireAnt, it will work everywhere else, but like any compatibility testing, you should test in all the major clients to make sure your feed is working right.

ALERT Because the standards for video blogs and podcasts are still changing, not all blog applications support them yet, and for those that do, some assembly is required. FeedBurner is the fastest way to turn an ordinary blog into a video blog or podcast—all you have to do is include an `<A HREF>` link to an MP3 or video file in your blog entry and FeedBurner will do the rest.

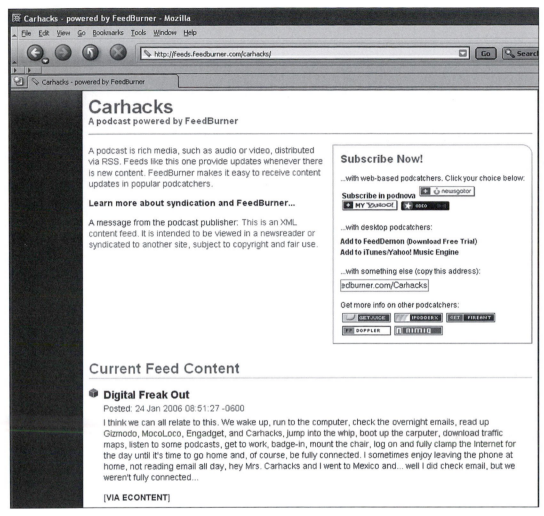

Figure 1-7
FeedBurner feed page for carhacks

TypePad buys you a more direct route for the $5 a monthly fee. There is no need for Feed-Burner as the hosted blog application publishes the correct enclosure XML as soon as you hit the publish button. That little bit of code rendering on the server side does a few things: it allows your newest posts to be live in iTunes and other aggregators instantly while eliminating the need for a middleman.

Although you may be able to host small image files with TypePad, you'll need to find a spot to host your media files. Your ISP will likely offer some space, but like most ISPs, they get cranky and pull the plug on very popular downloads from user directories. There are free places to put your image files such as the Internet Archive, Our Media and Blip.TV *http://www.archive.org/*, *http://www.ourmedia.org/* and *http://blip.tv/* (more on this in Chapter 12 Hosting and Bandwidth).

Once the media is uploaded to its permanent home and you've tested the direct media link, publish the post in TypePad and test out the URL in iTunes. **Figure 1-8** shows you how to subscribe to your podcast using the *feed://* URL from your FeedBurner link or your blog software. If it works and the feed pulls without any issues, you should see your blog in the Podcast area of iTunes. If you don't see it, or if an exclamation mark shows up next to your feed, then backtrack each step to ensure each step of the process worked. That your multi-media files are working; that you're using FeedBurner if the blog software doesn't natively support podcasts; that FeedBurner recognizes your blog's RSS feed, and so on. **Figure 1-9** shows an overview of the completed process.

If you test each step as you do it, it will be easier to find problems in the setup. Make sure the video you upload is the small 5 MB encoded video and not the 5 GB master. Ensure your HTML tags, if you used any, are coded correctly. URLs are often long and can have special characters in them, but it's critical to remember two rules: there are no spaces in file names, and upper/lower case letters are not the same. Make things simple by using all lower case for all files and for spaces use the dash "-" or underscore "_".

Once you've found a good rhythm and have a repeatable process, it's a good idea to document that process, if only to write down the settings for the hardware and software you used. What frame rate and picture size did you use; what are the usernames and passwords for the sites you just signed up for; what are the XML feed URLs for the site; and what is the base URL for content feeds and any other data that would come in handy if you were struck by an errant five pound walnut and forgot some things. Hey, it could happen.

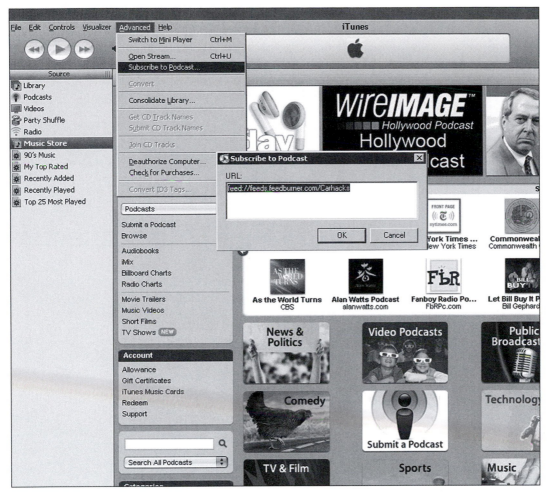

Figure 1-8
Subscribing to a podcast feed in iTunes

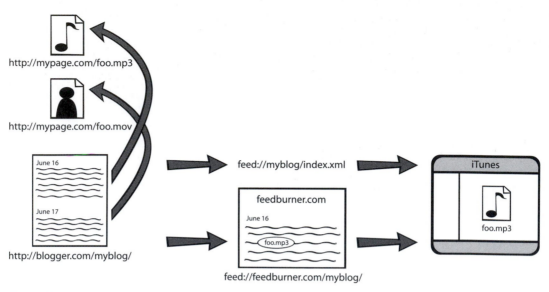

Figure 1-9
Making a podcast

Conclusion

Along with a bit of trivia, this chapter detailed the process of podcasting into a few simple steps: content, content hosting, blog setup and posting, blog XML feed URL, and subscribing in iTunes or another blog aggregator. If you already blog, you should realize quickly that there's almost nothing to adding podcasting or video blogging—you just upload a multimedia file to a website, link to the file, and make sure your feed supports enclosures. If you've turned your blog into a podcast in the process of reading this chapter, you're probably excited to see it in iTunes, but wondering where all the flashy pictures and titles and other metadata are. That's the subject of (Chapter 6, New Skills for a New Technology).

CHAPTER 2

Podcasting and Video Blogging Basics

Podcasting and video blogging are natural extensions of the text-based weblog.

Weblogs, or blogs, have grown from a convenient web-page updating tool to a vast cultural phenomenon. There isn't an old-media outlet—newspapers, television, magazines, you name it—that hasn't come up with some sort of "blogging strategy" in response to their popularity. Blogs have become part of the social fabric, much as web pages did in the 1990s.

Blogs are fundamentally a means of communication, a modern twist on an ancient format, the diary. Similarly, the proliferation of simple, portable, ubiquitous tools for recording speech and filming everyday events has created new forms beyond still photography. It is therefore not surprising that the sounds and moving pictures so effortlessly captured on handheld devices have combined with the one-to-many medium of the web-based journal.

This chapter discusses the fundamental concepts of multimedia blogging and its differences from traditional web-based streaming. This chapter covers:

- the anatomy of a blog,
- a brief history of blogs,
- multimedia in the blogosphere,
- media standards emerge, and,
- podcasting and video blogging grow up.

Anatomy of a Blog

Before we continue on the key concepts of podcasting and video blogging, we should cover the basics of a blog.

One of the benefits of a blog is that it's a standardized format, so audiences don't have to re-learn site navigation like they do for every website. Not every blog has every element; personal diary blogs have far more links to other sites and blogs than blogs attached to a major news organization, for example. **Figure 2-1** shows the basic layout of a blog.

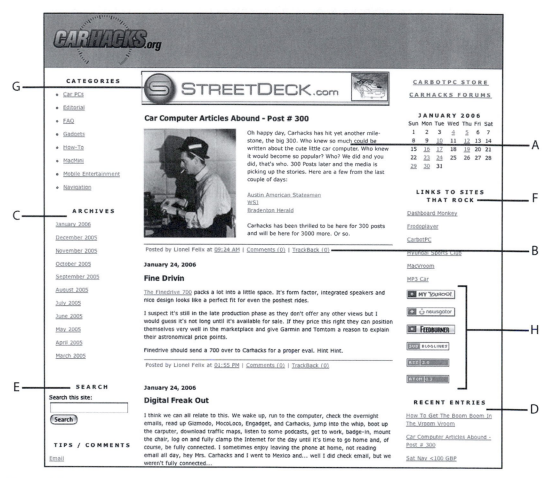

Figure 2-1
The anatomy of a blog

Most blogs are arranged in a 2- or 3-column format. The center of the blog is usually the area for sequential text. The side areas contain navigation features relating to the blog, links to other blogs, and additional semi-permanent, nonblog content such as advertisements.

A.   As you can see, the center of the blog is usually the area for the sequential text and picture *posts* or *entries*. Each blog post contains the text, pictures, and links relating to that story. Some blog entries are merely a web link with a comment, while other entries can be pages long.

Blogs often embed pictures with each entry, to provide an interesting image that relates to the subject of the text. Other blogs use the same set of icons to represent recurring topics or categories.

Some posts end with a free-form list of categories or *tags*. These are part of a system for *tagging* blogs, labeling them with subjects or categories that can be used to organize blogs around similar topics and facilitate finding them. Tags are good for labeling what wouldn't be found in a normal keyword search of the blog—for instance, an entry on the blogger's cat might be tagged "pets" or "animals," even if it did not have those words. Clicking on the tag will bring you to a list of all blogs on the system in that category or having that tag.

B.   Each entry has several associated links. The *permalink* (sometimes shown as a time stamp) is a permanent URL to that specific blog entry that will be valid after the entry goes into the *archive*, which contains all the historical posts after they fall off the main page.

The *trackback* is a system where blog A can reference a post on blog B, and blog A's weblogging system will automatically notify blog B (through a small message called a *ping*) that references it. Thus, the trackback link, when correctly used, lists other blogs that elaborate on, reference, or speak about that blog entry.

Most blogging systems include a *comments* link, which allows visitors on that site to comment on that entry. Blogs are a very interactive medium, often encouraging readers to comment on the posts.

C.   The *archive* and associated links (such as specific months and years) bring up all the blog entries from that time period, narrow or wide. Many blog systems also have a mini-calendar showing the current month, where each day hyperlinks to any posts for that day, allowing visitors to see at a glance which day's posts were made.

D.   The recent posts section is just that, a list of the most recent posts summarized in a very small format, so no scrolling is required to look at the headlines.

E.   The search function on blog pages does much as one would expect, bringing up any blogs that match the search criteria.

F.   Many blogs, especially personal blogs, have a large list of links to other blogs that the blog author frequents. This list of blogs is called a *blogroll*.

G. Not unique to blogs, many high-traffic websites generate income through advertisements.

H. A defining feature of blogs is their ability to be *syndicated*. This means that blogs follow a standard format that can be automatically downloaded, blended with other blogs, and shown on other websites as part of a newsfeed. This also means that readers can use *aggregator* programs or websites to pull together all the blogs they read into one interface.

When a program, another blog or a search engine pulls down blogs automatically, this is called a *subscription*, although no payment is involved, just periodic updates on a schedule.

Subscription is achieved through a format called *RSS*, which stands for *real simple syndication* or *rich site summary.* You will often see a stack of small, colorful rectangle icons on the side panels of a blog. Some of these link to an RSS *feed*, which is a file containing a list of all the recent posts with the web page clutter removed. This feed is what aggregators and other programs use to summarize the blog and extract its entries for syndication.

A variety of software and web-based aggregators have developed a one-click method of subscribing to a blog. iTunes, Yahoo!, and other aggregator links are also provided in this format. Simply clicking on these will activate the appropriate program and add this blog to your RSS aggregator. Its sort of like pressing "record" on your remote.

Sometimes, these icons are used for nonsubscription links as well, because graphics add visual interest.

Inside the Industry

 The universe of all blogs, considered together, is humorously (but not facetiously) referred to as the *blogosphere*.

As blog software has developed, new features have been added, especially in the areas of tracking, reporting, searching, and cross-linking between blogs. Because many blogs rely on one of a handful of software programs, features (such as tags) are quickly deployed once they are standardized. Features such as integrated Flash-based media players are available on some of the newest blog hosting services, and it is only a matter of time before multimedia features become standard fare for blogs.

A Brief History of Blogs

Blogs (a shortening of *web logs*) became popular through their inherent simplicity of use and linear, journal format. As personal web pages became more and more complex and disjointed, they fell out of favor. The time, effort and barrier to entry made them difficult to start and update. Even with easy-to-use tools, a majority of web users were not going to design and create their own web page. The blog sprouted out of the gap left between the complex toolsets and complex web page hosting requirements. Blog sites like blogger.com and typepad.com have a rich set of page templates that allow you to setup fonts and colors only once, and then create content forever more.

What made the concept more compelling is the nature of linear posting, one after the other. New posts take the top spot over old ones. People could share their lives, as they happen, as they post them. Citizen journalists jumped on the technology as it works perfectly for their format: new news on top of older news, and so on. Fire and forget. Never having to worry about managing the content. Once it's up, it just gets pushed back, self-archiving.

Posting to a blog is as easy as writing an email. Blogging was the liberating form that allowed informational web pages to move completely past mechanics and focus on the message.

Blogs technically have been around since about 1997 but didn't gain popularity until 2001. Dot-com booming and busting left little room for a technology that seemed to have evaded the over-hyping era. As blogs gained momentum as personal, topical and political view outlets, people were already thinking about where the technology was headed.

Multimedia in the Blogosphere

As with anything on the web, evolution never sleeps. Text was great but pictures were better. Soon blog sites allowed picture uploads, giving more life to posts. And one of the first multimedia variants of the blog format was the *photoblog*, where each blog entry consists primarily of a picture or pictures, with some brief commentary. Another variant of this is the *moblog*, or mobile blog, containing pictures, text, and small video and sound clips sent directly from a mobile phone.

While photoblogs became popular quickly after blogs, audio and video blogs took longer to emerge. Most blogging software quickly added tools for uploading and hosting pictures. Since pictures don't take up that much bandwidth (tens of kilobyes), they could be hosted right with the blog without being a financial burden.

Audio and video were a different story. The first barrier to entry for audio blogging was cost. In the first days of the 21st century, the majority of US Internet was still dial-up, and the cost of hosting blogs was enormous. Added to this was uncertainty about the legality of distributing online music; witness the saga of Napster. The licensing terms for even legitimate Internet radio were nowhere near settled, and MP3 hadn't yet become the de facto standard.

For video, these legal bandwidth and standards issues were ten times worse. Streaming, an attempt to prevent copying by keeping the data on the server and doling it out to media players in small, jerky chunks, was the state of the art for online video. Watchable video, generally ten times larger than audio when compressed was really limited in distribution to broadband viewers on college or corporate networks. And it was anyone's guess if a video standard would ever emerge.

Media Standards Emerge

After the genie was put back in the bottle on MP3 file sharing and the Internet radio licensing terms were settled, things got a little more predictable, if restricted. Napster was sued into submission, and later emerged as a "legit" pay service; and a late entrant to the media player market called the *iPod* was released followed by a music store that quickly helped prove out the downloadable music market. Over these couple of years, MP3 did finally become the de facto music format, and a growing population of camera phones and digital recorders helped finally put MPEG-4 video back in the standards race.

With the growing popularity of blogs shadowing the popularity of mobile music players, the audio blog was born. People with iPods and people with blogs collided in that, "You got your chocolate in my peanut butter, no, you got your peanut butter on my chocolate!" sort of way.

As blogs became more popular, engineers and content creators started tinkering with the format, seeing if they could add audio and video. A multimedia *enclosure element* was added to the blog standard to enable these rich-media blogs. Like the first land-crawling creatures slogging their way out of the sea and breathing air, the enclosure element was the critical element that allows audio blogging and video blogging to work. (Without it, it's just a link.)

Tools were quickly developed to get the enclosures from the blogs directly to iPods and other portable devices. Apple quickly adapted their iTunes software to read, download and synchronize audio blog and (later) video blog enclosures, which they naturally called *podcasts*. This accelerated mainstream market interest in rich-media blogging and increased the use of the podcast label to describe it.

In its most basic form, a *podcast* or *audio blog* is simply an audio file referenced as an *enclosure* by a blog that can be downloaded. *Video blogs* are the same thing, but the enclosure is a video file. These files are not streamed, they are downloaded. That means that a normal web server can host the files. Whereas CNN might stream their video to you to keep the video on their own servers, the enclosures included in podcasts and video blogs can be copied to your computer (by applications such as FireAnt) for you to consume at any point in time. They can also be automatically aggregated from various sources into a single web-based feed, sort of like email, so that you don't have to go to all the source websites to consume them; they're all right there at the top of your Earthlink, MSN, Yahoo!, or Google personal home page.

Audio Blogging and Video Blogging Grow Up

Although the technical development of all multimedia blogging built on the technology of RSS enclosures, the media of audio blogging and video blogging have been developed by different groups of people.

Audio blogging was catalyzed in 2003 by the posting of some MP3 lectures to an existing text blog. The key influencers of audio blogging standards were very active in the blog community, and built upon the emerging MP3 player market in general and iPod's predominance in this market in particular. The technical similarities between audio blogging and the downloadable music market, as well as the "mainstream" music industry experience of the early influencers, pushed audio blogging in

Author's Tip

In this book, for the sake of simplicity, we have lumped most audio-only blogs, be they mobile phone moblogs, news programs or music blogs under the term *podcast*. Similarly, we have explicitly categorized all blogs with video, be they vlogs, v-logs, "vodlogs," and video podcasts as video blogs. Although a podcast can include video, in this book we will usually say *video podcast* when we're talking about video in the iTunes music store or for the iPod.

the direction of high-production value, radio-like broadcasts (see **Figure 2-2**). And the rising dominance of the iPod and Apple's quick support of audio blogging helped solidify its new name, podcasting.

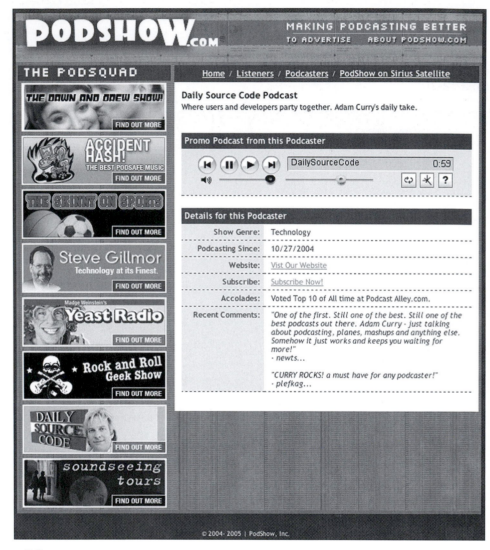

Figure 2-2
Podshow.com

Video blogging developed in the same time period as audio blogging, but in a different community. The pioneers of video blogging, or *vlogging* developed it less as an alternative to radio and more as a new art form in the style of "cinéma vérité." Many of the video recording devices available for impromptu recording—such as cell phones and digital cameras—record at a very low resolution. But, these same tools are much less intrusive than a tripod and a large video camera, and they lend themselves to documentary, newsgathering, and artistic filming. Even some video bloggers with a formal video production background have eschewed polishing their productions, preferring to present "life in the raw" in their blogs (see **Figure 2-3**).

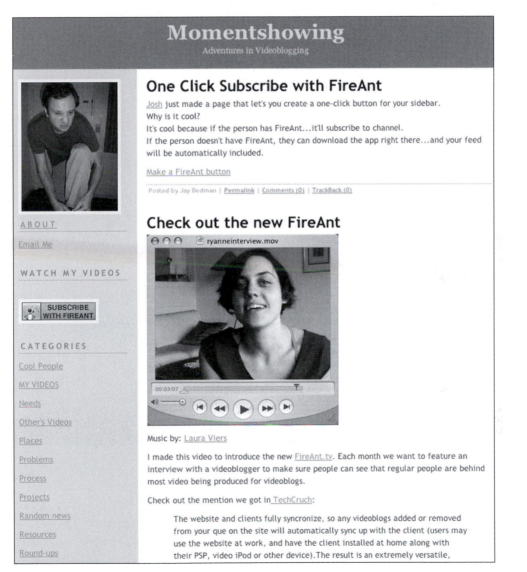

Figure 2-3
momentshowing.net

This does not mean that all video bloggers do this. In fact, the most successful video blogs, although having a "raw" look, are well scripted and filmed on carefully designed, if spare looking sets. For film school graduates with directorial backgrounds, it can take a lot of work to make a video blog look like it doesn't take a lot of work (see **Figure 2-4**).

Figure 2-4
rocketboom.com

Conclusion

Blogs quickly evolved into the most popular format for delivering news, diaries, and online journals. Blogs are the "web portal" of the 21st century, and have permeated all areas of online publishing.

In addition to their popularity with people, blogs are easy for computers and automated systems to read as well, because of their use of RSS (really simple syndication) standards. Thus, blogs can be automatically searched, merged, sliced-and-diced, and downloaded without human intervention.

Audio and video can be attached to any existing blog. With the right tools, this video can be automatically downloaded to audience computers or portable media players.

Audio blogs and video blogs have their own evolving style and conventions.

The next chapter will focus on the many popular uses of podcasts and video blogs.

CHAPTER 3

Podcasting and Video Blogging Uses

The technologies that have recently converged to allow instant publishing of text, video and audio have all been swimming around the Internet for years. In fact there are only a few new elements in this recipe, so often the case with wonderful things. Like the great primordial ooze, the Internet is teaming with millions of elementary particles, merging, growing, dying and being re-used. Once in a while, a little bit of lucky cohesion happens and something great happens. P2P applications and MP3 encoding came together and a digital music revolution was born, in spite of much hand wringing by record producers predicting the end of the music world.

In the case of video blogging and podcasting, long ago in Internet time, XML met with web news aggregators and from that, RSS was born. Soon after that, the humble blog, a stronger, more defiant variant of the nearly extinct home page, began to take shape. The little blog organism found a strong host in large RSS reefs like Blogger.com. Soon images could be added, then audio and video. Then one day, the great Apple iTunes gazed upon the podcasting creature, and the Apple smiled and said, "It was good."

This is not the end of the story, in fact it's just the beginning. The tools, processes, services and uses join together, becoming bigger, stronger, more unified, converged. What takes five tools and three services today will soon be part of a suite of connected tools. If you look at how difficult it was to manage digital video eight years ago and compare it to what can be done with Premiere, Avid or Vegas today, it's a wonder we made it work at all. There are so many uses for podcasting and video blogging that a list is only a primer to get the thought process going. We are already seeing massive short video clip libraries that grow by thousands of clips each day. A new vlog and podcast goes live hundreds and thousands of times each day. Mobile podcasting and vlogging is cut down to an easy single-step process. It is truly a brave new world.

This chapter has two main goals: to get the reader familiar with podcasting and video blogging media formats and how they differ from traditional streaming media, and to suggest new uses of rich-media blogging. This chapter will cover:

- Getting familiar with rich-media blogging
- Personal and special interest uses
- Mainstream media uses
- Corporate uses

Getting Familiar with Rich-Media Blogging

One of the most important hands-on things to do to get familiar with this new medium, and the point so often missed, is to thoroughly survey the landscape yourself. You probably don't want to be one of those clichéd Hollywood types that doesn't read the scripts, never watches the movies, but talks about "buzz" while waving their hands.

It's really difficult, if not impossible, to understand how the medium works from just reading a book. Now, it's not really impossible—in fact, we're trying to help you do it right now. But, the quickest way to get familiar with the format, content length, production quality, advertising approaches, and other essential attributes of podcasting and video blogging is to "channel surf" the rich-media blogosphere for a week until you're an expert on what's playing.

As mentioned earlier, audio blogs and video blogs have a somewhat different heritage. Audio blogs are more often found emulating radio, and are viewed by some as an online extension (and TiVo-ification) of that medium. Thus, it is natural that you will find many newspapers, radio stations, and TV news networks adding podcasting content to their web presence. Similarly, anywhere radio stations wish they had more exposure—public radio, AM radio, and small-municipality stations—they are turning to not just streaming audio but podcasting to increase that reach.

Because of the heavy investment in podcast delivery technology made by Apple to increase the utility of the iPod, the easiest and smoothest way to sample podcast content is in iTunes. To do this, download iTunes, go to the Music Store, and click Podcasts (see **Figure 3-1**). You will find well-presented, abundant, professional quality podcasts. No iPod is required, and the podcasts are all free (clicking *subscribe* costs nothing, despite the connotations of the word).

Figure 3-1
iTunes podcast directory

Sampling the video blogging waters can be a bit more of a challenge. In the same iTunes podcast directory, you will find a number of "video podcasts," which represent some of the most popular shows, but are by no means a comprehensive view of the medium like their audio selection. In addition to wandering around in iTunes, you should search for a topic that interests you at *http://www.mefeedia.com/feeds/* or *http://www.vodstock.com/*.

Probably the most useful tool for finding, subscribing to, and viewing video blogs will be FireAnt, which you can download for the Mac or PC at *http://fireant.tv/* (see **Figure 3-2**).

Figure 3-2
Subscribing to FireAnt

Personal and Special Interest Uses

Blogs have opened up an enormous hole in the news universe. Unlike print, the Internet can be anywhere and everywhere in milliseconds. The digital age has brought us closer together, but the Mainstream Media has had the monopoly on who gets to know what and when. With blogs and subsequently podcasts and video blogs, having your own news outlet is as easy as making a home video, encoding, editing, uploading and posting. Moments later, the world can see what you have to say. The major differences are the established readers and the volume of content. That said, major media has seen the value of a broader, more diverse and independent journalism base.

Author's Tip

Video Blog Sampler Plate

Here's a list of video blogs representing a range of content. Check all of them out and watch at least an episode or two to get the flavor of the video blog pacing, format, and presentation.

http://noservicecharge.com/videoblog/

http://davemedia.blogspot.com/

http://viviendoconfallas.blogspot.com/

http://www.tikibartv.com/

http://node101.org/

http://www.Backstaging.com—how to film video blogs

http://stevegarfield.blogs.com/

http://www.mnstories.com/

http://www.rocketboom.com

http://mediamatters.org/

Inside the Industry

Sites like Wonkette.com under the Gawker Media umbrella (a large blog only collection of sites), Rocketboom, and Engadget have developed their following through little more than compelling content and word of mouth, yet their audience rivals major news outlets. That has not gone unnoticed by larger conglomerates, which then cut deals with some of the bloggers for exclusive content and syndication.

In most cases, the citizen journalist podcaster focuses on a much narrower scope than larger outlets, by *narrowcasting*. Where a paper, such as the *LA Times* has a calendar section, an LA entertainment podcaster might focus on events that cater to their own personal tastes and can give a better level of detail and insight into the subject matter. Unfortunately, most staff writers at larger publications and TV news shows have to quickly get up to speed on topics they know little or nothing about, whereas industry individuals are already at the ground level on these topics and can speak with authority.

CNN can do an article on newer cell phones shown at CES, but Engadget can dissect the phone offerings at CES down to their basic elements, which caters to people who want to know more than cursory details about color and approximate size and shape. CNN will never be able to have an on-staff cell phone junkie, but the blogosphere is happy to play host to dozens of those who, in turn, can offer that level of expertise to their audience. Although most staff writers do have an area of expertise, it's often quite broad; their skill is in writing, not knowing the arcane details of CDMA vs. GSM. Writing skills are important, but offering the audience real depth is the real value and that's where the larger outlets can't compete.

Blogging organizations like Gawker and Weblogs, Inc. have capitalized on the concept of serving up what people want in the niche they're interested in. Where podcasts and video blogs succeed is in the relatively editor-less creative environment, allowing them to cover the subject matter they know, and in their own voice, without having to worry much about making big sponsors upset. That doesn't give them license to fly off the handle and say terrible things without the risk of losing some of the audience and sponsors, but there is significantly less of that to worry about. The focus is on the content, not on making nice with corporate interests.

Inside the Industry

 Four Types of Content

Eric Rice, a noted multimedia blogger, views content creation as happening for one of four reasons:

1. Personal
2. Art
3. Information/education
4. Performance

In his view, text, picture, audio or video blogs are just different ways to communicate something for one of these purposes, whether it is done for money, fame and recognition, or for cash.

In his encouragement of new media creators, he emphasizes a focus on the message, not the medium.

Trying to decide if one is a blog, or a video blog, or a vlog, and what category one should belong in is just getting caught up in the mechanics of it all. The fact that all these tools exist today allows new, hybrid media forms to be created, and artists should simply use the tools and get on with it.

The ability of a podcast to exist outside of major corporate control, even in the case of Weblogs, Inc. and Gawker, means there is a lot more editorial freedom. Imagine the world of *Rolling Stone* in the age of Hunter Thompson. *Rolling Stone* got away from the "If you don't have anything nice to say…" format of mainstream media because their audience was ready for flavor, depth, and insight, rather than the tepid inoffensive and bland coverage offered by other music magazines. The same holds true for podcasts; if the audience wants a talking head giving you the news in bite size chunks with words that never exceed five letters, they have the local newscast.

Citizen journalists involved with video blogging also have the luxury of much lower over-head. No 3-camera studios, unionized crew or satellite feed to pay for, just the tools they may already have on their computers. That's not to say production should be done with the lowest tech available; it's quite the contrary, it's just as important to know that in this uni-verse the content matters more than a scrolling lower third graphic and fancy glass news desk. In fact, that would likely end up looking corny unless irony is the desired effect.

User-generated content for personal and niche use runs the gamut of expression itself. Popular forms include:

- diary podcasts to journal life,
- documentary work, both journalistic and artistic,
- media fact checking, with precise audio and video evidence to hand,
- informational, on any subject imaginable, as a 21st-century Internet "portal,"
- educational, from elementary to university to online, and,
- religious, using new media as a pulpit with global reach.

Mainstream Media Uses

Blogs completely blindsided conventional media. The wave of alternative media sources put the fourth estate (the press) in the position of having to make a decision that could have lead to their demise or a new era of news reporting. They just didn't know what answer would lead to what end. In a short period of time, bloggers who followed the basic rules of reporting floated to the top and became credible in their own right. The ability for someone to sprout a news organization could have been realized with older technology, but it just didn't stick.

The linear blogging format combined with feed syndication was the perfect hook for the public. It's not surprising that it was such an instant hit, it conformed to the way we are used to getting news. We read from top to bottom, in columns or side-to-side with headline tick-ers; we're liner content devourers. Big unwieldy web pages and their over stylized nav-bars had become so bloated with content, pop-ups and advertisements that people started to give up.

Many news outlets tried to charge a subscription for their online content and were answered with a vitriolic backlash. The broadsheets were losing their public appeal, their demograph-ics were falling up the age scale and the blood seemed to be in the water.

Interestingly, the news didn't die. Blogs didn't take over, and people still buy the *New York Times* from newsstands. What did change was quite significant. Bloggers in respectable numbers had proven themselves as reliable writers, editors and fact checkers. A blogger can post a story in minutes, including links to relevant data, photos and editorial while still maintaining journalistic integrity and fact-checked sources.

In a short amount of time, bloggers were embraced as the new addition to the fourth estate, yet not one held to the same standards as the bastions of stiff and staid media. Although bloggers break news, make headlines, and do embarrass larger media outlets to some degree, the real competition is in editorial content. The massive editorial bureaucracy that makes up larger papers, magazines and news television sometimes sucks out creativity, humor, anger and empathy. This leaves readers with bland we-don't-want-to-risk-offending-anyone material that doesn't offend but barely entertains and certainly takes a fency stance on hot issues

Inside the Industry

An Editorial Voice

Bloggers, on the other hand, have a position and their viewership subscribes to that view, that set of beliefs, that editorial voice. Younger viewers have left the big three-point-five networks for *The Daily Show* to get their news and editorial needs met. Those same people are also not reading the *New York Times* or other "big" news sources. They're getting their news and editorial online from those that share their voice.

Podcasts and video blogs allow for a new level of depth in reporting and editorial content. It's a place where the audience is captured more by the slant given to a topic by a particular personality. On-air news personalities can offer extra commentary or depth on a topic they covered on the air that day. That value-add adds a compelling element to the broadcast and allows viewers to feel closer to what's happening. That said, if the video blog looks too professional and well-produced, people may look at it as not so much a video blog, but just extra clippings or some sort of commercialization of the online content.

Therein lies the rub. Why spend money on a tie-in that's not going to generate revenue and why can't it look like the rest of the content? The public has established expectations even on things as new as podcasts and video blogs. Although that taste evolves over time, the current expectation is that the content is a departure from conventional in-your-face corporate-speak media. At the same time, people will tolerate interstitial ads to support the podcast.

There is a lot to be said of an online archive of aired programming. The BBC has been working feverishly to bring the majority of their back-catalogue online and available to anyone who wants to download it, and that includes news shows. Archival footage allows the public to go back into time and hear what a political candidate had said in the past, whether a previous prediction was on target or even if they themselves were on TV. Although the demand for footage may be low, there is a value in being able to defer to an online archive when asked rather than having to load tapes and print copies.

Following are potential mainstream media uses for video blogs and podcasts:

- **News and Journalism**
    - Provide a blog for on-air talent to go deeper into subject matter
    - A place for talent to editorialize
    - Linear archive of news shows for people who might want to see a previous broadcast
    - Outtakes and raw feeds to give an "insider" look to viewers
    - Consolidate and modernize the rich-media initiatives of an existing news site
    - Improve syndication and reach of information
    - Co-opt user generated op-ed content

- **Entertainment**
    - Provide teaser and backstage content
    - Get a steady link (through blog subscriptions) with fans of specific shows
    - Facilitate getting users to watch TV shows
    - Generate buzz for an upcoming movie release
    - Repurpose otherwise perishable material for Internet
    - Collect user-generated content for re-syndication as a bundle

> ### Author's Tip
>
> Podcasts can also take the form of a downloadable version of the aired shows in an archival format. Once the show has aired, there is still a value to the audience that didn't get a chance to see it. Consider it a variation of video-on-demand. This is also a good opportunity to drive ad revenue through running new ads or keeping the ads that ran in the aired show. Advertisers might not be able to guarantee that their ads are not skipped, but they already know that, as we live in the age of TiVo and cable company distributed PVRs.

Corporate Uses

Most companies have methods in place to keep their employees informed about happenings within the organization, restructurings, new business directions, marketing initiatives and sales reports. They can appear as intranets, company meetings, newsletters, emails or even shouted over the PA system. Some make use of a combination of outlets. The purpose of internal communication is that it gets the right information to the people that need to get it. As is the case with most of these types of communications, people ignore the vast majority of them and the message is lost.

Informing Employees

Smarter organizations are more creative about how they get the information to their employees. Some of the tools being used are the podcast and the video blog, retooled to fit their environment.

Intranets are often put together in haste in order to satisfy a certain need, which grows into a tangled nest that can often turn people off from using them, thereby, obfuscating the important data through messy menus and lists of links. The blog format can solve at least one of the problems that stop communications from getting lost in the cacophony.

The dreaded company meeting, an event met by most people with feelings of nausea and can, in some cases, trigger the fight or flight reflex. Taking a cue from Xcasting, keeping it brief, informational and somewhat entertaining is key. The other key is to make it available off-line for those who cannot attend. Webcasting is good, but only for the people who are not at the meeting and are somewhere they can tune in.

Informing the Board

The same can be done for stockholder and board meetings. Private intranets can be set-up to allow other senior managers to access board meetings so they don't have to rely on minutes and notes taken by attendees. Employees are often told of what happens in these meetings, but giving them the ability to virtually sit in on them gives the employees a better feeling of inclusiveness.

As is the case with many board meetings, sensitive material is discussed and that material isn't fit for the general public. Nowhere is it written that the content cannot be edited. In the case of a board meeting, simple cutting should be able to remove any sensitive bits and the process doesn't take much in the way of resources. Even if the board meeting is a little too in-depth, stockholder meetings are often public, yet their contents rarely make it back to the employees in much more than small outtakes. Publishing the stockholder meeting videos would allow employees to feel more a part of their company.

Where the video blog becomes even more compelling is in the area of a weekly or monthly address. Many CEOs simply don't have the time to host a regularly scheduled meeting with their employees, yet they need to keep them informed.

A CEO can videotape a short-format, weekly address that is posted like a podcast to the intranet, which will allow anyone at a computer, or connected to an RSS-enabled device to see or hear them talk about issues that matter to the organization. The big company meeting is good for getting out a lot of information at once, but the podcast is more personal. It's often viewed on a desktop system or on a personal media player and the employees tend to pay more attention. Don't tell me you don't drift off when the sales folks start talking about their exciting new CRM (customer relationship management) system.

CEOs don't have to have a monopoly on the short-format video blog. In fact, the more departments that get involved in regular postings, the more likely people will stay tuned in and listen to what's posted next. The key is to keep it brisk and informative. Droning on and on about dry policy changes is a good way to turn people off. Think creatively about how best to communicate all kinds of content, even the dry stuff so that people don't tune out.

The fact is, we've all become media consumers and simple things such as corporate communications have to compete with the deafening din that surrounds people. We have become selective about what we are willing to let in. TiVo has proven that people want to control what is marketed to us, and employers have to remember that there are a lot of things that are vying for people's attention. It's incumbent upon the corporation to recognize their need to provide communications that people will consume without threat of brute force or a pink slip.

Demonstration Videos

Instructional videos are useful not only to new-hires, they can help get existing employees up to speed on new safety and security issues, technical instructions and operational practices.

Most corporate environments have three methods for getting people up to speed on "how things work":

1. Direct instruction and documentation
2. Peer assistance
3. Do it yourself (DIY)

The last two are less than optimal ways for people to learn the ropes. The simple things people take for granted in the workplace are foreign to people new to the business, as well as employees changing offices or jobs within the organization.

The blogging format lends itself to informal but instructive presentations. For example, most people don't need to know the gory details of the multifunction copier, but they do need to know how to copy, collate and print double-sided. All it takes to clear up the mystery is an administrative assistant, a video camera and 3–5 minutes of live demo. That's all most people need, yet the act of instruction has to take place over and over again, thousands of times as that knowledge is passed on. Rather than lose all of that productive time, do it once, tape it and make it available in the archive.

Finance can do the same for expense reports and capital expense requests; HR can do it for filling out vacation requests and leave of absence information; IT can do the same for checking Web mail, or what to do when "the network is down"; security can make short videos on not letting strangers into the building, asking for assistance to your car at night and filing out a theft report.

There are no departments in an organization that can say they think everyone in the business knows everything they should know. There is a way to get the information to people and it does not need to come in the form of a bound tome of pedantic and condescending legalese. This is an opportunity for departmental leaders and technical ground-level people to show that the human side of the company is looking out for them.

Publicity, News and Commercials

There is a special level of disconnect an employee feels when their company runs a new commercial and they only find out about it by sitting in front of the TV and seeing it by chance. People want to feel more connected to their company, and by showing previews and offering archives of the publicity and advertising aspect, the company can allow their staff to feel included in the goings on. When someone works for months and months on a project that "means so much to us all," only to be left in the dark once their part is done does nothing to inspire them. Getting the most out of people takes sensitivity to their needs and being informed of things like media mentions, new commercials, and other public video and audio clips can engage and fire up the people that work to make the end product.

External Communications

Companies from a broad range of industries can create a more dynamic customer experience for their products, support functions and publicity through the use of podcasting or video blogging. There is a compelling aspect to keeping an online archive of audio and video content kept in a linear function. Super bowl commercials are often collected on websites and get huge traffic numbers. People may have seen something in a commercial and can't exactly remember a detail they were interested in. Through the video blog, they can re-run the ad. Interestingly, setting up an site will run less than the cost of a single airing of an ad on television.

Inside the Industry

 As Apple has proven through their movie trailers website *http://www.apple.com/trailers*, people are interested in upcoming products (in this case, movies) and will even go out and download advertising content. When Adcritic.com offered up their archive of commercials to the public, they discovered a very large audience that was happy to browse commercials.

Although commercials may not be the height of entertainment content, a significant number of people are interested enough that there is a value in making content like that available through a vlog. Radio commercials fall into the same category.

Ads are not the only content that can add value for the customer. Customer support, often a large chunk of overhead can be overwhelmed by support calls, most of which are similar in detail. As stated earlier, videotaping tutorials, troubleshooting, configurations and posting them in a prominent place can reduce support calls by allowing people to help themselves. If self-serve podcasts and video posts can reduce calls by 5% in a support organization of 500, the value is clear.

ALERT Phone support can often be tricky, but with the use of video, things like locations of buttons, UPC codes, and configuration windows can be shown to people. Using a simple concept like "How do I make a video clip that shows someone how to do task X that is simple enough that even the most inept person can follow it?" can have a direct impact on the cost of support.

The concept can be applied to support pages that report on events such as outages, delays, updates, and other timely things. This model works even better in the linear format of podcasts and video blogs. For example, weather radar, traffic cameras, ski-slope conditions and ocean surf can be described, but seeing it completes the picture so to say. Even municipalities can get in on the action by posting city council meetings, city news and events, and tourist attractions for visitors interested in the city.

When companies connect directly with their customers in a more intimate way, they often respond well and with their wallets too. When announcements are made, they often come in the form of a press release. The press release is not going away, but it has fallen behind. Using product clips and CEO commentary puts a more human face on the communication.

Product managers can talk about exciting things coming up, HR can talk about the need for new positions and how to apply, sales departments can offer information on new outlets selling their products, and support can talk about their new customer support video blog. The human face this can put on a corporation is very similar to the commercials you see on TV where companies use their own staff to talk about how great their products are. This method is more direct and timely. That's the key, there is new information and people get a subscription to the feed. That kind of brand permeation is invaluable, as it's far less spam-like than newsletters which few people actually read and the feeds are controlled by the end user so no opt-out administration is required.

Potential corporate uses of multimedia blogging forms include:

- **Internal communications**
    - Keep employees informed of new initiatives
    - Disseminate internal training, demonstration, and sales, with increased employee uptake
    - Disseminate relevant external news clips to staff
    - Ensure employees see company commercials
    - Inform employees of media mentions
    - Create a video newsletter at local management level, to increase team communication and esprit
    - Replace functionality of "bulletin board" with more visual and audio interest

- **External Communications**
    - Improve press release production value and quality
    - Increase public relations message integrity
    - Put a human face on your company with a less "formal corporate" communication channel
    - Keeping customers in the loop with an alternative to the standard press release format
    - Serializing products in development to get people interested in it before release
    - Facilitate intra-industry communication outside of conferences

Conclusion

If you go to the magazine rack of a large bookstore, you'll find hundreds of magazines on more topics than you knew existed—and there's probably a handful of podcasts or video blogs on all of those subjects. Like blogs, multimedia blogs are unlimited in scope because almost anyone with a video camera or even a telephone can make one. With decent production values and good writing, small organizations can develop a large and dedicated following for their content.

You should really sample lots of podcasts and video blogs so you can get to know the undocumented conventions of the new format. You wouldn't want to craft your company's television strategy if you rarely watched TV. iTunes has a great podcast directory. Once you find a few video blogs that interest you, your search should get easier, as many provide a never-ending cornucopia of links to other blogs.

Offering multimedia content blog feeds to customers, citizens and potential clients offers a different kind of up-to-date chronicle that will always ensure that people feel closer and in-sync with things that matter to them. If people say something is missing, go out with a camera, shoot it post it and it's done. Low overhead and linear format works in a familiar news pattern (newspapers), freshness and content drive traffic, but the format allows for archival footage.

Keeping the message somewhat informal will allow people to feel that they're not being marketed to in a slick sort of way. We are bombarded by "fancy" advertising from all angles and this is an opportunity to get eyeballs through not being fancy, through being real. Whatever the message, however, it's often updated. Podcasting can offer a great outlet for media, news, publicity, support, company information or just plain entertainment.

Now that you've figured out something you might want to say, the next chapter will get into the software and hardware people can use to receive your message.

CHAPTER 4

Tuning In to Multimedia Blogs

This chapter is about getting your hardware, software and content to work together.

The technology universe is in a constant state of flux. As we get access to more and more bandwidth, disk space, and computational speed, the content keeps coming in at an unrelenting and ever increasing flow. Where we were once excited to wait a minute or so to view a choppy RealVideo stream in a postage stamp window, we are now downloading TV-quality video over our cable modems.

Our desktop and laptop computers are not the only ones benefiting from these advances; our phones, cable boxes, media-center systems and PDAs are also enjoying access to downloadable multimedia content. Mobile phones became more than simply a phone with a small cache of phone numbers stored in memory when manufacturers started to add interfaces and advanced features such as SMS messaging and Internet access. In fact, mobile phones are now supplanting PDAs, cameras and even MP3 players.

As mentioned in earlier chapters, *RSS*, or real simple syndication, is the language used by blogs to let the world know when a new post (or in this case, audio or video file) is available. In response, RSS reader-client applications called *aggregators* or *podcatchers* fetches these new episodes for later enjoyment.

This chapter will go through the various aggregators and RSS readers available today. You may be perfectly happy with viewing or listening to the enclosures right at your computer, but if you're one of the millions of people who can't leave the house without their mobile music or video player, keep reading.

This chapter serves several purposes. One is to help the reader get podcast content onto the device of their choice, or to choose a device that can get the content they want. The other purpose is to illustrate just how wide a range the potential audience is, and consequently, how many content formats a media blog may need to support.

This chapter covers:

- Receiving multimedia blog enclosures automatically
- Web-based aggregators
- Win and Mac clients
- Linux and friends
- Email-based clients
- Mobile clients
- Installation

Multimedia Blogs: Feeds and Enclosures

The basic technology for receiving podcasts is easy to explain: a blog has links to MP3s or video files, and special software automatically downloads these enclosures for later viewing. If you view a multimedia blog online, it's not that different than a traditional "rich-media" web page—basically it's a web page with audio or video in it.

To get the full benefits of the time-shifting and space-shifting content revolution that is overtaking the land, you need to get software that automatically *aggregates* your content, either gathering it up on a single web page for your perusal, or better yet, downloading it to your computer or mobile device so you never have to wait for it when you click play.

Each aggregator client is going to have its own set of unique (or not so unique) set of features and user interface. The user interface is a personal preference thing. If you like it, great; if not, see what else is available. The whole experience should be good and there are enough options out there that you can be choosy. Download a few, try them out and once you pick one, uninstall the rejects.

From a viewer's perspective, a multimedia blog involves four pieces: the RSS feed, the client, the enclosed media content, and a media player (see **Figure 4-1**).

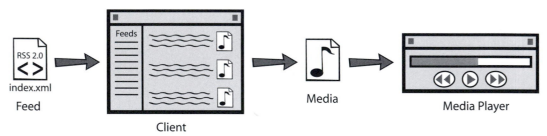

Figure 4-1
Four basic parts: feed, client, content, player

The basic process of subscribing to a feed, in almost all of these programs, is:

1. Find the RSS 2.0 feed (e.g., index.xml) and copy the URL (e.g., "*http://www.carhacks.org/index.xml*")

2. Add the feed to your aggregator by pasting the URL into your reader application.

3. Tell your software (as applicable) to "subscribe" (automatically download feeds and enclosures).

Finding the feed for a site may be very simple or quite difficult depending on the website designer. If viewing a website through a standard browser, most sites will have a cluster of their "feed flags" (**Figure 4-2**).

Figure 4-2
Feed flags

These flags are links to one of two things: the direct feed XML, which when clicked on looks similar to HTML code or a link that takes you to one of a number of web-based feed viewers such as MyYahoo!, Bloglines, Newsgator or PodNova. There are many more and the one you choose will depend on your personal preference. The link that goes directly to the XML code is meant for your client reader, i.e., *http://www.carhacks.org/index.xml* (see **Figure 4-3**) should be copied and pasted into the RSS reader.

Standard browsers frown on code they can't parse so they throw their hands up if no MIME type is specified for the XML by the web host. The reader on the other hand is happy to parse that XML code. When setting up any reader it will ask for a link to the feed. Sometimes, but not often, handing the reader a link to the main site will work. In most cases, that will just make the reader confused and it will tell them that no feed is available. Some readers can search for a good feed, most will not. It's best to give it what it wants so everyone is happy.

Author's Tip

Each application is going to require its own install procedure. Desktop/laptop installations are typically straightforward and only require running the downloaded executable. Mobile devices can be more challenging and may require syncing, rebooting or some sort of file transfer process. Be sure to read the install instructions—the instructions you generally ignore before clicking on the cool new download.

The application may or may not come with pre-loaded feeds. A good way to test out the device is to give it a few good, known feeds. Here's a small sampling of different types of feeds:

http://www.rocketboom.com/vlog/index.xml for a video feed;

http://www.cnn.com/services/podcasting/newscast/rss.xml for an audio podcast; and,

http://www.gizmodo.com/index.xml for straight-forward blog content.

If it all works and the files play, you're in business!

If the link points to one of the web-based RSS clients, it will take you to that client site, expecting a login or sign-up as a new member. If you only read feeds through Bloglines, for instance, a link to add the feed to MyYahoo! will not do you any good. If no link exists to add directly to your web-based reader (assuming you use that type), then go back to the direct XML link and paste that one in.

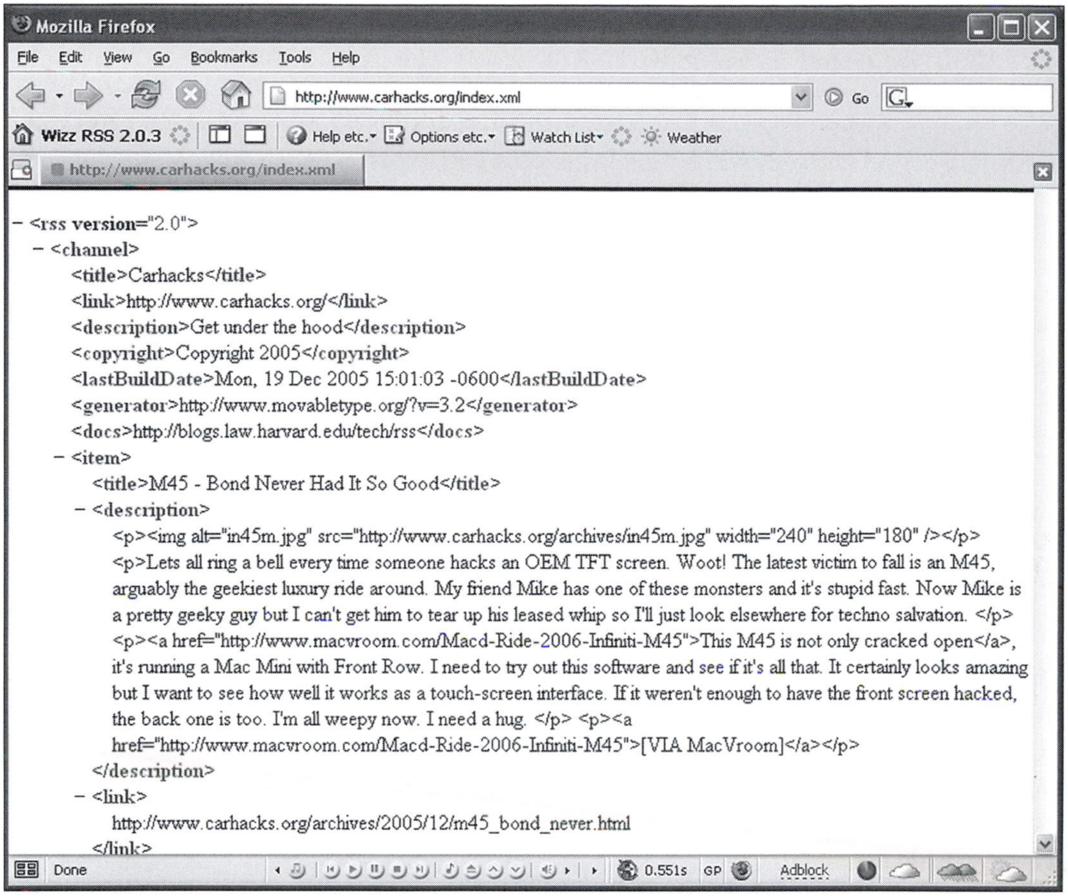

Figure 4-3
RSS 2.0 index.xml

Author's Tip

Depending on the platform being used to view the blogs, additional *codecs* (audio and video compression software) may be needed to view enclosure content. QuickTime is a native format on Apple computers but not Windows, and is very popular because of the iPod, so you should install that program first: *http://www.apple.com/quicktime/*. If you're on a Mac, the most popular non-QuickTime format you're going to see is Windows Media. You can get a Mac-centric player for Windows Media at *http://www.flip4mac.com/wmv.htm*.

If you think you have the right players installed and you're still having no luck playing back audio or video blog content, you might be able to find a player that solves the problem at *http://www.free-codecs.com*. They provide Windows-installer packages of codecs for most file formats out there.

Web-Based Aggregators

The fastest way to start subscribing to RSS feeds is to sign up for a web-based client. There are many different ones to pick from and at their most basic level they do the same thing. As mentioned before it's important to vet them for their RSS 2.0 ability, otherwise they will not be able to deliver enclosures and that defeats the purpose of subscribing to feeds such as Rocketboom.

Newsgator offers a simple, easy to use RSS feed aggregator that is happy to properly parse RSS 2.0 feeds. It can be populated by little "add to NewsGator" buttons, take a direct XML URL, or let you search for and select sites it has within its own database of sites. *http://www.newsgator.com* (**Figure 4-4**).

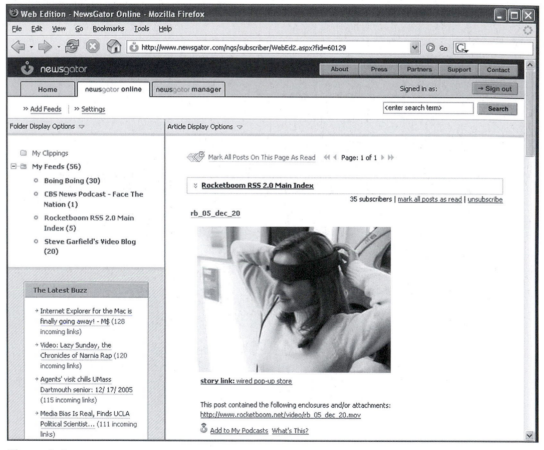

Figure 4-4
Newsgator

MyYahoo! was one of the first true personalized portals. Its very customizable content windows are a tweakers delight. Local weather, popular photos, news headlines, stock quotes, all in one places. (In fact Dan Libby of Yahoo! created the first version of RSS in 1999.) Yahoo!, not one to rest on its purple laurels,has greatly expanded its use of RSS across all its web properties. This is a great solution for those already familiar with MyYahoo! or people who want more than just feeds as part of their "digital dashboard" (**Figure 4-5**).

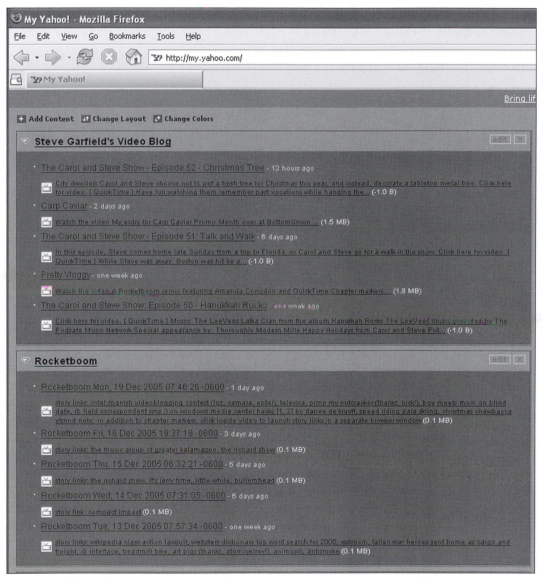

Figure 4-5
MyYahoo!

Bloglines was one of the first web-based RSS aggregators. Its simple and useful interface makes it easy to manage your subscriptions and download content. Enclosures are clearly marked, and as is the case with all web-based RSS clients, you can log-in and check your subscribed feeds from anywhere in the world (**Figure 4-6**).

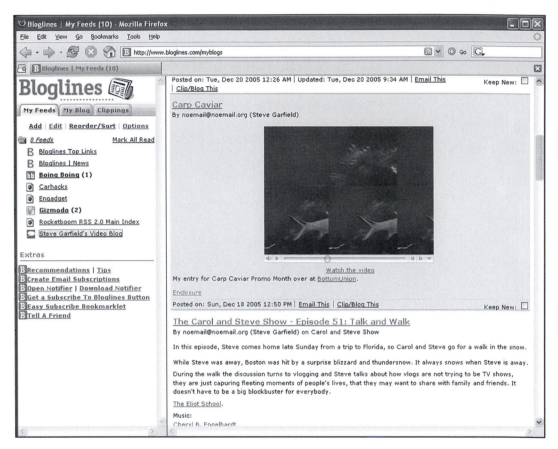

Figure 4-6
Bloglines

Never one to be left out of the reindeer games, Google has a web-based RSS reader. In typical Google fashion, they depart from the standard RSS reader user interface format and have devised their own take on it. The layout may be a little jarring for those with established expectations of what these clients should look like (**Figure 4-7**).

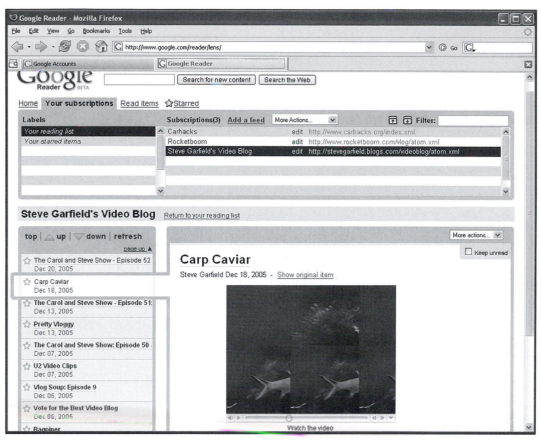

Figure 4-7
Google

When choosing a web-based RSS reader, it's important to feel comfortable adding, deleting, viewing and navigating within the client. Each one has its own look and feel. Some are more feature rich than others. At the most basic level, they all provide the same things, it's just a question of how you want it presented.

Local Clients

Client-side applications give you the benefit of being able to pre-download enclosures so they're ready for immediate viewing in fast succession. Where web-based clients demand that you click and wait, client-side applications pre-fetch your content and play it in an included window. It's a much neater and tidier process. Client applications have the benefit of being able to dictate finer points of the user interface giving you more sliding bars, adjustable windows and many tweakable options.

Once downloaded to your computer you can add and subtract feeds, save media and even take it along for a ride with your laptop with applications that gives off-line access to downloaded feeds. A long plane ride can feel shorter as you wile away the flight reading, viewing and listening to various posts you subscribed to and downloaded.

Applications like FireAnt and iTunes are available for both Mac and PC platforms, without much, if any variation between their respective operating system versions.

FireAnt (*http://www.getfireant.com*) established itself as a video blog RSS client. Its look and feel are similar to standard RSS readers, but it has built-in video and audio playing capabilities, which allows you to do all of your reading, viewing and listening from a single interface. Its built-in ability to pre-fetch your content makes FireAnt a useful tool for those with slower connections, although podcasts and video blogs are not optimized for anything slower than broadband connections. It's available for both Mac and PC platforms (**Figure 4-8**).

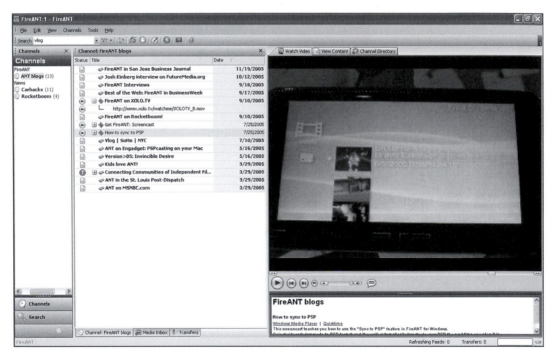

Figure 4-8
FireAnt

iTunes (*http://www.apple.com/itunes*) for Mac and PC has focused on the enclosures and cares little for the rest of the content. Videos and podcasts can be subscribed to, but the text part is not as easy to access. After all, it's meant to sync the enclosures to their product and their product isn't a text device. Adding a subscription is hidden in a menu under advanced, but once added, iTunes goes right for the XML and starts pulling content. It's great if you're on a hot connection and want to download everything, but it even manages your bandwidth, pausing downloads for shows you haven't watched and clearing out old shows you have automatically according to your preferences. Whatever it lacks in features it makes up for in sheer simplicity and ease of syncing. Its best use is for sites like Rocketboom where the video is the entire content (**Figure 4-9**).

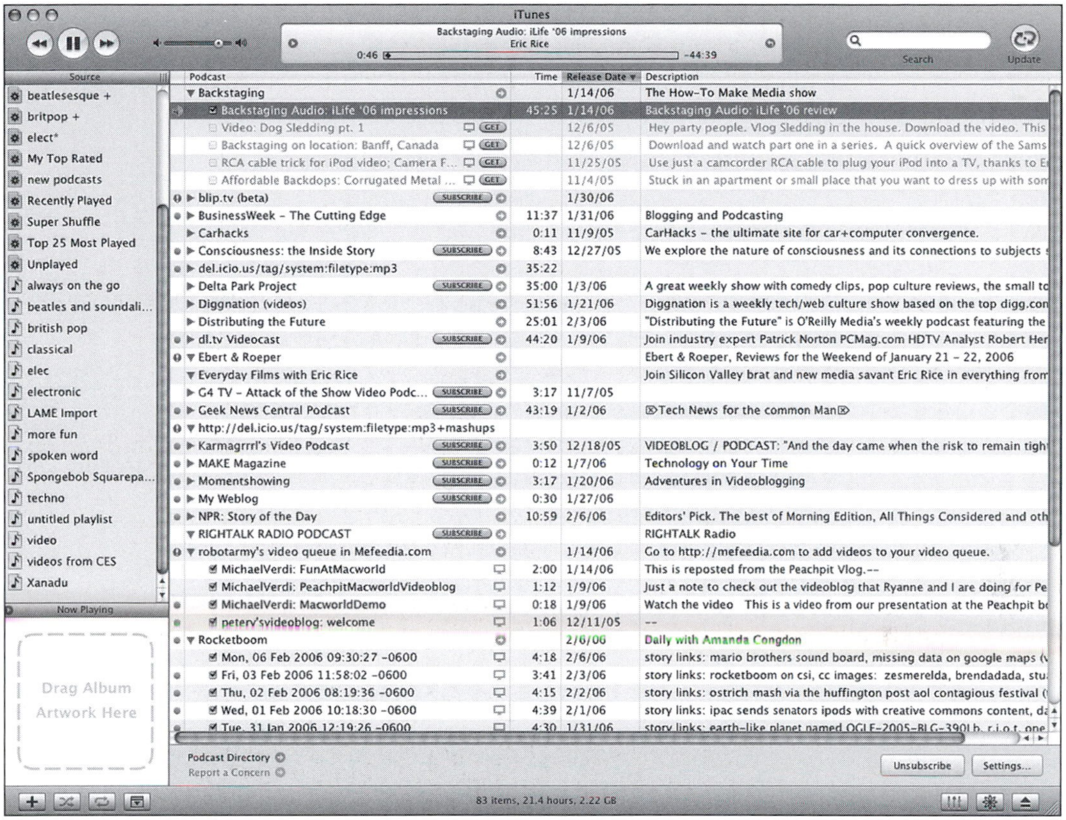

Figure 4-9
iTunes

Pluck (*http://www.pluck.com*) designed their reader to work within Firefox and IE as an add-on. This differs from readers like Bloglines and MyYahoo! in that the software and add-on is part of your browser application, headers and content is downloaded to the locally installed add-on. Working within the familiar browser allows you to jump in and out of blogs and standard web pages transparently (**Figure 4-10**).

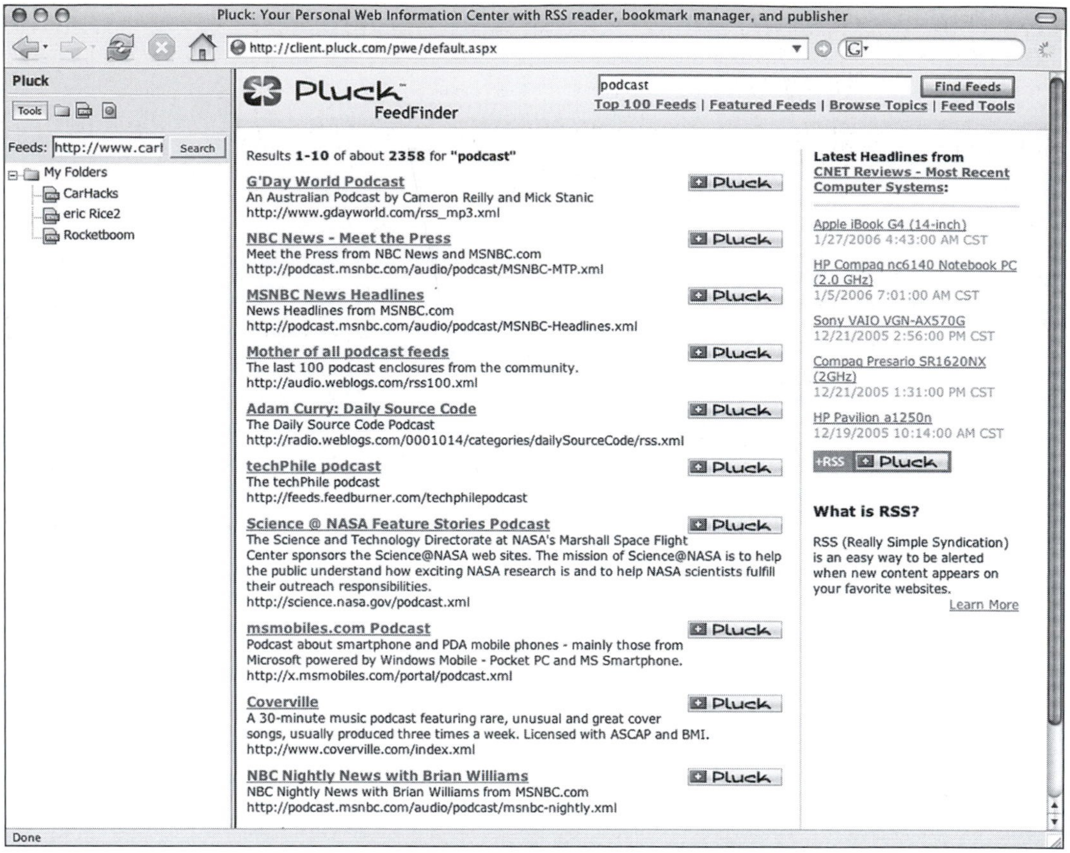

Figure 4-10
Pluck

jPodder (*http://www.jpodder.com/*) focuses on enclosures and the ability to integrate and interact with iTunes and Windows Media Player. The key here is that it simplifies getting the downloaded enclosures to your portable media device. jPodder comes in Linux and Windows versions.

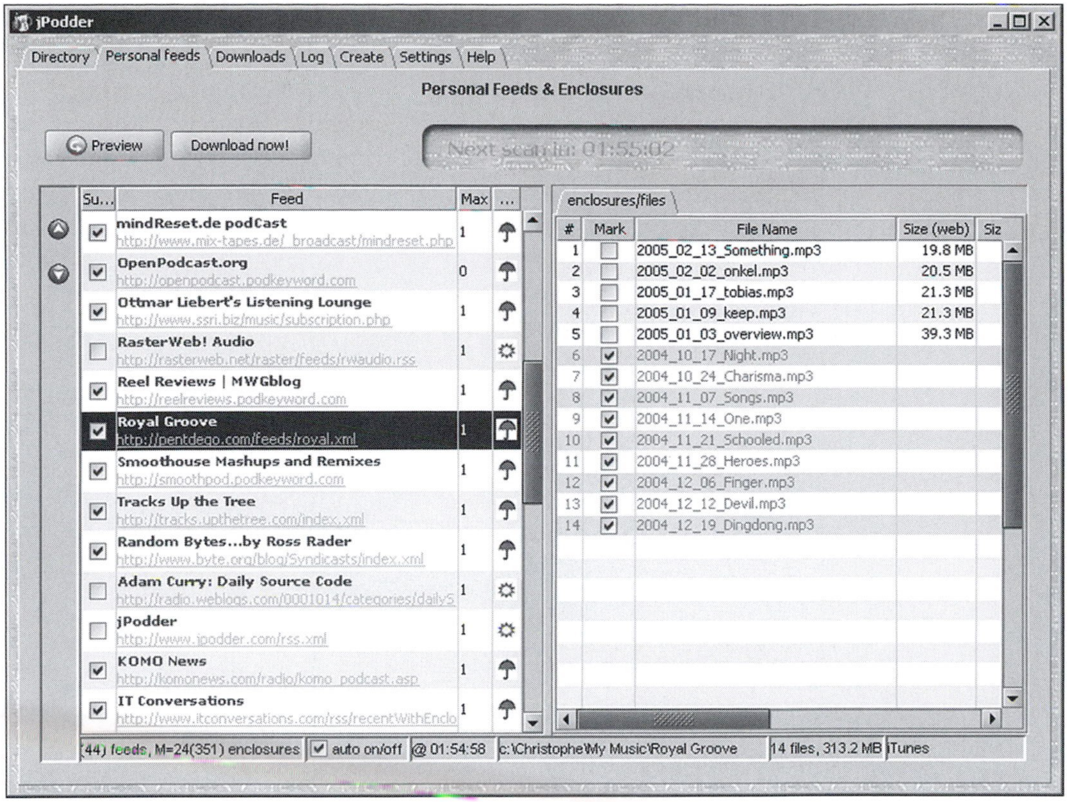

Figure 4-11
jPodder

Transistr (*http://www.transistr.com*) is looking for a fight. "iTunes, come out and plaaaaaeeeay." Transistr is challenging the incumbent iPod sync/music player/enclosure application to a feature for feature showdown. Interestingly enough, Transistr is looking pretty good against iTunes. Basic features such as the inability to read text within feeds and hyperlinks within show-notes leaves iTunes wanting. All of the features of a stand-up RSS 2.0 compliant reader and the ability to sync with an iPod makes this a very good choice for both Mac and PC users who want it all.

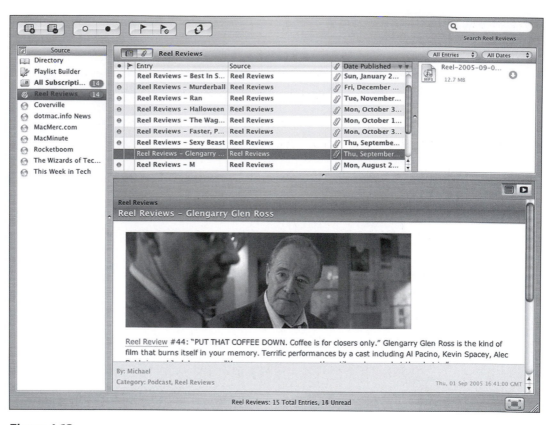

Figure 4-12
Transistr

4. Tuning In to Multimedia Blogs

Linux and Friends

If you lived in a Linux world, your car would have been designed by people from all over the world, working on separate parts, none of whom have ever met each other and likely never even spoke on the phone, yet when it was done, it would be the fastest car on the road and have the best gas mileage. Unfortunately, you might have to assemble the car yourself.

Good natured open-source taunts aside, there are a several robust and very professional looking RSS readers available for Linux/Unix platforms.

Lifera (*http://liferea.sourceforge.net/*) gives you the meat and potatoes, viewing text and downloading enclosures. (**Figure 4-13**)

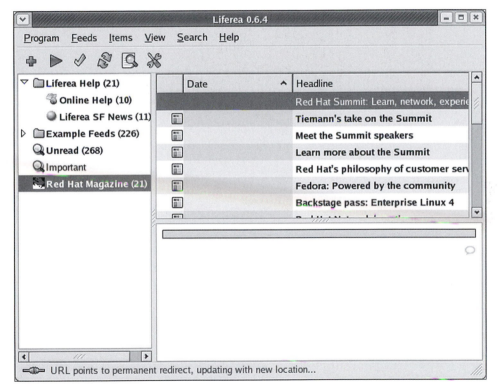

Figure 4-13
Lifera

Castpodder (*http://www.castpodder.net/*) is designed specifically for fetching podcasts on Linux. (**Figure 4-14**).

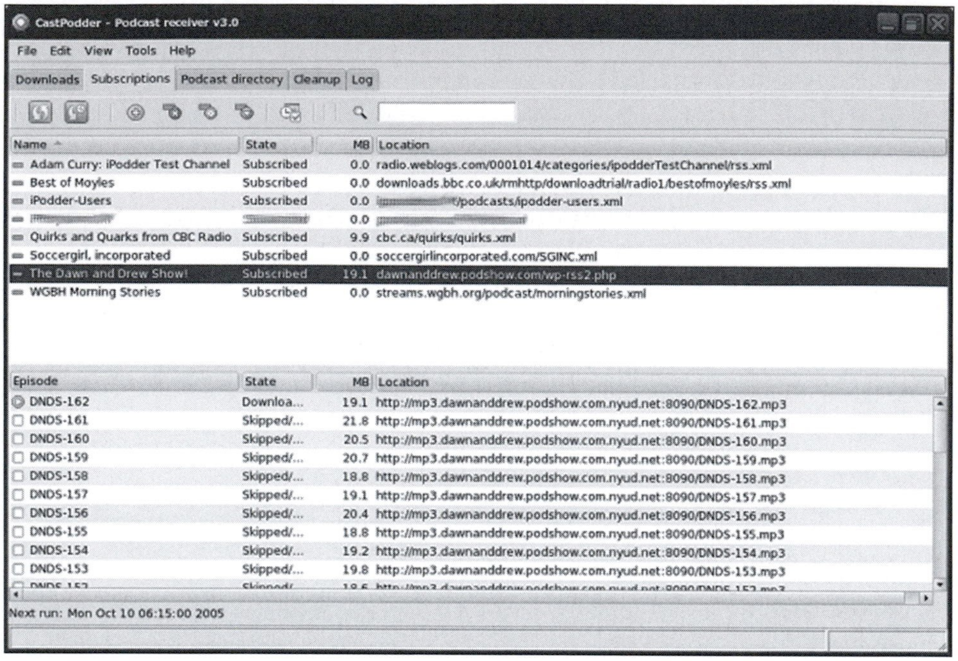

Figure 4-14
Castpodder

RSSOwl (*http://www.rssowl.org/*) wants to be one thing to all people, a robust RSS reader that handles enclosures well. Solaris users are in much the same boat as Linux users with regards to the dearth of applications for the desktop. RSSOwl comes in Linux, Solaris, Mac OSX and Windows flavors although it will be more of a draw to the Solaris and Linux folks considering the number of client options for Mac and PC. Its design follows the RSS reader template of panes, folders and links (**Figure 4-15**).

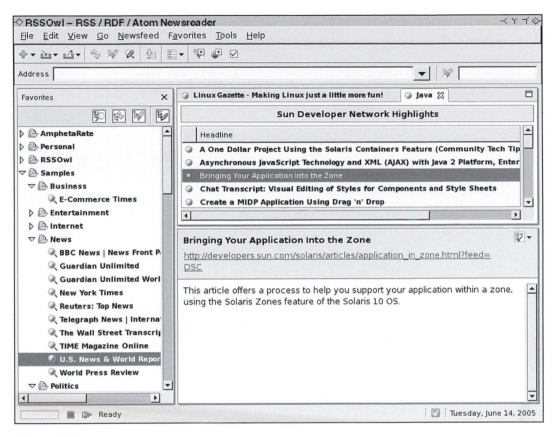

Figure 4-15
RSSOwl

Email Clients

Attensa (*http://www.attensa.com/*) brings all of the features of an RSS 2.0 client right into the familiar Microsoft Outlook application, allowing the obsessive-compulsive mail reader to stay within their soothing womb-like environment for blog consumption. Once installed, Attensa will be happy to download your enclosures and show your RSS feeds in the same way Outlook would display emails (**Figure 4-16**).

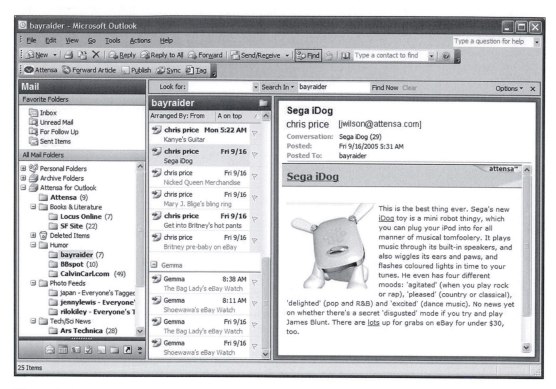

Figure 4-16
Attensa for Outlook

Mobile Clients

People on the go can't be stopping every 10 minutes to boot-up and download the latest Engadget podcast. As more phones include Internet connectivity and larger color screens, consumers are asking for pared-down ports of some of their favorite tools. Email, the killer app was first. Attachments begged for viewers and so came the avalanche of new features. Most smarter phones use one of three operating systems; Symbian, Palm OS and Windows Mobile. Each has its strengths and each implementation, unlike computer-based operating systems, is somewhat unique. Different screen sizes and resolutions, memory capacity and speed come into play.

Bloglines (*http://bloglines.com/mobile*) offers a mobile version of their web-based client that lets you have all the fun without installing software. It's a good option if the IT folks frown on you installing applications on company equipment.

FeederReader (*http://www.feederreader.com/index.html*) is a well-reviewed, full-featured podcasting client for the Pocket PC (**Figure 4-17**).

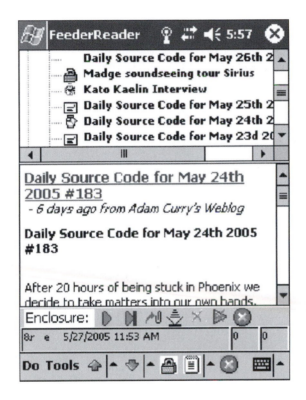

Figure 4-17
FeederReader

Egress (*http://www.garishkernels.net/egress.html*) is an extremely feature-rich RSS client. It plays enclosures, updates on-the-fly, and even offers a zoom-in function. Just because you hand in the laptop for a hand-held doesn't mean you can't have it all (**Figure 4-18**).

Figure 4-18
Egress

Author's Tip

The FeedReader website has a nice list of media players that you may need to play back video enclosures at *http://www.feederreader.com/mediaplayers.html*.

Small phone users need not suffer. Wildpalm offers RSS 2.0 client software for Symbian Series 60 phones called Headline (*http://www.wildpalm.co.uk/HeadLine.html*). What does that cover? More than 20 Nokia phones, and a handful of Siemens, Sendo, Sony, Ericsson and a few Nokia Series 80s. What might surprise you is that the software does support enclosures and can, depending on the phone, play them directly through the earpiece (**Figure 4-19**).

Figure 4-19
HeadLine

The handhelds with the most software under the sun are the Palm devices. The Palm 650 is a cult-like object that melds the functionality of a PDA with a phone and wireless Internet. The platform begs for a good RSS reader. As you would expect, there are many available, but Quick News (*http://standalone.com/palmos/quick_news/*) stands out. Like the other mini-readers, it offers fully-functional enclosure support and content pulling on the go. Palm 650 owners are not the only ones who can benefit from this software, it works on the majority of Palm-based devices.

Figure 4-20
Quick News

Conclusion

Given that podcasting and video blogging are, in Internet time, still quite young, it's encouraging (and telling) to see that aggregators are already available on so many platforms. From media center PCs, to iPods, to mobile video players, TiVos, and mobile phones, it seems like everything with speakers or a screen will soon be able to receive podcasts and video blogs.

The next chapter will go into more details on the new skills (such as RSS) that a traditional web designer will need to create rich-media blogs.

CHAPTER 5

Monetizing New Content Delivery Models

The purpose of this chapter is to go over the various successful ways that podcasts and video blogs are being *monetized* (MBA-speak for making money) today. And even if your podcast is not for profit, or is a marketing or PR initiative for an existing company, the concepts of audience scale, targeting, and advertising discussed here will apply.

You may not have money in mind in starting a podcast. Fame, artistic achievement, entertainment, marketing, PR, a desire to get a message out may be the real reasons behind your efforts. But, even if you have the money and resources to continue to feed and house your podcast, you may ultimately want it to grow up and start making a living on its own.

This chapter will discuss the business models for multimedia blogs themselves, as well as the ecosystem developing around blogs. It will cover:

- Success criteria
- Mainstream media advertising
- Business models for podcasts and video blogs
- Ancillary business models

Mainstream Media Invasion

Anyone even half-interested in keeping up with Internet technology trends has heard of blogs. What they may not know about is the tremendous technical and business influence these weblogs have had on the streaming media industry and how they are significantly changing audio and video delivery on the Internet.

The commercial Internet is now a mature ten years old, and we have reached the tenth anniversary of streaming media as well. RealAudio's first webcast ushered in an era of online digital media distribution, but that era has proceeded haltingly, and after the dot-com bust, the concept of creating original audio or video programs for web audiences seemed doomed.

In recent years, however, financial barriers have been falling at an increasing pace, and a few recent pivotal developments have opened the door to new technical distribution models and a host of new business opportunities.

When Apple Computer achieved market dominance in the portable music player market as well as the downloadable music market, and added "podcatching" and podcast capabilities to iTunes, they launched a directory of over 3,000 podcasts. That number is greater than 25,000 today. But more interestingly, Apple launched this service with a host of "mainstream" and free audio content from not only independent audio bloggers, but also mainstream sources such as ABC news, BBC, *Newsweek*, and ESPN. By mid-2005, audio blogging had now emerged as a viable mainstream form of radio program distribution.

Similarly, by the end of 2005, video blogging had taken root in the blog ecosystem. The major blogging tools began adding audio and video features; tens of millions of venture capital dollars began flowing to startups relating to user-generated video content, and several "video blog celebrities" had already been formed and were getting their first content deals.

Success Criteria

With online media initiatives, there are a variety of ways to measure success and not all of them are financial. For many years, streaming media has been largely subsidized by marketing budgets, for lack of a viable online pay-per-view model. The return on investment of streaming media has been largely calculated based on the viewership or listenership of the event, and the resultant press and PR coverage.

Now, though, just as the Internet-based audiences were growing large enough to support ad-driven video, narrowcasted podcasting and video blogging are making these techniques even more effective by reaching the audience more precisely.

But this assumes that all success is somehow financial. As the recent tongue-in-cheek Citibank ad campaigns have ironically illustrated, *human* interest is an essential and oft-forgotten commodity.

There is a dichotomy between the commercial and nonprofit proponents in the podcasting/ video blogging movement, but the same tension has existed for each of the Internet communication technologies that preceded it in recent years. Mainstream media stories, in their analysis of emerging communication technologies, bounce between the dual themes:

- "Look how *email* is changing the culture?"/"How can *email* be used in business?"
- "Look how *websites* are changing the culture?"/"How can *websites* be used in business?"

- "Look how *instant messaging* is changing culture?"/"How can *instant messaging* be used in business?"

- "Look how *blogs* are changing culture?"/"How do blogs fit into business?"

And so it goes. Each of these technologies changed the culture; eventually, each of these technologies also became a tool for business. In every case they eventually absorbed into the communication landscape and are taken for granted.

So it will go for multimedia blogs.

Inside the Industry

Keeping It Real

If you Google the term "video blog," you're likely to find the prominent positions occupied by blogs without a profit motive. The true pioneers, the nurturing mothers and fathers of the "vlogging" movement, have been promoting it since its inception for every reason *but* money.

Steve Garfield's blog, (*http://stevegarfield.blogs.com/*) includes a "Vlog Soup" sampling of popular video blogs, a very popular "real" reality show (The Carol and Steve Show), as well as politically involved calls to action and citizen journalism.

Ryan Hodson (*http://www.ryanedit.com*) and Michael Verdi (*http://www.michaelverdi.com/*) are some of the most active promoters of vlogging as a means of self-expression, of journalism, and documentary, creating what they call *social media*.

Along with Jay Dedman (*http://www.momentshowing.net/*) and Josh Kinberg (*http://www.joshkinberg.com/*), one of the developers of FireAnt, they created *http://www.node101.org*, a nationwide network of "nodes" where individuals can go to learn video blogging for free.

This quote on node101 sums it up nicely:

> "Media is a conversation, not a lecture. Active participation is required."

Ryan and Verdi also produced *http://freevlog.org/*, a site with an incredibly simple tutorial on how *anyone* can begin vlogging for free.

This kind of passionate energy for video blogging is remarkable. It has no business model, nor does it have an "exit strategy."

These are very commendable activities by some very commendable people.

And the fortunate thing is, while many new media of yesteryear were quickly co-opted and taken back out of the hands of the people, there's really nothing that can stop video blogging from being everything these pioneers envision it to be.

Mainstream Media Advertising

In looking at business models for podcasts, it is very useful to look at the world from an advertiser's point of view. If you are already familiar with advertising business models, this section will be very elementary. But if you are coming from a content creation perspective, it will help you better understand how to make a podcast commercially appealing.

There are many different advertising channels in the world today: Internet, direct mail, television, magazines, newspaper, and radio, not to mention billboards, tie-ins, various sponsorships, and anywhere a screen can be snuck in such as buses, taxis, supermarkets, and elevators.

When you subscribe to a magazine or cable TV, you may naively believe that you are the customer. But you aren't. Your *eyeballs* are the product, and the customer is the *advertiser*. As you know, broadcast television (in the US) is subsidized 100% by advertisers. All you need to do to pay for TV is to have a sex, an age, and a zip code. For instance, Forrester Research estimates that an episode of *Desperate Housewives* brings in $11.3M in advertising revenues, which means that each viewer is delivering 45 cents of value to the show just by (hopefully) watching the advertisements.

Even basic cable and satellite "pay" TV is primarily supported by advertising revenues. Premium cable is theoretically supported by viewer subscriptions, but only exists on top of an ad-supported basic cable service.

A similar situation exists in magazine publishing. While a few magazines are entirely subscriber driven, most rely heavily on advertising and many trade magazines are funded by advertising alone. And, if you've listened to commercial radio recently, you may notice how aptly named it is.

Thus you can see the goal of these media channels: deliver valuable content to build a large, happy, desirable audience, and then rent that audience to the advertisers.

Author's Tip

The other dominant methods of paying for content are subscription and direct purchase; whether it takes the form of physical media or a digital download. And in fact, Google, Apple, and many other companies are quickly developing their own online marketplace for digital media downloads.

Subscription models for online media have never fared as well as advertising. Nonetheless, there are examples of podcasts (such as *http://thisweekintech.com/*) supported entirely by "tip jar" voluntary subscriptions.

Advertising Lingo

Advertisers are in the business of selling products. Their job is essentially to convince people to buy goods, services, or ideas. Advertising is a part of *marketing*, which encompasses the entire process of developing a product, building awareness of the product, and building a large customer base.

Advertisements are specialized for different demographics. A demographic can be defined as a "group of like-minded consumers." In order to not have to create a unique message for each and every different consumer, advertisers lump large groups of people together and create a message that should appeal to the majority that group. For instance, you may have heard of the "18–34 Male" demographic, or the "soccer mom." An almost synonymous term for demographic is market segment. Carving up these segments isn't an arbitrary process; a good deal of statistical science goes into selecting appropriate groupings.

Traditionally, advertising has been delivered through a mass medium. In this term, mass means "large" and mass media (or mainstream media) are communication channels that reach the majority of a culture, country, or even the whole planet. In practice, that means that mass media reaches millions of people. CNN is an example of a mass media news program. Newspapers, considered together and getting news from the same sources, are a mass medium. Movies, television, nationally syndicated radio programs, magazines, etc., all make up the mass media.

Ad inventory is the term used to describe all the time slots or blank pages or banner space available for ad insertion. As a general rule, there are more advertising dollars available than there is good advertising *inventory* available to supply that demand. Ad inventory has a variety of characteristics, such as size, frequency, length, and reach (local or national). A particular magazine, show, network, newspaper, or website provides potential ad buyers with a *rate card*, a list of the various advertisement slots and packages they have available and how much each one costs.

How are these rates set? These depend on the type of ad, but for the most part, advertisers base their rates on the number of *impressions*, or individual viewings or listenings, the ads will generate. A radio station in a large city may claim that it has a million listeners, but if your ad plays at 3 A.M., chances are it will generate only thousands of impressions. Magazines, however, have a chance of generating as many impressions as there are subscribers and purchases, and then some—because the magazines may sit around on coffee tables and be read by others.

Being able to quantify and back-up what kind of audiences are getting these impressions is the whole name of the game in selling advertising. This is generally done through audience surveys. Be it magazines, radio, or television, systems have been developed to survey and sample the audience and then extrapolate those numbers across the entire population. For instance, the Nielson Media Research ratings system samples the viewing habits (through paid reporting as well as automatic tracking) of a small subset of the approximately 110 million households in the US. It then applies these surveyed numbers to estimate the total number of people watching any given show. With over 100 million households, shows that grab less than a million viewers show up with a zero percent rating *point* on the Nielson scale.

Off-line vs. Online Advertising

When advertisers look at a mass medium, they know that their message is going to get out to hundreds of thousands or millions of people. The more general the medium, the more the message has to be something with broad appeal, like potato chips or beer or razors or cars. Anything advertised in a national magazine should be something available nationally. National ads inventory is the most expensive, and thus is very useful for goods and services national in scope as well as major brand building. Some advertisements are merely to remind people "hey, we exist" and to reinforce brand names.

Local advertising media are less expensive to advertise in, and are naturally more effective for local goods and services. However, while a local commercial, print ad, or newspaper ad may be limited by geography, it is still a broad demographic.

Advertisers try to increase the effectiveness of their messaging by *targeting* specific demographics. The value of a medium's ad inventory depends on how well they can quantify their audience, and on how demographically clustered their audience is.

Here's an exaggerated example: Few men purchase cosmetics. ABC's *Monday Night Foot-ball* is highest ranked in the adult male demographics. Thus, advertisers do not put ads for lipstick on *Monday Night Football*. Similarly, *Oprah* is watched primarily by women. An advertiser trying to market a product purchased primarily by men would not purchase ad spots during *Oprah*.

These are broad demographic examples. A very specialized instance of a demographic and specialized ad inventory would be a trade journal for house builders. National brands like *Home Depot* might advertise in it, but they would probably ensure the message in the ad was written for building professionals, not do-it-yourselfers.

Traditional mass media (video, radio, newspapers) are referred to as *above the line* by advertisers. These media are characterized by their broad but fuzzy reach to consumers. Although above the line advertising can reach millions, it does it in a scattershot manner and can only target demographics, not specific classes of customers or market segments.

Below the line advertising includes more means of communication to the customer that have the potential for more effective targeting. Mailing lists, carefully culled from a specific group, such as "people interested in knitting," have always been more effective means for niche industries to advertise. While a television advertisement for yarn in a soap opera slot would probably find knitters, it might also hit a lot of nonknitters and waste impressions on noncustomers. However, a yarn catalog sent to a list of confirmed, card carrying knitting club members would see the highest possible return—assuming the knitters did not object to the advertisement.

Inside the Industry

There are a variety of terms for niche advertising—*narrowcasting* is often used to describe podcasting from the perspective of an advertiser seeking highly quali-fied potential customers of their goods or services.

Believe it or not, there is rarely enough ad inventory to supply all the willing buy-ers. And it is a well-remarked fact that Internet-based ad spending is increasing rapidly year over year, with online becoming the majority of many advertiser's allocation.

Podcasting and video blogging are a vast potential source of additional, quali-fied, and novel online advertising opportunities.

Business Models for Podcasts and Video Blogs

Unlike web pages, which were a brand new content form and medium, audio and video are well-established forms, and thus we are seeing a familiar medium in a revolutionary new distribution channel.

Like all new hyped technologies, we have to put podcasting and video blogging to the test: How do these new technologies make us money? Often times, the new technologies that everyone is excited about are not, in their own right, a business model or industry. This was arguably the case with the "peer-to-peer" technologies that emerged around 2000 (think Napster). Many businesses were started, but in the end, peer-to-peer was an enhanced distribution technology that lowered the costs of distributing media, not a sustainable new business model. Content distribution was the actual business, and standalone peer-to-peer businesses didn't make sense.

Video blogs and podcasts are different. They are more than enabling technologies—they are new distribution channels. And, because they lower the barriers to entry for content creators, they are potentially disruptive to existing channels. Podcasting directly to mobile devices is a tangible threat to both terrestrial and satellite radio. And video blogging finally delivers on the long-awaited promise of an Internet-based alternative to television.

Author's Tip

While economies of scale are necessary to fund blockbuster movies, they aren't necessary in the creation of niche content. In fact, the community-driven nature of podcasting and video blogging allows group participation and collaboration (in the form of feedback, or topic suggestions) that are absent in larger one-to-many mainstream media. This participation also possibly explains why a lower production value, as compared to mainstream content is completely acceptable. The community is to a greater or lesser extent guiding the outcome of the show.

Podcasting, video blogging, and blogs in general are very interesting to advertisers because they are a new and exponentially growing medium. Advertisers are looking for "eyeballs" (or earballs in the case of podcasts?) and whether these new media are taking away from TV and radio or simply adding to them, the advertisers want to be anywhere there is an audience.

The difficulty, so far, for advertisers, is the scale of blogs. Advertisers are used to spending large chunks of money to target hundreds of thousands to millions of viewers. However, most podcasts and video blogs target a much smaller audience—thousands to tens of thousands of viewers. The runaway success podcasts count audiences in the hundreds of thousands.

Inside the Industry

 One of the terms used frequently in discussing the financial opportunities in podcasting, video blogging, or blogging in general is the *long tail* (**Figure 5-1**). The theory is this: By plotting the audience or popularity of millions of pieces of content (such as the back catalog of a record label, or all the books available on Amazon, or all of the millions of weblogs), a number of items will rank extremely high (platinum albums, bestseller books, hit weblogs), and the majority of the other items will create a long "tail" with an exponentially decreasing popularity or demand curve. However, treated cumulatively, and properly aggregated, the volume of demand of this "niche" content can rival or even exceed the demand for the hyperpopular content.

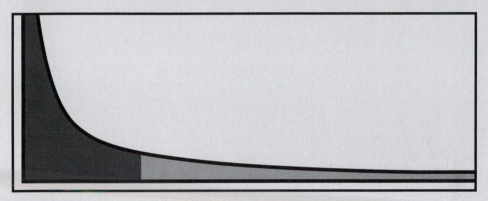

Figure 5-1
The long tail

New business models that can, through efficiencies of scale or digital delivery, supply large volumes of niche market content have a chance of making a viable business out of it.

The term was coined by Chris Anderson, Editor in Chief of *Wired* magazine. Additional information on the topic can be found at *http://www.thelongtail.com* and in the book *The Long Tail: The Radical New Shape of Culture and Commerce.*

The business models that have sprung up around these new content delivery systems fall into two basic categories: helping and supporting podcasters with tools and services, and the creation and monetization of original audiovisual content itself. In fact, as with any new medium, many of the ways to "make money in podcasts and video blogs" have more to do with the ecosystem and ancillary effects on existing businesses than the medium itself.

Original Content Creation and Licensing

The biggest opportunity for these new delivery models is in content creation itself. Never before has it been this easy or cost effective to launch a radio or TV show. The costs of professional audio and video production are as low as the cost of a good computer. (Arguably, Reality TV has actually lowered people's expectations of production value, making camcorder-based content edgy, cool and "authentic").

Brand new video news shows such as rocketboom.com are garnering hundreds of thousands of viewers and establishing a new format for online journalism and programming. The resulting media buzz about these podcasters is also helping to build market awareness and broadening the market. Newspaper stories are anointing these "new stars" of podcasting and video blogging and validating the new medium (regardless of the fact that it needed no such validation). Countless other shows such as Tiki Bar TV (*http://www.tikibartv.com/*) and Diggnation (*http://revision3.com/diggnation*) pop-up on iTunes, FireAnt and other blog aggregators, bringing their own huge audiences with them.

There are also some promising trends in the television space. Home theatre PC software from both Apple and Microsoft has the capability of downloading and playing video blogs and podcasts. Mobilcast (*http://mobilcast.com/*) is taking podcasts to mobile phones (**Figure 5-2**).

Audible has had one of the most effective and secure downloadable audiobook businesses for years, and TiVo has even begun adding delivery of video blog programming directly to their set-top boxes over a broadband connection—completely bypassing traditional delivery channels. Each of these systems has all the ingredients for direct sales of episodic content—digital rights management (DRM); tracking; customer information and a credit card. Most of them, notably Apple, have already demonstrated their ability to sell content directly to consumers, but have not yet opened that capability to podcasters.

Figure 5-2
Mobilcast

Google (*http://www.google.com*) is a notable exception. Although they don't have a hard-ware presence, Google was one of the first to launch a completely free hosting service *and marketplace.* Anyone can upload a video, and after it is screened for objectionable content, it is hosted for free, unless it becomes very popular, in which case Google will charge *viewers* a small fee to cover delivery costs.

With Google's entering the user-generated content hosting space, it is probable that Google's search and portal competitors will follow suit. (**Figure 5-3**).

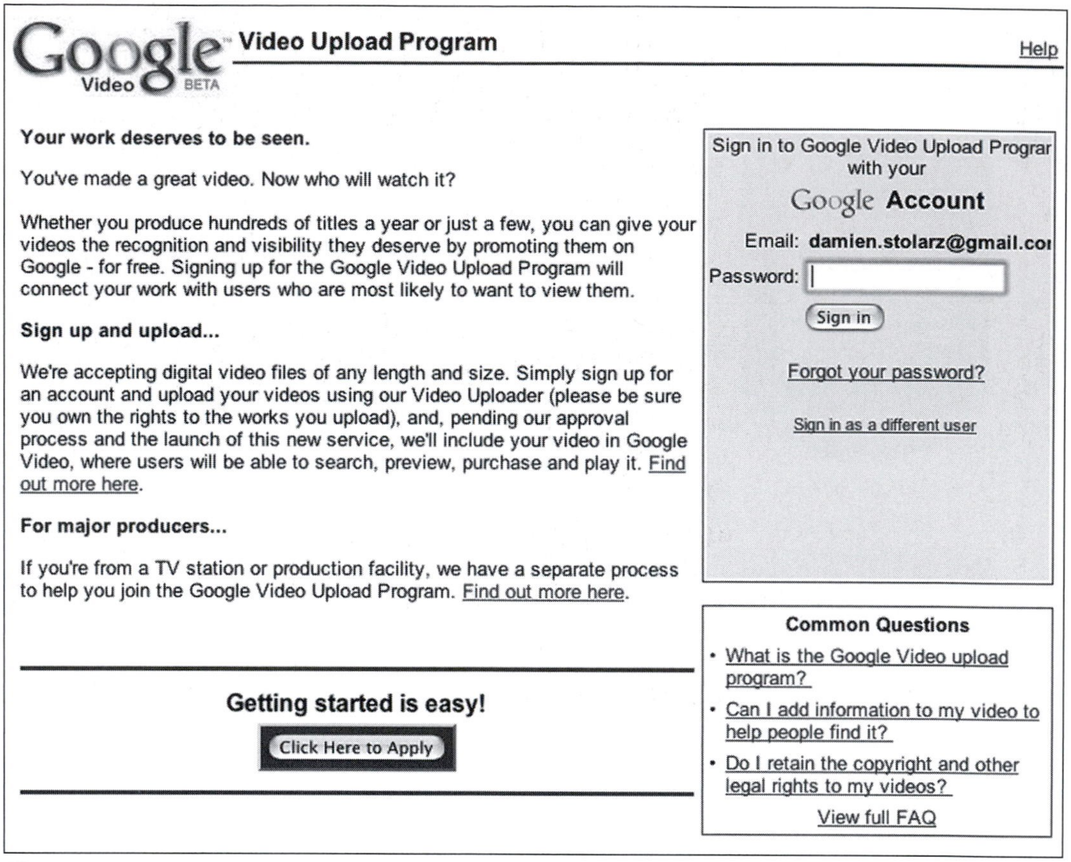

Google Video BETA **Video Upload Program**   Help

Your work deserves to be seen.

You've made a great video. Now who will watch it?

Whether you produce hundreds of titles a year or just a few, you can give your videos the recognition and visibility they deserve by promoting them on Google - for free. Signing up for the Google Video Upload Program will connect your work with users who are most likely to want to view them.

Sign up and upload...

We're accepting digital video files of any length and size. Simply sign up for an account and upload your videos using our Video Uploader (please be sure you own the rights to the works you upload), and, pending our approval process and the launch of this new service, we'll include your video in Google Video, where users will be able to search, preview, purchase and play it. Find out more here.

For major producers...

If you're from a TV station or production facility, we have a separate process to help you join the Google Video Upload Program. Find out more here.

Sign in to Google Video Upload Program with your
Google **Account**

Email: **damien.stolarz@gmail.com**
Password: [   ]

(Sign in)

Forgot your password?

Sign in as a different user

Common Questions
- What is the Google Video upload program?
- Can I add information to my video to help people find it?
- Do I retain the copyright and other legal rights to my videos?

View full FAQ

Getting started is easy!

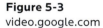
Click Here to Apply

Figure 5-3
video.google.com

Right now, the direct payment possibilities of all these services are in their infancy. The focus today seems to be on stabilizing the technology.

But all of these early efforts point to a future where audio and video content can be created—and monetized—without satellites, cables, or circular disks.

Launchpad to Mainstream Media: "Getting Signed"

One of the business models of video blogging and podcasting is to "get signed" (or "sell out" for the cynical) to a greater or lesser degree.

There is endless debate about the existence of mass untapped and unsigned "talent." Even if you discount this, most professional actors and performers have months of downtime that could be utilized. Combine the never-ending demand for high-quality content and a new, inexpensive means of reaching and building an audience, and there is a whole new way to get original content projects greenlighted.

One indirect use of podcasts for revenue is to distribute podcast content for free, building a large audience of viewers, and then go mainstream by signing a content distribution deal with a mobile phone carrier. Most new mobile phones are shipping with multimedia features, and mobile content consumption is a big part of most carriers' future revenue plans. This is quickly creating a market for speech-based audio and short-form video content—just the kind of content that podcasters specialize in.

Several years ago, the MP3 and P2P evolution lowered the barriers to entry for independent musicians, and sites such as CDBaby (which does on-demand pressing of one-off CDs) permit musicians to exist at any scale. In many ways, the content efforts and growing pains of podcasters and video bloggers are analogous to those of unsigned artists and local bands. They release albums; they build a following; they refine their content through interaction with their audience. They find areas where they can make some money, so they can keep doing what they love. And for some, they hit it—get "discovered"—as the audience they've built becomes interesting and valuable to an existing mainstream content provider or label.

Advertising vs. Subscription

There are many potential ways to leverage podcasting. Streaming media has long been used as a relationship-building and marketing tool. Unfortunately, brand promotion is a better way to spend money than to make it. For right now, the primary method of making money with podcasts is advertising.

For the first several years of the commercial Internet, many wondered whether it would be subscription or advertising models that funded content-based websites. For the most part, advertising won, with subscription models coming in a distant second. People are used to getting online information for "free," and many online businesses have failed in an attempt to ignore this expectation.

Although a number of "walled garden" subscriber-supported sites exist, the majority of web sites are focused around collecting demographic information and using this to enhance their ability to sell advertising. And podcasting follows this tradition. But there are several major differences between podcasts and traditional media that make them uniquely interesting to advertisers.

Inside the Industry

Podcasting vs. Traditional Media

Although many television shows have an associated website, the TV set is the primary destination. With podcasts, however, there is a strong web-based community relationship between the audience and the show. Many podcasts and video blogs grew out of and maintain an associated text-based blog, and blog software allows audience members to give feedback on each show. This feedback loop is immediate and very accurate.

No Nielsen ratings or statistical extrapolation is needed to find out fairly precisely how many downloads a show had. And this information is available in real time—as soon as a show is downloaded, these statistics can be analyzed. There are a few blind spots: with shows that are automatically downloaded by aggregators, there is no mechanism (yet) to track whether it has been watched, but solutions to even this problem are being actively developed by the podcasting software authors and portable media device manufacturers.

Advertisers have been shifting a majority of advertising budgets from traditional media such as magazines, radio, and TV to Internet in increasing numbers, and podcasting is likely to accelerate that trend. Podcasting can make up in targeting what it lacks in volume. Narrowcasting to groups of thousands of like-minded audience members, with their tight demographic clustering, can provide a captive audience of great value to advertisers. In traditional media, it usually takes millions of viewers or hundreds of thousands of listeners to keep a show supported. But podcasts with only ten thousand listeners have been able to generate meaningful advertising and sponsorship revenues.

There was a long period of time when Internet-based CPMs (cost per mil, or thousands, of ad impressions) were wildly variable, as usual in any immature market. Click-throughs, banner ads, and interactive Flash ads were all new and hard to price under existing cost-per-impression models. This created confusion for advertisers and slowed their spending. Fortunately, companies are rising to the challenge of standardizing podcast ad rates, or at least the metrics in their rate cards.

Because many podcast and video blog ads are essentially the same as radio and TV commercials, they are inherently more familiar to ad buyers. Podtrac (*http://www.podtrac.com*) is one company that has come in to serve as a link between podcasts and advertisers. By precisely analyzing a podcaster's demographic and creating an industry-standard rate card for advertising and sponsorship, they are helping to formalize and standardize the rates that podcasters charge (see **Figure 5-4**).

Figure 5-4
Podtrac.com

Fruitcast.com is offering ad insertion and tracking for podcasts. They automatically add pre-roll audio advertisements to many podcasts, and then track when those are downloaded by listeners. They then sell this created ad inventory, across multiple podcasts, to advertisers. This allows advertisers to do a smaller number of more expensive ad buys that they are more accustomed to. (**Figure 5-5**).

Figure 5-5
Fruitcast.com

Audible.com has introduced a new service, WordCast (*http://wordcast.audible.com/wordcast/*), which uses their copy-protectable and highly trackable audio format in podcasts. Audible's .aa format (similar to Apple's AAC) is supported by iTunes and the iPod and many leading portable media players. What is significant about their offering is that, for prices ranging from fractions of a cent to about 3 cents per listener, they will give you highly granular, third-party audited listener tracking and reporting. When .aa files are consumed on the computer or portable devices, the actual duration of the listening—including whether the entire program was listened to or not and whether ads were heard—is positively reported back to Audible. The feat requires the participation of many elements—the mobile media player, the aggregator application, and Audible's back-end tracking infrastructure. But the result is an unparalleled granularity in impression and program tracking, whenever the digital media player is connected to the computer. (**Figure 5-6**).

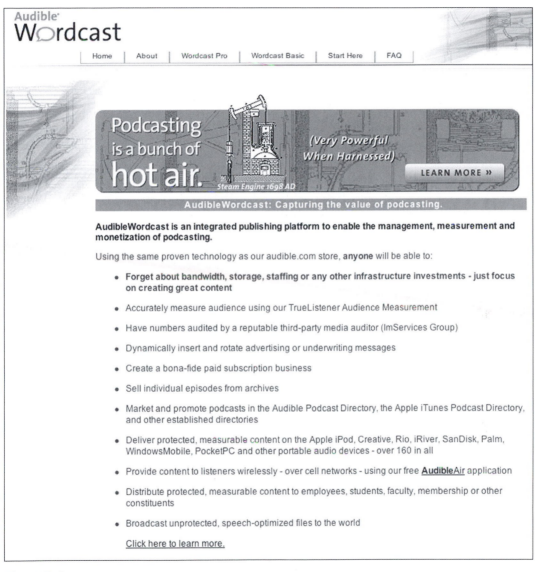

Figure 5-6
wordcast.audible.com

Revver, founded by Ian Clarke of earlier P2P fame, has a simple model of ad insertion for video blog monetization. They embed an ad at the end of your video ("Revverizing" it). You can then distribute the video freely wherever you want. When and if viewers click on the ad, this is reported to Revver, who collects revenue from the advertiser and splits the revenue 50/50 with the video poser. If an affiliate helps, by hosting or providing viewers to the video, they get 20% of the transaction as well. (**Figure 5-7**).

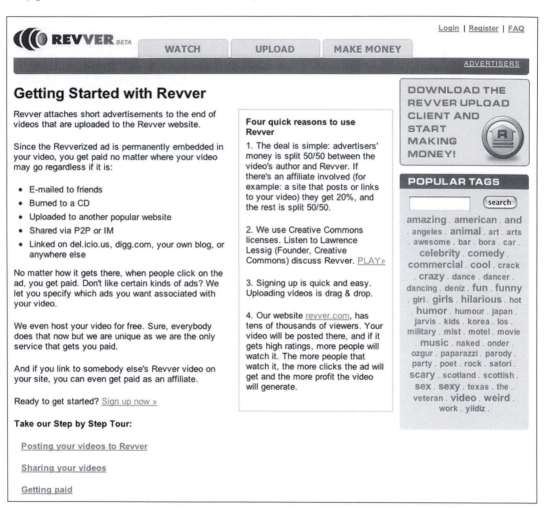

Figure 5-7
Revver

Sponsorship

Sponsorship is another method for monetizing podcasts. Part of the podcasting ethos, carried over from blogging, involves an authenticity and honesty with the audience. The medium has established a reputation for straight talk without hidden advertising. Product and service recommendations on blogs and podcasts produce results, because the audience trusts the personality behind the blog.

ALERT ! Many podcasters will not take ads or will only take ads for products they already use and recommend for podcasts. However, the upside of this is that podcast audiences understand that podcasters need to make some money, and are very tolerant of sponsorships.

Podcasters will speak about a sponsor's product (and how they use it) as a not-so-subtle but acceptable form of advertising. For instance, podcaster and video blogger Eric Rice (ericrice.com) integrates sponsorships from a variety of sources for software and hardware tools he actually uses to produce his shows. For his audience of fellow podcasters, his recommendations are highly regarded, providing him with many sponsorship opportunities and negligible audience backlash. Some podcasters will even speak honestly of the products' drawbacks to ensure they are not diluting their credibility, and smart advertisers accept this as a necessary part of utilizing the new advertising medium.

Tip Jars and Subscriptions

Veteran radio personalities such as Leo Laporte (thisweekintech.com) are transcending their old-media radio shows with the global reach of a podcast, bringing in over $10,000 a month through a *voluntary* PayPal subscription. Leo opted not to accept advertising in his podcast (which also airs on traditional AM radio), instead relying on a "tip jar," a link to a one-time or recurring PayPal payment to support the show (**Figure 5-8**).

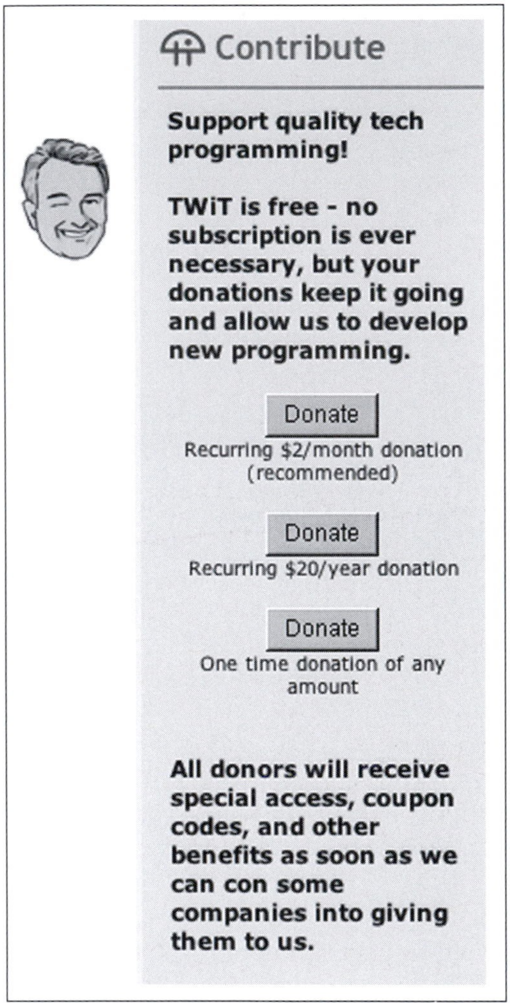

Contribute

Support quality tech programming!

TWiT is free - no subscription is ever necessary, but your donations keep it going and allow us to develop new programming.

Donate
Recurring $2/month donation (recommended)

Donate
Recurring $20/year donation

Donate
One time donation of any amount

All donors will receive special access, coupon codes, and other benefits as soon as we can con some companies into giving them to us.

Figure 5-8
TWiT's Tip Jar

The use of CafePress (*http://www.cafepress.com*) on-demand blog-branded merchandise, affiliate programs, and PayPal tip jars are well established for blogs, and have carried forward as a staple podcasting and video blogging funding approach.

Co-Opting Models

If a new medium is cheap and accessible to anyone, it's certainly easy for incumbent media players to enter.

Mainstream news outlets, already having finally embraced a proactive "blogging strategy," were ready for podcasts. Interestingly, the podcasts provide a means for traditionally print-only media, such as the *New York Times*, to begin producing audio content and extend their brand even farther outside their traditional scope.

Advertisers are also discovering the medium as the ultimate in opt-in messaging. BMW (*http://vodcast.bmw.com/*) launched a video blog, with full RSS support that allows customers to automatically receive advertisements that they asked for.

To build interest in the new *SuperMan Returns* movie, director Bryan Singer began an incredibly well-produced "behind the scenes" video blog throughout 2005.

The marketing, positioning, and branding power of podcasts to a fan base of customers are only beginning to be explored.

Ancillary Business Models

Many aspects of podcasting and video blogging leverage the existing streaming media business infrastructure: audio and video hardware, software, A/V production, storage and hosting. Some aspects are new or require a complete revisit of traditional services: aggregation, advertising, tracking and reporting. And most importantly, because these new channels have distribution costs orders of magnitude lower than radio and television, there is an early window for a number of runaway successes in original content creation.

Production Tools

Podcasts are essentially radio programs. They are listened to on computers but more usually on portable media players. The production process before audio engineering is primarily the same, so goods and services that targeted the radio industry have a great deal of potential growth in consumer radio production.

Because anyone can "create their own radio station," the amateur and prosumer audience for microphones, audio equipment, audio engineering, and other technologies is rapidly increasing. However, because the delivery format is MP3 and not FM radio, the audio engineering required to get the best sound is different. Thus, new business opportunities exist in helping podcasters create the best sound for their podcasts.

Similar opportunities exist in video production. Low-cost tools that accomplish what the "big boys" use to produce popular television content will find a much larger audience. As in any mass-production situation, a vast increase in potential market will enable price drops and bring semi-professional equipment down to consumer prices. The popularization of the medium and the potential for anyone to make their own "Daily Show" will doubtlessly increase the sales of greenscreens and chroma-keying software in the near term.

Hosting and Bandwidth

One of the major side effects of time-shifted audio and video (see the sidebar: the Return of Downloads) is that podcasts, and to some degree, video blogs are extremely insensitive to bandwidth problems. That means that the extensive (and expensive) multicontinental networks built-up by premium content delivery networks are largely unnecessary to support a podcast. In fact, in many cases, all that is needed to host a podcast is reliable bulk bandwidth. Flat-fee hosting providers such as Cogent (cogentco.com) and providers that sell "dumb pipes" are completely sufficient for podcasts.

ALERT A small consumer podcast could easily be hosted on the bandwidth of some cable modems or fiber to the home connections. When any commercial reliance upon these new media enters the picture, server uptime is critical—and it isn't free. Only a hosting solution with 24/7 support and a satisfactory service level agreement of guaranteed uptime will be suitable for most commercial podcasts.

It's also worth noting that not all video blog and podcast audiences will be time shifting their content—in fact, most blog-based audiovisual content still has a large portion of its audience experiencing it directly from a Web page, through *progressive download* (watching while downloading). If the majority of the audience is likely to come directly through the web page and not through iTunes or some other RSS podcatching solution, it still increases audience satisfaction to have a good video-hosting or content delivery partner.

One of the biggest challenges to streaming media in the past has been the "paradox of popularity." Most hosting companies charge *more*, not less, when more bandwidth is consumed, sort of like going over the minutes in a mobile phone plan. Fast growth of a podcast's audience usually results in an insurmountable bandwidth bill. Some hosting companies (Liberated Syndication (libsyn.com) is a prime example) have begun experimenting with flat fee hosting models—charging a based on storage, regardless of the popularity of the podcast.

About a dozen new aggregators and hosting services, funded with new venture capital, are even willing to host this content for free (or for a paltry sum) in exchange for access to the content and some rights to capitalize on it. Nonprofits such as ourmedia.org will host audiovisual content for free if it is made available under appropriate licenses, several of which permit commercial use of the hosted file. But many standalone video blogs and podcasts are not interested in giving up licensing, advertising, or distribution rights to their content in exchange for bandwidth.

So although a comprehensive global content delivery network is not needed, quality bulk bandwidth, skilled system administration and new, more granular and less explosive billing plans are. There may be a lucrative angle for smaller ISPs and collocation facilities to begin specializing in podcast and video blog hosting.

Inside the Industry

The Return of Downloads

Since the dawn of connectivity, there've always been two kinds of content: interactive content that you can get right away, and downloaded content you have to wait for. In the "waiting" category there are two basic kinds of wait: get-a-cup-of-coffee waiting, and let-it-download-overnight waiting. In the early 1980s, text chat and forums were "real time," but downloading programs took a while. By the 1990s, AM-quality streaming audio was instant, but CD-quality audio required a download. Today, many audiovisual experiences are a click away, but DVD quality movies and television shows still have to be queued up for overnight download.

Just a few years ago, comparisons between television broadcast and Internet delivery would declare TV the clear winner every time. Television delivers hundreds of high-quality channels in real time. The only way to serve high-quality content over an Internet connection is to make viewers suffer a lengthy download. The only way to provide Internet viewers with "instant gratification" was with costly streaming servers and lower quality versions of the content.

Today, the advantages of streaming over downloading (real-time content delivery and slightly better content protection) are losing relevance as consumer content consumption habits change. With the advent of digital video recorders, people are becoming so acclimated to time shifting that the difference between TV and Internet video experience is blurring. Shows are often watched a day or two later than they air. When combined with program guides and automated downloading, the Internet video experience can be just as convenient and high quality as a personal video recorder. The estimated one-third of Internet traffic made up by audio and video file downloads over P2P networks is a testament to this fact.

Software Tools
While a large number of consumer applications exist for video editing and music recording, these applications mostly focus on producing DVDs and CDs as their output. The process of producing audio and video and getting it uploaded it to blog hosting sites in the right format is a complex process for the average blogger.

Although the big players in blogging software are already established, the opportunities to create add-ons that work with these services abound. One company (videoegg.com), created a web-based plug-in that simplifies video blog creation and integrated this with the leading blog hosting software. With dozens of blog creation software packages and perhaps thousands of blog hosting services, each with their own community of users, providing audio- and video-blogging tools to the millions of active bloggers is a sizable opportunity.

Conferences, Books, and How-To Guides
Cynically speaking, it is often the conference companies and early publishers that make the most on new technology fads. However, podcasting and video blogging are a permanent part of an emerging mobile media landscape and aren't likely to vanish as last year's news. Thus, there is a good deal of profitable work to be done in evangelizing these new technologies and educating people in their effective use.

Go to Amazon and type in the keywords "podcast" or "video blog". You'll find, among a plethora of books (including this one), several downloadable e-docs, including other articles on the subject, available for purchase. This is another way that people are monetizing rich media blogs.

Search Engine Optimization
Even the SEO (search engine optimization) industry has jumped on board, and are exploring ways on how they can increase traditional web traffic by exploiting the new medium.

Another popular angle for getting on the bandwagon are the number of informative guides about how to drive traffic to your site using podcasts and video blogs.

Aggregators, Search Engines, and Portals
Search engines and web portals are rather mature Internet industries and a new entrant had better have a clever new twist to break into these. But new technologies beget new market entrants, and while "we're a search engine—but for podcasts" may become a start-up's epitaph, there are a variety of promising portal plays in this new media playground.

Podcatching and mediablog aggregation will quickly become a feature on almost any portable media device, but there are plenty of opportunities to be found in "digital plumbing," the dirty work of getting all this content converted to the right formats for the myriad of personal devices (from video iPods to Playstation Portables to new home consoles and media center PCs).

With the new medium, an influx of pure content creators has come that don't want to worry about the mechanics and just want to get their content to a large audience. In this area, quite a few start-ups have come up to collect and aggregate user-created content and give these individuals their 15 megabytes of fame.

Many popular blogs and podcasts are focused on a particular topic or area. The same web-based evolution of consolidating these niche portals into comprehensive but focused content offerings can be repeated in the audiovisual space. Niche-focused websites can begin expanding into podcasting or video blogging, either by creating new audio and video content or by simply finding relevant podcasts and striking revenue-sharing deals with their creators.

The same ecosystem of tagging and rating services that grew up around blogs has plenty of growth opportunity in this new blog-based audiovisual media. And the differences between blogging, podcasting, and video blogging present opportunities for these services to specialize their product offerings for both the creators and consumers of these media.

Because of the long and deep tradition of audiovisual content creation, the most likely candidates to try to co-opt and "own" the new medium are the incumbents—television and movie studios, radio and television stations, cable and satellite companies—anyone with capital who has long controlled the creation of new media and who can turn on a firehose of original content without much effort. The other likely suspects are the Internet giants—the Googles, Yahoo!s, Apples and Microsofts of the world who would love to steal the distribution business from these incumbents. Although charging with these elephants is not for the faint of heart, it's entirely likely that a new company could own a meaningful piece of this new landscape when the dust settles.

Podsafe Music and Video

An interesting opportunity in the podcasting community exists due to outmoded licensing structures. In a nutshell, while a straightforward and reasonably priced music license exists for online *streaming* media, such as web radio, it is very unclear how to get a license to include big-label music in a *downloaded* podcast. As a result, the audio jingles and background music and the mood music for video blogs, must not be under RIAA restrictions, i.e., *podsafe*.

Unsigned bands, indie musicians, and other creators not under contract to a record label can produce high quality music and offer it under any licensing terms they want. An entire community has sprung up around aggregating and creating podsafe music for podcasts; a simple web search for "podsafe" will turn up a dozen or so music providers.

One market need that has not yet been addressed is that of podsafe video. Sites such as archive.org have large collections of older public domain video and some new Creative Commons media, but there are few (if any) commercial video stock footage providers with a pricing structure accessible to video blogging. This is another growing, yet untapped opportunity.

Conclusion

For companies whose core competency is not content creation, ROI may be measured in other ways.

Podcasting and video blogging are now a permanent feature of Internet media. Because they are new, there is a window of opportunity for content creators and the product and service vendors that support them. Although "mainstream" media have tremendous resources, their ability to co-opt the new channel is hampered by their unfamiliarity with the medium.

For every podcast with a direct profit motive, there are dozens more done for marketing, relationship building, or pure self-expression. Just as with blogs, the content is put out for free, and revenue is only sought once the audience grows and the bandwidth bills get too high.

Many experts have sounded off about what are "viable podcasting business models" and the consensus is that going up against Yahoo!'s, Apple's, or Google's podcasting strategy is a bad idea. Nonetheless, there is plenty of room for many companies to create the product and service ecosystem around blogging and podcasting.

Many traditional media companies are responding to the expansion of online media by creating digital rights management (DRM) systems to allow copy-protected viewing of their video assets online. But right now, there is no clear path to similar technologies for video blogs and podcasts. For the near term, the primary means of creating revenue and subsidizing the creation of these media is advertising.

Like every "new" technology, there are many precursors, and critics will try to point out how podcasting and video blogging are not new. In some ways they are quite right; for instance, online sites such as iFilm have had serially updated video for years. But to discount the revolutionary effects they are having on mainstream or existing media channels would be missing the point: technology standards and evolving consumer habits have combined at this fortuitous time to create an important, inexpensive, popular and rapidly expanding new form of content distribution.

CHAPTER 6

New Skills for a New Technology

Even if you're web-savvy, the learning curve for multimedia blogging can be a bit steep. This chapter is about the new technologies you'll need to be familiar with.

Podcasts and video blogs are built on blogs. Even if you've going straight to podcasting or "vlogging" and have no interest in maintaining a text-based daily journal, you'll need to learn about them. Blog directories, blog search engines, and blogging syndication are all used by bloggers and podcasters alike. And many blogs are now "hybrid"—a combination of text, pictures, documents, audio and video.

This chapter covers:

- **Blog Basics**
  - XML vs. HTML
  - Push technology
  - Enclosures
  - Streaming vs. downloads
- **The Blogosphere**
  - Automatic updates
  - Comments
  - Pings and trackbacks
  - Blog indexing and search ranking
  - Tags
  - Blog directories
  - Feeds revisited
  - Show notes and chapters
  - Web page embedding

Blog Basics

Blog is short for *web log*, a date-stamped, serial news and content distrubution and display format. Blogs can be viewed from a web page or special blog-reading software. Blog pages are served up by *blogging* software that runs on the web server. The two most popular blog applications are WordPress and Movable Type, but there are dozens of other blogging systems. Blog applications are similar to other database-driven websites like forums and content management systems (CMS).

Inside the Industry

World Wide Web

A web *host* is a computer, sitting somewhere in the world, connected to the Internet and capable of serving up web pages. A small company might have a single computer *hosting* their web page. A large company, such as Google, might have thousands of computers, in different locations around the world, serving up their pages.

Google's *URL* (uniform resource locator), *http://www.google.com*, points to Google's hosting facility and more specifically, to one of their web servers.

The mechanics work like this: Someone opens up their browser and enters a URL. Their computer looks at its own tables to see if the address is local, if not it asks a *DNS* (domain name service) server. The DNS server looks up the *IP address* or addresses that correspond to that server, provided by a *domain registrar*. For example *http://www.google.com* might get translated into *http://64.233.167.99* (Google.com translates into a different address depending on which of its thousands of servers will be taking that request).

Once the IP address is found, the computer can make a direct request for the default page. The default page is the page served up by the server on the other end when no page is specifically requested. In many cases the default page is *index.html*.

Once the page is sent back to your computer, the page is *rendered* (interpreted and displayed) on the client side. The page, made up of HTML, is processed by your browser. Inside the HTML are links to pictures, such as *http://www.google.com/images/google_sm.gif*, and these are retrieved as well by the web server, using the same *hypertext* transfer protocol (*http*). Links are requested; pictures are pulled and displayed in your browser.

Links inside the HTML page can be on the same server or come from some completely different server, which is called *hyperlinking* (perhaps named because its linking is all over the place?). This "hyper" linking connects all the web pages (or in our case, blogs) together in a metaphorical *World Wide Web* of pages.

Pages and Feeds

There are two main ways that podcasts and video blogs are consumed. In the first scenario, a web browsing human goes to the web page associated with a blog (such as *http://www.carhacks.org/podcast/*) and reads it. If there is audio or video in the blog, they then click the audio or video link. This causes the web browser to launch the appropriate media player (for instance, an MP3 player for podcasts, or a video player such as QuickTime, Flash, or Windows Media for video blogs—see **Figure 6-1**).

Carhacks Podcast

MARCH 20, 2008

StreetDeck navigation on sub-$200 ultramobile PCs!

StreetDeck's 2008 NAV solution is now available on the ultra mobile PC platform, you can take it in and out of the car. We recorded a demo of the nav system which you can see here.

Posted by dstolarz at 04:50 AM | Permalink | TrackBacks (0)

MARCH 19, 2008

Long awaited Prius "tribrid" SUV finally released - larger than an H4!

SEARCH

Search this blog:

[Search]

CATEGORIES

* podcast

ARCHIVES

* March 2008
* March 2007
* March 2006
* February 2006

RECENT POSTS

* StreetDeck navigation on sub-$200 ultramobile PCs!
* Long awaited Prius "tribrid" SUV finally released - larger than an H4!
* Interview with Chuck Holbrook, creator of Streetdeck
* Major manufacturers - GM, Ford - switch to Ethanol cars
* New BMW nav system uses telepathy

Subscribe to this blog's feed [What is this?]

Figure 6-1
A podcast webpage

Fundamentally, *podcasts* and *video blogs* are simply blogs with links to audio or video. In this podcast-as-a-web page scenario, there's not a whole lot of new technology here; the page is essentially a rich-media, database-driven website (**Figure 6-2**).

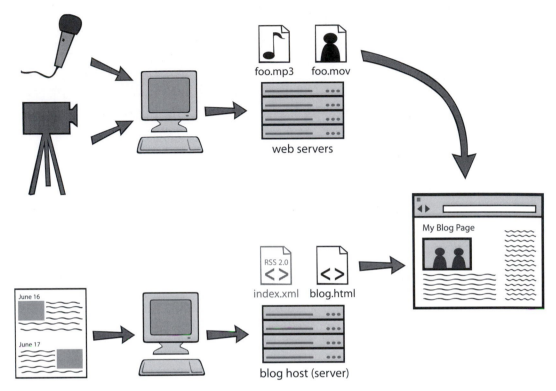

Figure 6-2
Multimedia webpage flow

Have you ever looked at raw HTML? You know, the text within brackets:

⇒   <title>My nice Web page</title>

HTML is used to "mark up" web pages and tell web browsers how to display a web page. Well, *XML*, the eXtensible markup language, is a human-readable successor to HTML that can be reliably interpreted by programs as well as people. It looks sort of like HTML but can be used to describe almost anything.

While HTML is great for web pages, XML is great for delivering structured data—lists, extra information, status updates—between computers.

At the simplest level, the HTML "language" is already specified and locked down, whereas in XML you can make up new bracketed elements to store and convey any information you want, such as <genre>Techno</genre>.

Because XML is so flexible, it is used to make new file formats, such as the news feeds that power blogs.

You'll see the term XML bandied about all the time, and then you'll hear about some other alphabet soup acronym being an XML file. Don't get confused by it all, just know that an XML-based file is a bunch of made up words in brackets that solve some computer communication problem or another.

The second way that blogs and multimedia blogs are consumed is automatically, by software, through a *feed*. In this case, a different URL, such as *http://www.carhacks.org/ podcast/index.xml*, provides a clean, uncluttered (to a computer at least) summary of all the pertinent information about the blog feed. All the graphical niceties, the frames, formatting, banners, bells and whistles are absent; just the facts remain. Modern web browsers, such as Internet Explorer 7, Firefox, and Safari are able to view these feeds and display them in all their stark glory. **Figure 6-3** shows the XML file for a feed, and **Figure 6-4** shows the feed as understood by the Firefox web browser.

```
- <rss version="2.0">
  - <channel>
      <title>Carhacks Podcast</title>
      <itunes:author>Carhacks Podcasting Team</itunes:author>
      <link>http://www.carhacks.org/podcast/</link>
      <description/>
      <language>en</language>
      <copyright>Copyright 2006</copyright>
      <lastBuildDate>Mon, 20 Feb 2006 06:50:40 -0800</lastBuildDate>
      <itunes:image href="http://www.damienstolarz.com/blog/carhacks.jpg"/>
      <itunes:subtitle>Because your car isn't good enough.</itunes:subtitle>
    - <itunes:summary>
        This is a lengthy summary. the reason it's so lengthy is because, well, i dind't have anything to say. So i just blathere
      </itunes:summary>
    - <itunes:owner>
        <itunes:name>Carhacks</itunes:name>
        <itunes:email>lionel@carhacks.org</itunes:email>
      </itunes:owner>
      <copyright>Copyright 2006</copyright>
    - <itunes:author>
        <itunes:name>Carhacks</itunes:name>
        <itunes:email>lionel@carhacks.org</itunes:email>
      </itunes:author>
      <itunes:link rel="image" type="image/jpeg" href="http://www.damienstolarz.com/blog/carhacks.jpg">Carhacks</it
      <itunes:category text="News"/>
      <itunes:category text="Video"/>
      <itunes:category text="Technology"/>
    - <image>
        <url>http://www.damienstolarz.com/blog/carhacks.jpg</url>
        <title>Carhacks</title>
        <link>http://www.carhacks.org</link>
      </image>
      <itunes:link rel="image" type="video/jpeg" href="http://www.damienstolarz.com/blog/carhacks.jpg">Carhacks</it
      <generator>http://www.sixapart.com/movabletype/?v=3.2</generator>
      <docs>http://blogs.law.harvard.edu/tech/rss</docs>
    - <item>
        <title>test mp3</title>
      - <description>
          <p>test mp3 is </p> <p><a href="http://www.damienstolarz.com/blog/test.mp3">link</a></p>
        </description>
      - <link>
          http://www.carhacks.org/podcast/2006/02/test_mp3.html
        </link>
      - <guid>
          http://www.carhacks.org/podcast/2006/02/test_mp3.html
        </guid>
        <category/>
        <pubDate>Mon, 20 Feb 2006 06:50:40 -0800</pubDate>
        <enclosure url="http://www.damienstolarz.com/blog/test.mp3" length="2708973" type="audio/mpeg"/>
```

Figure 6-3
An XML-based podcast feed

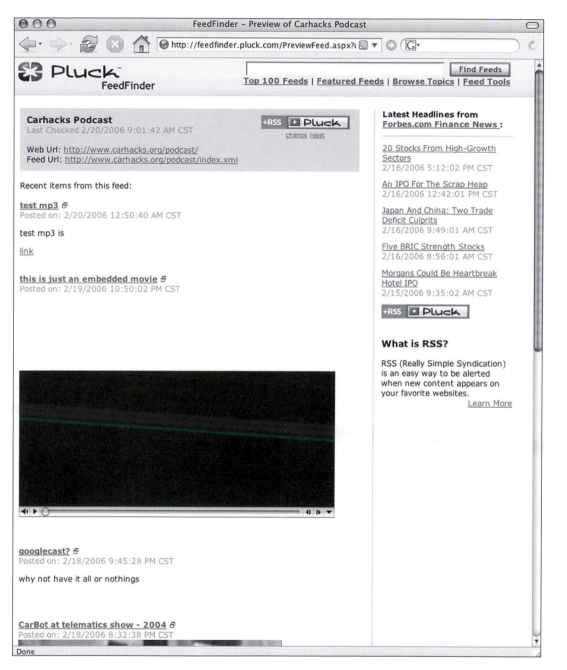

Figure 6-4
A podcast feed in Firefox

Inside the Industry

Push Technology Reborn

Unless you are expert in blogging technology, you may not be intimately familiar with the terms RSS and Atom. RSS, which stands for "really simple syndication" or "rich site summary" (or various other things depending on whom you ask), is a new computer communication standard that powers frequently updated news-based websites (i.e., weblogs or blogs). Atom is another standard that achieves the same effect. While these feeds are a fairly flexible new technology, the "push" technology concept behind it is not so new. A company called PointCast had gained great popularity in the mid- to late-1990s with its real-time news delivery software, which "pushed" out new information on a periodic basis.

You can think of RSS and Atom as the new "HTML for blogs." While the graphics and text that make up web pages are delivered to web browsers via HTML, these "feeds" contains all the recent stories that make up a news site or a blog, without all the graphical clutter. RSS and Atom are based on XML, a human-readable *eXtensible markup language*, which is why feeds often end in ".xml".

If you use a modern web browser, such as Firefox or Safari, you may have already noticed the RSS features built into the browser. And most of the major search portals, such as Yahoo!, MSN, and Google, have added features to allow you to aggregate all the news feeds you subscribe to and present them in an easy-to-browse list. Multiple RSS feeds can be blended together to create a new feed, and this feed can be shown on multiple other web sites (hence, syndication). Similarly, individuals can create their own personalized "diet" of information by selecting RSS feeds from a number of sites and have the information automatically retrieved. Using an RSS aggregator, the software that blends all these feeds together for a client, hundreds of websites' worth of information can be easily absorbed in under an hour.

Why all this focus on XML feeds? Well, just like HTML, RSS and Atom are now becoming part of the essential "glue" that holds the Internet together. One of the technical reasons its use is growing so quickly is that it solves an age-old problem for web pages: automatic retrieval of website updates. While search engines scour web pages for information, it's very hard to extract the exact part of a web page that is "new" or changed. RSS is a standard language for asking a web page "tell me what has changed on your site since I visited it last." RSS even has ways of telling an automatic process how frequently to check back for changes so that site traffic is kept under control (see **Figure 6-5**).

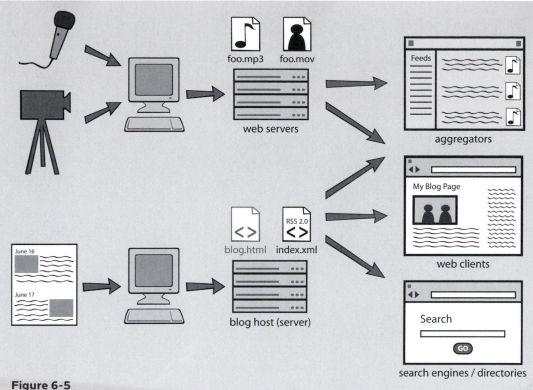

Figure 6-5
RSS feeds aggregators and search engines, and powers news sites

The key difference between a video blog/podcast, and a mere "rich-media" site, is the serial, subscription nature of podcasts. People expect blog content to be frequently updated. If they like the blog "channel," they are likely to come back for more. And with RSS, the viewers and listeners are explicitly requesting to be informed when the content has been added to, updated, or changed. This "opt-in" to the content creates a stronger (and in some cases, more trackable) affinity between the content consumer and the content source. And even if people aren't consciously using RSS or even aware of what it is, the websites they visit for frequently updated content are powered by RSS. Good technology fades into background and allows the experience to shine through.

Audio and video aggregator sites have been trying to serve as the Internet equivalent of a TV Guide for years. RSS feeds into the "TiVo" cultural transformation of time- and place-shifting content. It allows web content to be placed in front of the user more transparently, so that when they are just looking for something to listen or watch, it's already there on their home page, on their computer or on their portable device.

So if blogs are just web pages and podcasts are just blogs, what's new?

Enclosures

When blogging was first getting popular, a variety of client applications (*aggregators*) were developed to retrieve blogs automatically and download them into the background, so that fresh information was already waiting when the weblog reader came to their computer.

As blogging expanded, people began adding a variety of multimedia elements to their blogs just as they would to a web page, such as pictures and sound clips. A natural extension of blog technology in the form of enclosures, allowed these additional files—such as pictures, PDFs, MP3s, or video clips—to be automatically downloaded as well.

The next pivotal technical step—automatically transferring downloaded audio files to a portable media player, like an iPod—was called *podcatching*, and the process of producing and publishing a serialized MP3-encoded audio show for automatic download was dubbed *podcasting*. As blogging matured, a number of bloggers began adding video recorded snippets of their life very much in the style of the personal diary blog. The enclosure worked for video files too, and new *podcatching* aggregators begin to automatically download these video files (**Figure 6-6**).

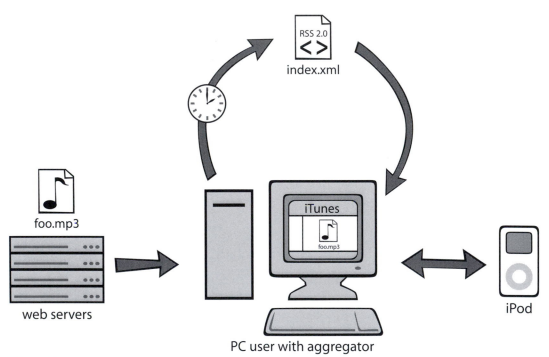

Figure 6-6
Automatic download of enclosures

Enter the Blogosphere

Although feeds are useful for automatic downloads, that's not the only thing they're good for. In fact, feeds have fundamentally transformed the speed at which information is conveyed online.

For many, there is just too much information online. It's impossible to take it all in. Web pages are updated all the time, and a lifetime could be spent just checking in to see if a colleague, friend, family member or company has updated their news feed.

For years, there have been attempts to create a standard "Has this web page been updated?" tool. In the late 1990s, web browsers had a "check for changes" features on web pages. However, even with these technologies, the process took too long, and anyone trying to check-up on the hundred must-read websites still couldn't keep up.

Blogs, in the form of personal journals, multiplied this problem even more. Whereas millions of people had personal web pages, blogs took these millions and allowed them to update their sites by the day, by the hour, by the minute. This could have resulted in complete information overload, but fortunately, blog feeds solved the problem.

Automatic Updates

The solution that feeds provide is simple: You don't have to read the whole web page to see what's updated; just ask, and the web page feed will give you a tidy summary. This has tremendous implications for the way information is sorted and gathered.

Feeds are a sort of "ticker tape," a summary of new posts to a blog. News web sites are a natural for this sort of technology, because they can have hundreds of reporters, each creating their own feed, and then blend these feeds together to create a "master" feed that goes on the main web page. Feeds can be categorized, so that "tech" and "international" news can be viewed individually.

Feeds even have a built-in mechanism for limiting traffic to a site. Whenever a feed is read from a website, it includes a sort of "snooze" button, telling the requester when to check back again. If the blog is updated daily, it will say "check back tomorrow." If, however, it is a news site, it might tell the requester website or program to check back in a few minutes, as breaking news is updated all the time.

Comments

Another way that blogs have increased the connectedness of the Internet is through a commenting feature. Almost all blog software includes a comment feature so that readers can join the conversation. While forums and other websites have had these sorts of features for years, the blog is a different conversational format: one main author, many commentators. Most blog tools have several options you can set, so that comments can either be immediately posted, or they can be screened (for inappropriateness or spam) and then approved by the blog author.

Pings and Trackbacks

Pings are tiny, efficient messages that are used by computers on the Internet to check up on or signal each other. (The term has even moved into colloquial speech, as in "ping me this weekend and we'll see if we can hook up.")

Blogs rely on *pings* as an update mechanism. They make the web more connected and real time. Ordinarily, if site A links to site B, site B would not know for a while about the link. With a ping, site A can immediately tell site B, "hey I linked to you." This *trackback* mechanism allows conversations to occur not just within a blog site (as with comments) but also between blogs.

Trackbacks work like this: blogging software will generate a unique trackback URL for each blog post. If blog A wants to comment on blog B, blog A will write its post and include the URL from blog B in a special trackback field in the blog entry tool. When this is done, behind the scenes, blog A will ping blog B. Now, if you go to blog B, you will see a link back to A.

This is one of the tools that enables blogs to Internetwork.

Blog Indexing and Search Ranking

Traditionally, (we're talking about 10 years of tradition here), web searching has been implemented by web spiders or crawlers. Google, Yahoo!, Ask Jeeves and other sites "crawl" the web, by having thousands of computers request every web page in their database, follow every link wherever it goes, copy the entire page, compare it with the copy of the site that they looked up on the last crawl, and sort it into a big index so they can answer search queries. Because of the enormous task this is, search engines can't be completely up-to-date—except for certain special types of information (like news and blogs), search engines may only update their index every couple of weeks. So although they fake it well for topical changes, search engines (even Google) are far from real-time.

Blogging speeds this process up. Blog sites can be queried at much faster rates because they always provide a concise summary of their changes. As a result, a new generation of *blog search engines* and *blog directories* have emerged. Examples include:

- **Search**
    - Technorati.com
    - Blogdex.com
    - Daypop.com
    - Popdex.com
    - Tailrank.com
    - Memeorandum.com
    - Google Blog search
- **Directories**
    - Blo.gs
    - Weblogs.com

These systems are able to provide literally up-to-the minute results. This works in two ways:

1. Once these search engines know about a blog, they can simply subscribe to the feed, checking up on it frequently and efficiently to see if it has changed.
2. These engines get pinged and updated by the blogs themselves. Most blogging software is pre-configured to ping several of these. (For instance, Movable type pings Technorati, Blo.gs and Weblogs.com by default).

There are even "meta" services that will ping all the important blog search engines on your blog's behalf every time you post, so your blog doesn't have to on its own, such as Ping-o-matic (**Figure 6-7**).

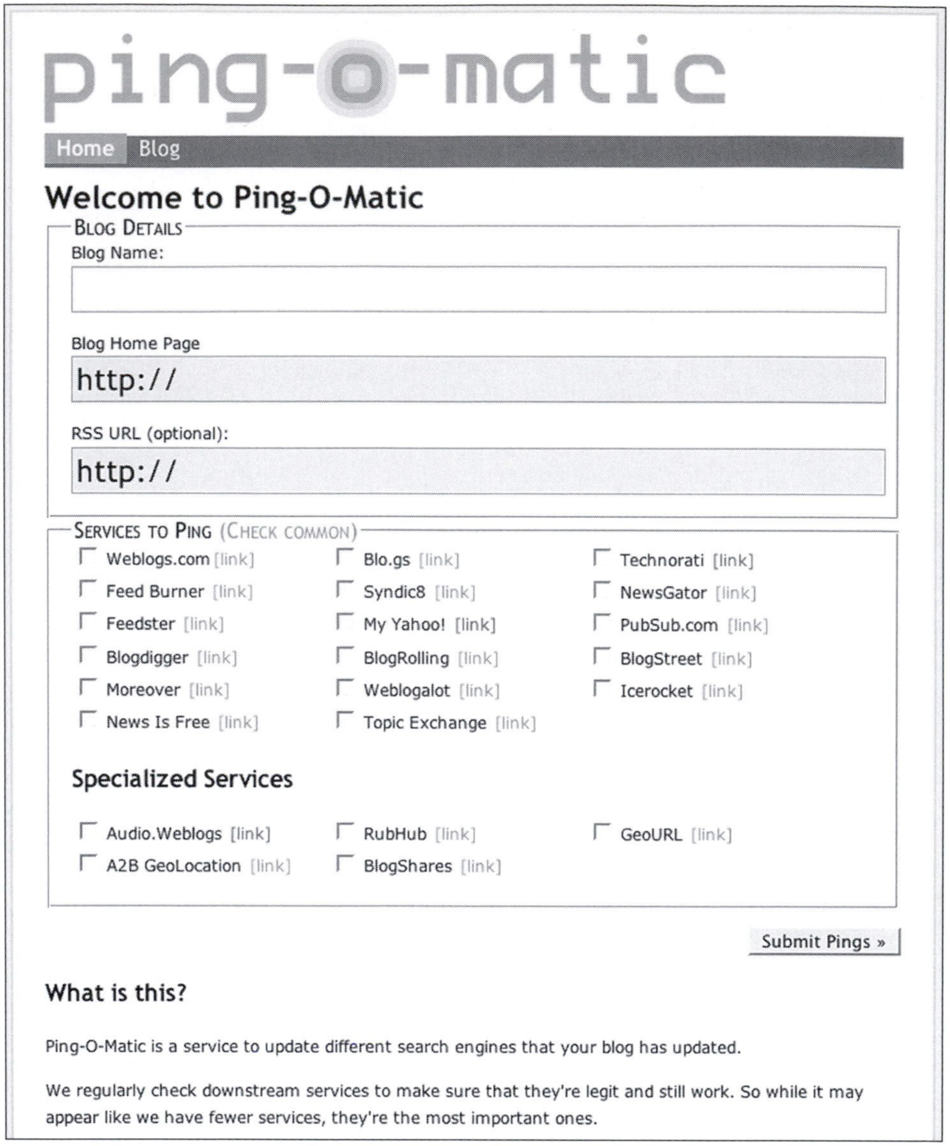

ping-o-matic

Home | Blog

Welcome to Ping-O-Matic

BLOG DETAILS

Blog Name:

_____

Blog Home Page

`http://`

RSS URL (optional):

`http://`

SERVICES TO PING (CHECK COMMON)

☐ Weblogs.com [link]　　☐ Blo.gs [link]　　☐ Technorati [link]

☐ Feed Burner [link]　　☐ Syndic8 [link]　　☐ NewsGator [link]

☐ Feedster [link]　　☐ My Yahoo! [link]　　☐ PubSub.com [link]

☐ Blogdigger [link]　　☐ BlogRolling [link]　　☐ BlogStreet [link]

☐ Moreover [link]　　☐ Weblogalot [link]　　☐ Icerocket [link]

☐ News Is Free [link]　　☐ Topic Exchange [link]

Specialized Services

☐ Audio.Weblogs [link]　　☐ RubHub [link]　　☐ GeoURL [link]

☐ A2B GeoLocation [link]　　☐ BlogShares [link]

[Submit Pings »]

What is this?

Ping-O-Matic is a service to update different search engines that your blog has updated.

We regularly check downstream services to make sure that they're legit and still work. So while it may appear like we have fewer services, they're the most important ones.

Figure 6-7
ping-o-matic

Because these engines have complete up-to-the-minute data, they can then compete on their ability to sift out the data trends. For instance, if over a several hour period the word "pentagon" keeps appearing with increasing frequency, because it's being heavily blogged, then you can assume that something important is happening at the Pentagon. Similarly, if a particular website or blog URL keeps coming up in blogs, then you can assume there's something exciting about that link. Web search engines do the same sorts of things, but can't keep up in real time. Blog search engines can.

Here's what Technorati.com says about indexing and ranking:

> A few years ago, Web search was revolutionized by a simple but profound idea—that the relevance of a site can be determined by the number of other sites that link to it, and thus consider it 'important.' In the world of blogs, hyperlinks are even more significant, since bloggers frequently link to and comment on other blogs, which creates the sense of timeliness and connectedness one would have in a conversation. So Technorati tracks the number of links, and the perceived relevance of blogs, as well as the real-time nature of blogging. Because Technorati automatically receives notification from weblogs as soon as they are updated, it can track the thousands of updates per hour that occur in the blogosphere, and monitor the communities (who's linking to whom) underlying these conversations.
>
> (from *http://technorati.com/about/*)

Tags

Tags are a recent practical innovation to categorizing group information that is seeing a lot of success on the web today. Categories are hard to create and maintain. If it's just you storing your own personal data on your hard drive, then you can keep it in whatever structure you want that makes sense to you. However, when people are trying to find information online, their minds are organized differently, and they would never look where you put it.

(Note that these tags are not the same as the words in brackets such as <img> found in HTML and XML files, which are called *elements* but also sometimes called *tags*).

Group tagging solves this problem. This concept has been pioneered by services such as *http://del.icio.us* (a bookmark sharing/tagging service) and *http://flickr.com* (a photo sharing service). Basically, whenever links or pictures are uploaded, the uploader has a chance to add tags, single words with no space. For instance, I might tag a picture *kids* but also *wedding* and *Maui* if the picture had all those elements.

On Flickr, many uploaded photos are shown to visitors as they are uploaded, and everyone has a chance to tag the photos as well. This group assignment of meaning has been called *folksonomy* (modeled after the word *taxonomy*, a formal categorization system), because many *folks* are organizing and categorizing the data together. In this example, the kids/wedding/Maui picture might also be tagged with *beach*, *sand, sunset, Kapalua* (because someone recognized the specific beach), and so on. Now, that picture is *very* well tagged.

All of this rich *metadata* (information about information) helps tremendously when the uploader or others are trying to find information. The large community of people viewing and adding tags to content increases the quality of the metadata.

Now, this same idea applies to blogs. As an example, someone might go on a tirade about a new application being released and having many bugs. They might not use the word "rant" or "tirade" but that would be an accurate description for the post. Or, a long post about semantics or software or baking might not contain the main word that sums up the salient category. So tags, when applied by either the author or others, can tremendously help the information find interested parties.

Technorati.com is a blog search engine that has done a lot of work on tagging blogs. They have created a *microformat*, a way of enhancing HTML code by literally adding meaning to it. Their microformat is a simple link that you can put into any blog post to add a tag to it.

In HTML, when you insert a hyperlink, you can specify the *relationship* of this URL to the current page by inserting *rel=* in the link. The tag microformat simply consists of adding rel="tag" and a URL. This indicates to search engines that the last word of the URL listed is a *tag*.

For instance, if a blog was about podcasts, you could add the tag by simply adding:

```
<a href="http://technorati.com/tag/podcast" rel="tag">podcast</a>
```

into the end of a blog post. The link to Technorati will bring up a page that has all *other* blogs that also added the same tag to their post. As a result, you can see, in close to real time, every blog of a particular category (see **Figure 6-8**).

Video sharing communities such as *http://youtube.com/*, although not technically video blogging (you can't download the videos) are using tagging extensively as well to help sort through thousands of choices.

Tags are one way to attach meaning and description (instead of mere formatting) to web pages and web-based information. This is referred to as the *semantic* web.

Author's Tip

You can get more information on tags, services that use them, and their use in blogging at:

http://en.wikipedia.org/wiki/Tags and *http://technorati.com/tag/*

Figure 6-8
The "podcast" tag on technorati.com

Podcast and Video Blog Directories

Pings handle the primary goal of getting a podcast or video blog to show up in the blogosphere. But search is not the only way, or even the usual way, that casual users find content. In fact, a lot of content choices are made by staring at a screen and picking whatever looks good.

The extremely busy home pages of news sites and ISP portals are an example of this. There are hundreds of links so that the viewer can glance around and click gossip, sports, stocks or weather depending on what they are interested in.

Imagine if this was the only way to get content for your TV: You turned it on, and there was a search box. You typed in a word on a keyboard remote control, and a list of shows playing now, matching that word were listed. Then, you selected one, and only then did any video show on the screen. That would be a pretty lousy interface, because you couldn't simply browse around (channel surf) and see what was on.

The search-engine video experience is not how most people watch video. And even online video services have realized this by offering dozens of thumbnails to video on every screen.

While there are many people who will go to a search engine to find a podcast on the topic of their choice, there are a far greater number that will download an application hoping that it will provide programming options for them.

There are a number of directories that offer podcast and video content with their own directory:

- **Applications**
  - iTunes (*http://www.apple.com/itunes/*)
  - FireAnt (*http://fireant.tv/*)
  - Open Media Network (*http://www.omn.org*)
- **Portals**
  - Yahoo! Podcasts (*http://podcasts.yahoo.com/*)
  - Odeo (*http://www.odeo.com*)
  - Mefeedia (*http://mefeedia.com/*)
  - Vlogdir (*http://vlogdir.com/*)
  - Podcast Alley (*http://www.podcastalley.com/*)
  - Podcast.net (*http://www.podcast.net/*)
  - Podcast Pickle (*http://www.podcastpickle.com/*)
  - Podnova (*http://www.podnova.com/*)

Most of these sites have a submission page and allow you to add your podcast or video blog. They require you to add some additional information, such as titles, website links, and categories. They have varying degrees of editorial processes; some will add the link quickly; others have staff that check over the blogs and see whether they pass content quality and suitability guidelines.

We're really in the wild west days of podcasting and video blogging.

There is so much web spam (fake or pure advertising websites) today, that search engines don't give much credence to sites submitted through their "add your site forms."

However, this is not the case with video blogs and podcasts. It actually takes a significant amount of resources, time, effort, and bandwidth to serve a podcast or video blog, and so submitting one to any of these directories is very likely to get accepted. If the content is good, they're likely to even feature it on their main page. Plus, in these early days, each of the above portals and directories depend on the availability of new content.

These portals will probably go through three phases:

1. Initially there is not enough content. All takers are added, regardless of the quality of the content, as long as it doesn't violate any rules.

2. Later, the directories that are doing the best will create a more selective A-list section, through an arbitrary undisclosed process, and sort of filter the riffraff or unlucky content off to the side. Content creators will complain about their sites not getting picked for the A-list.

3. Finally, there will be so much content that the portals have to start turning it away. At that point, the business models around these new TV-video-Internet-podcast portal/applications will mature, and some complex payola scheme will develop. Getting into the big portals like iTunes and Yahoo! will only happen via relationships or bidding or some other scheme.

Apple's process is probably the most vigorous of all. Apple requires special tags to be added to the RSS feed (which also work in Yahoo!'s portal) including a graphic to represent the whole podcast or video blog. But the work is worth it. In fact, because each of these portals are driving traffic to their directory and allowing you to have space in it for free, there's really no drawback to submission.

If you are creating a podcast, there's really no question that you should make sure first and foremost that it looks good in iTunes. You should also submit it to the iTunes directory so that people will find it when they search for it.

Figure 6-9
Apple's podcast portal in iTunes

Feeds Revisited

There are basically three practical ways to make a compatible feed for a podcast or video blog that contains the proper media enclosure elements:

1. Have your blogging application generate it.

2. Use a third-party service, such as FeedBurner.

3. Write it yourself or use an application, such as FeedForAll.

Feeds are normally generated by your blogging application. WordPress has support for podcasts built-in. Movable Type has a plug-in (*http://brandon.fuller.name/archives/hacks/mtenclosures/*) that enables them.

If you're using a host like Blogger.com or any blog system that doesn't already support enclosures, you can simply sign up for a free account at *http://www.feedburner.com*, give them your RSS 1.0 or 2.0 or Atom feed, and they will produce an RSS 2.0 feed with the appropriate enclosures, and even do subscription counting for you.

Writing RSS yourself and manually updating it is not hard at all, but you'll want to automate the process eventually. There is an application called *FeedForAll* (*http://www.feedforall.com*) that can be used to automatically generate feeds should you need to manually upload them. This is good if you are creating a feed for a blog that uses a web editing tool instead of a blog system, or if you are simply generating an enhanced feed for that blogging system.

Author's Tip

If you're going to be manually creating feeds, here are some sites that have feed validators and checkers to make sure the feed doesn't have syntax errors and conveys what it is supposed to:

http://www.nobodylikesonions.com/feedcheck/

http://feedvalidator.org/

http://www.feedforall.com/

Manually creating the feed is a great way to get familiar with the RSS 2.0 media formats, but that knowledge can then hopefully be used to update the templates in your blogging system so that it can automatically make the feeds for you.

Inside the Industry

Feeding Frenzy

Feeds are the critical element that makes blog syndication work. Unfortunately, there is a bit of a standards war going on about feeds.

There are three kinds of feeds that you're likely to see offered on a blog:

- RSS 2.0
- RSS 1.0
- Atom

When you go to blog sites, and look for subscription buttons, you'll probably find several of them. You would think RSS 2.0 was the next version of RSS 1.0, but they actually are completely different standards internally. Functionally, all the feeds say the same thing in different ways.

Atom is an Internet standard blog feed format, yet Apple, Yahoo!, and most podcast and video blogs rely exclusively on RSS 2.0.

Not only that, but there are two multimedia extensions to the RSS 2.0 specification:

- Yahoo!'s Media RSS
- Apple's iTunes RSS 2.0 extensions

The fortunate thing is, it's not like the VHS/Beta war, because this is software, not hardware. In practice, all blogging applications can spit out the three feed syndication formats, and most client applications and aggregators can interpret any RSS feed. Additionally, Yahoo! supports the iTunes extensions.

But the bottom line for podcasts and video blogs, as of this writing, are:

- Support RSS 2.0
- If you're going in iTunes, support those extensions
- Support the Media RSS extensions as well

This will give you maximum support that is supported by iTunes, Yahoo!, and pretty much any of the media blog aggregators.

Here's a feed example (from *http://podcasts.yahoo.com/publish/*) that illustrates the use of both iTunes and Yahoo! media extensions:

```
<?xml version="1.0" encoding="utf-8"?>
<rss version="2.0" xmlns:itunes="http://www.itunes.com/DTDs/Podcast-1.0.dtd"
xmlns:media="http://search.yahoo.com/mrss/">

<channel>
<title> Title of your site </title>
<description> A description of your podcast show </description>
<itunes:author>Your Name </itunes:author>
<link> http://www.yourserver.com/YourPodcastHomepage/ </link>
<itunes:image href="http://www.yourserver.com/YourPodcastPicture.jpg" />
<pubDate> Sun, 09 Oct 2005 21:00:00 PST </pubDate>
<language>en-us</language>
<copyright> Copyright Year Your_Name </copyright>

<item>
    <title> This is just a test </title>
    <description> A description of your podcast episode
</description>
    <itunes:author> Your Name </itunes:author>
    <pubDate> Thu, 16 Jun 2005 5:00:00 PST </pubDate>
    <enclosure url="http://www.yourserver.com/podcast_file.mp3"
length="3174554" type="audio/mpeg" /> </item>
</channel>
</rss>
```

This isn't the full list of elements, but it will get you going. The full list can be found in:

- Yahoo!'s Media RSS *http://search.yahoo.com/mrss*
- Apple's iTunes RSS 2.0 extensions *http://www.apple.com/itunes/podcasts/techspecs.html*

In practice, you will need to edit the RSS 2.0 generator code (or manually create the feed) and add each of the elements (Apple calls them "tags") in these standards to your feed. Each blogging application has its own way of customizing the RSS feed. **Figure 6-10** shows how to add these tags in Movable Type.

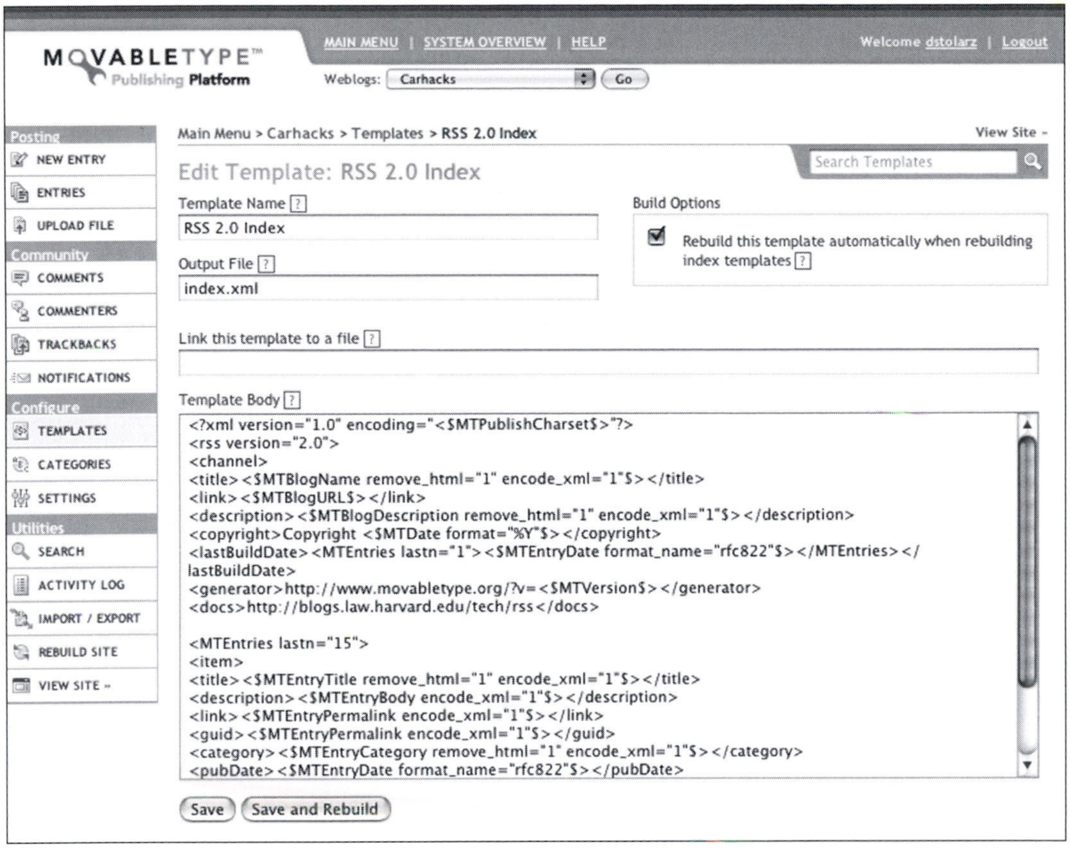

Figure 6-10
Editing the RSS 2.0 template in Movable Type

The general process is:

1. Find the template that generates the RSS 2.0 feed.
2. Add all the metadata you are going to support.

Show Notes and Chapters

There are various conventions and niceties for podcasts that help round out the experience. One very useful feature review, news, and information podcasts is show notes. (**Figure 6-11**). Show notes allow listeners who arrive via a web page to check the topics of a long podcast, see if they are interested, and if they are, allows them to follow the links discussed in the podcast.

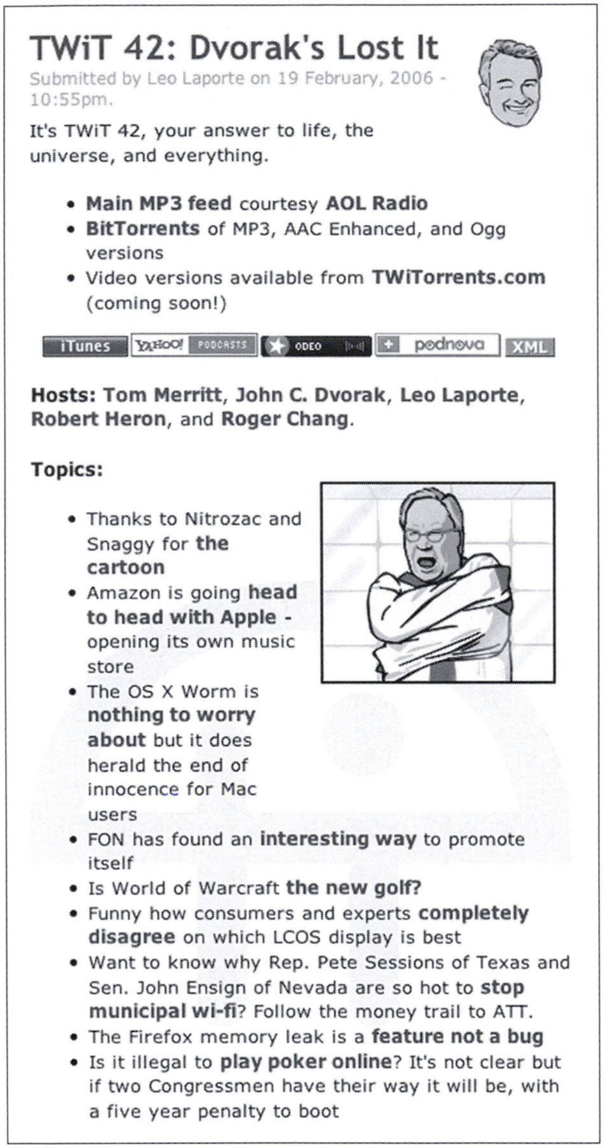

TWiT 42: Dvorak's Lost It

Submitted by Leo Laporte on 19 February, 2006 - 10:55pm.

It's TWiT 42, your answer to life, the universe, and everything.

- **Main MP3 feed** courtesy **AOL Radio**
- **BitTorrents** of MP3, AAC Enhanced, and Ogg versions
- Video versions available from **TWiTorrents.com** (coming soon!)

iTunes | YAHOO! PODCASTS | ODEO | podnova | XML

Hosts: Tom Merritt, John C. Dvorak, Leo Laporte, Robert Heron, and **Roger Chang**.

Topics:

- Thanks to Nitrozac and Snaggy for **the cartoon**
- Amazon is going **head to head with Apple -** opening its own music store
- The OS X Worm is **nothing to worry about** but it does herald the end of innocence for Mac users
- FON has found an **interesting way** to promote itself
- Is World of Warcraft **the new golf?**
- Funny how consumers and experts **completely disagree** on which LCOS display is best
- Want to know why Rep. Pete Sessions of Texas and Sen. John Ensign of Nevada are so hot to **stop municipal wi-fi**? Follow the money trail to ATT.
- The Firefox memory leak is a **feature not a bug**
- Is it illegal to **play poker online**? It's not clear but if two Congressmen have their way it will be, with a five year penalty to boot

Figure 6-11
This Week In Tech podcast show notes

One of the complaints about iTunes is that it does not support hyperlinked show notes, since you are in the iTunes application. However, Apple has created its own enhanced podcast format. Apple uses this to create their "New Music Tuesday" podcast. It provides chapter markers, which show up on the top of the iTunes application, as well as chapter marker artwork that displays in the bottom left, with hyperlinks. (**Figure 6-12**).

Figure 6-12
Apple's enhanced podcast with chapter markers

The drawback of this technique is that it requires you to encode the podcast in AAC, not MP3. You can solve this by doing multiple feeds, one with the MP3 for non-iTunes clients, and one for iTunes. If you are creating a video blog, however, you will probably already be dealing with multiple formats and their corresponding feeds.

Web Page Embedding

We've given a lot of attention to feeds and making sure that feeds work in iTunes. But what about good old users who just come to your blog's website? Well, there's already well established methods of making multimedia enclosures play nicely in a web page.

The following code is one standard way to embed a QuickTime movie :

```
<object CLASSID="clsid:02BF25D5-8C17-4B23-BC80-D3488ABDDC6B"
CODEBASE="http://www.apple.com/qtactivex/qtplugin.cab"  height="250"
width="480">

<param name="src" value="http://www.damienstolarz.com/blog/test.mov">

<param name="qtsrc" value="http://www.damienstolarz.com/blog/test.mov">

<param name="autoplay" value="false">

<param name="loop" value="false">

<param name="controller" value="true">

<embed src="http://www.damienstolarz.com/blog/test.mov"
qtsrc="http://www.damienstolarz.com/blog/test.mov" height="250" width="480"
autoplay="false" loop="false" controller="true"
pluginspage="http://www.apple.com/quicktime/"></embed>

</object>
```

Many video hosting sites such as Google Video and YouTube.com automatically generate the code you need to copy over to your webpage to embed their video player in a blog or web page (**Figure 6-13**).

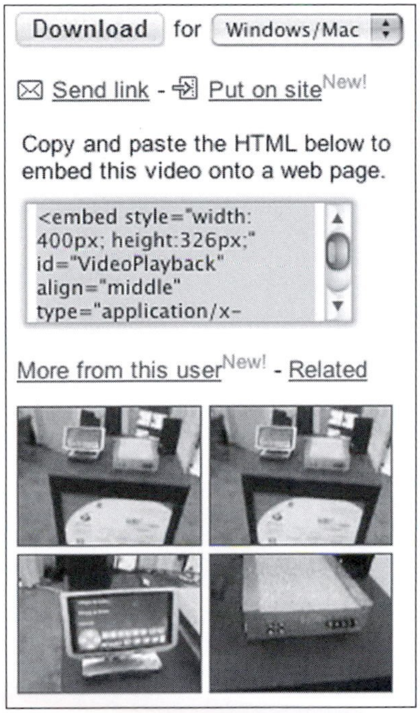

Figure 6-13
Player embed code

ALERT The drawback of many of these sites is they don't give you a direct link to download the file (YouTube), or if they do (Google Video), the link is not correctly formatted for blog software to correctly embed it.

Two very clean examples of clean video-blog webpage embedding can be found at:

- *http://www.audioblog.com*—This audio and video blog hosting service creates a seamless Flash player that you can embed in your blog—or they'll host the whole blog for you. Their system will even post the appropriate embed code to your compatible blogging system.

- *http://www.rocketboom.com*—These guys are the gold standard of viewer ease-of-use. You can go to their page and view source to see exactly how they embed their QuickTime and other files (they have a Windows Media feed as well).

Conclusion

The underpinnings of video blogging and podcasting are blogs. Blogs are powered by many two-way communication and syndication technologies such as comments, pings, track-backs, and immediate indexing into blog search engines and directories. Thus, blogs enable a global, real-time conversation to take place, and create an even deeper and tighter World Wide Web than before.

Podcasts and video blogs are nontextual media, and thus require manually-entered key-words, tags, and descriptive metadata to be effectively cataloged, searched, and displayed by aggregator applications and sites.

RSS 2.0 is the standard—right now—for multimedia blogs, based on Yahoo!'s and Apple's adoption. However, Atom is an Internet standard, and in the future Atom may take over RSS 2.0's role.

Taking full advantage of iTunes is worth the time, despite having to use proprietary tags. Yahoo! also interprets the same elements. Even if Microsoft follows up with yet another extension to RSS 2.0, supporting all the elements is not hard.

New blogging technology and standards (such as Technorati's tag microformat) are being developed all the time. Keeping up on basic text blog technology will make for better pod-casting and video blogging.

CHAPTER 7

Mobile Video Blogging and Podcasting

Mobile communications devices with video and audio recording capabilities have been around for a few years, offering us the ability to take snapshots, small videos and record audio snippets of everyday life. The quality of the recordings has often left something to be desired. Not good enough for home movies, family photos or professional voice recording, the functions were neat but not compelling, replacements for the equipment they emulated. But their true function—real time, conversational, and impromptu multimedia communication—has been revealed in *moblogging*.

Moblogging describes the posting of audio and video blog entries on the go, without resorting to a desktop computer. Moblogging can be done from mobile phones, PDAs, laptops or anything else that allows you to update your blog while "mobile." No special name has been given to adding video or audio to a moblog. Although coming up with another new word such as *movlogging* or *mopodcasting* might help if you're looking to lock-up all related domain names, moblogging is the word that has stuck.

This chapter will quickly get you moblogging from various connected devices. The common theme is that a moblog does not require plugging into a terrestrial Internet connection. This chapter includes laptops as a moblogging device because of the ability of laptops to work completely free of wired connections.

This chapter covers:

- Quick start moblogging
- Other moblogging options
- Laptop moblog
- Posting from PDAs

Quick Start Moblogging

A very quick way to get a mobile vlog up and going in a few minutes is to head over to *http://www.textamerica.com* and set up a *moblog* account. What makes this a great solution for just trying out the technology is that the sign-up and posting is so simple even the least tech-savvy person could be video moblogging in 5 minutes. The downside is the moblog is not enclosure-compliant, so only web viewers can see it—iTunes and other aggregators won't.

The sign-up (see **Figures 7-1** and **7-2**) process requires little more than a username, password the name of the blog and a short description line. Unlike most websites, Textamerica does not require an email validation so you don't have to wait for a confirmation email and special link to be sent to you.

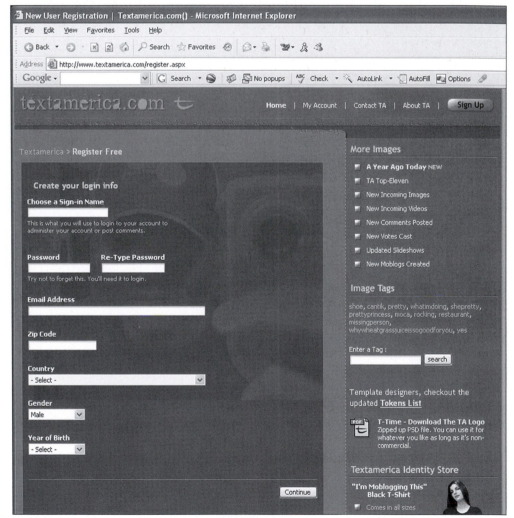

Figure 7-1
Textamerica.com sign-up page 1

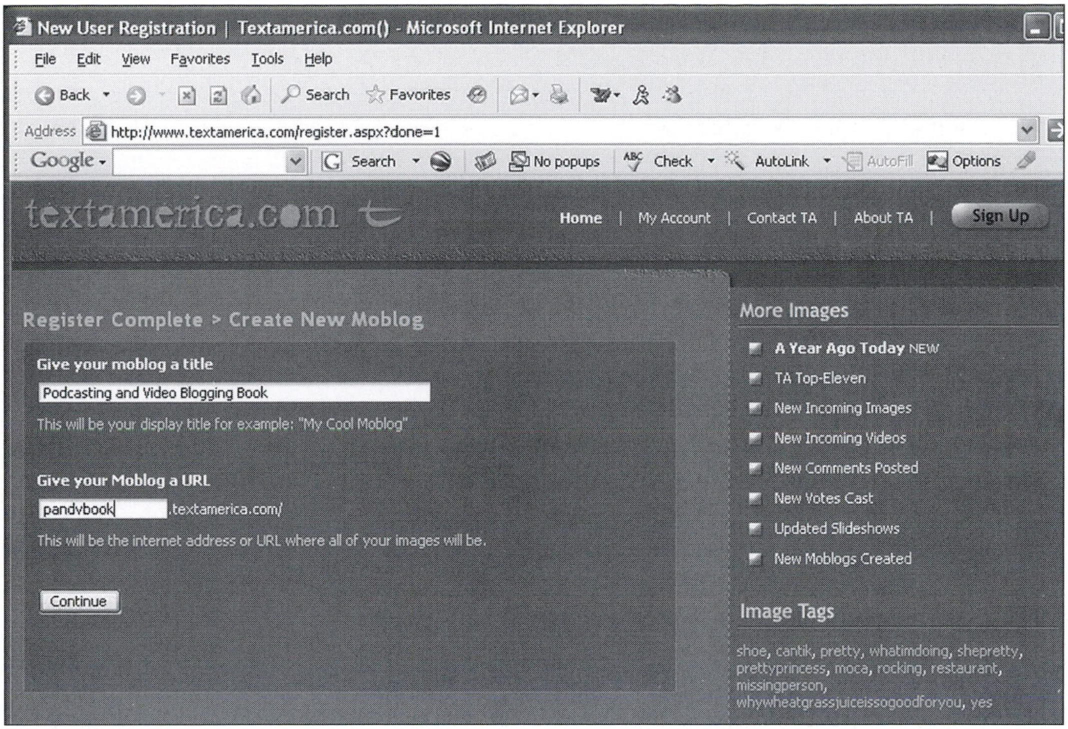

Figure 7-2
Textamerica.com sign-up page 2

Although the site is free, you can choose the $6.99 monthly option which gives you a lot more control over the look and feel of the moblog (see **Figure 7-3**). Once you choose your free site, it gets right to the heart of the matter. You're shown your new moblog URL and the address you use to mail MMS or email messages to and from your phone (see **Figure 7-4**). The moblog can support videos, photos and text but no audio files.

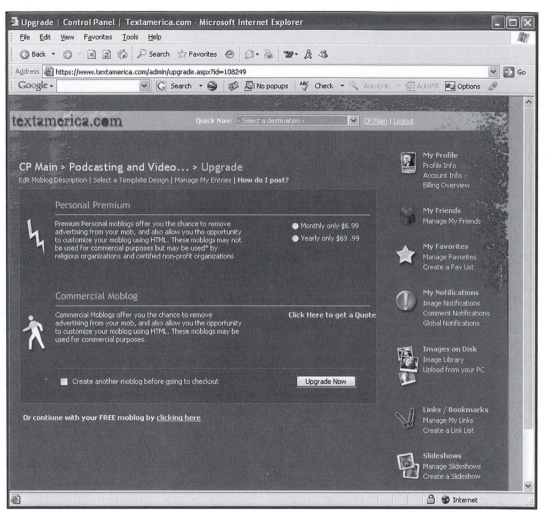

Figure 7-3
Textamerica.com site selection

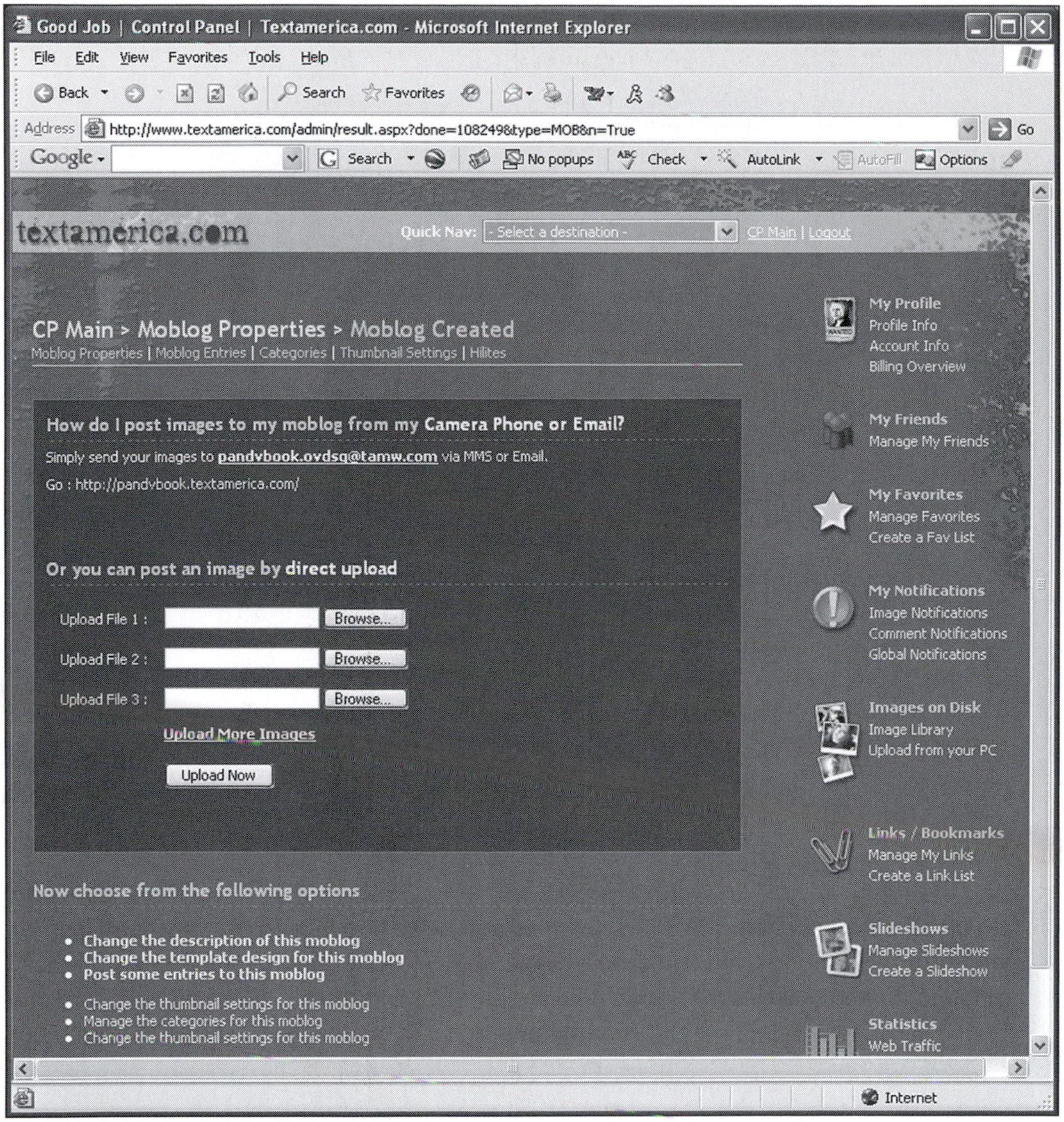

Figure 7-4
Moblog URL and posting email address

The supported file types are .JPG, .MOV, .3GP, .MPG, .MP4, .AVI, .WMV (these are defined in Chapter 11, Video Production) with a generous file size limit of 25 MB which covers not only your standard cell phone video and picture files but the 3GP format used by the Treo and WMV used by Microsoft Windows Mobile-based Smart Phones. Sending the file is as simple as shooting some video, saving it to your phone and sending it using MMS or email to the address provided on the administration screen of your Textamerica site (see F**igure 7-5**).

Figure 7-5
Capturing and sending video from Motorola V330

Author's Tip

Moblogging is so new that only a few all-inclusive tools are available, but it won't be too long until more robust versions come out that are RSS enclosure-compliant, i.e., produce a proper video blog feed, or translate the video to iPod and other media player formats. That will bring the mobility concept full circle allowing people to post wirelessly and let portable media player users view those videos on the go.

Once you've sent the file it might take a few minutes for the moblog to be updated, but the highlight is you don't have to do anything else. Once it's emailed, as long as you've sent the right file type to the right place, it works. Go to your moblog URL and see if the new post came up (see **Figure 7-6**). This is not limited to cell phone use, in fact you can post to the service through any connected device including a desktop computer.

What makes this a great tool is that anyone with a cell phone that takes pictures and video can use it from anywhere in the world. If you're hiking the Australian outback and take some video, you can post that video to your moblog as soon as you get signal. It's a great way for even the least technical person to share videos with their friends and family without having to go through the trauma of downloading the video to a computer and mail them. Even better, it's all available on the web within a few minutes without any intervention.

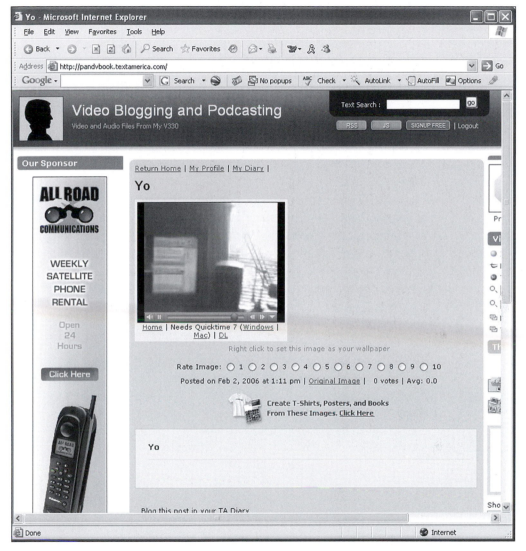

Figure 7-6
Uploaded and embedded video

Other Moblogging Options

There are a number of other post-my-mobile-video-to-a-web-page services that pre-date the current video blogging craze.

Vobbo.net

The Sweden-based mobilblogg.net is an essentially similar service that also provides free blog hosting and accepts posts through MMS and email messages. Unfortunately, it's also lacking in the RSS enclosure support department. A service called vobbo.net has a nice interface and does provide RSS feeds; however, they do not support enclosures, so it won't show up in iTunes or FireAnt directories, but you should expect that to be remedied in the near future as most sites that publish RSS XML are ramping up their enclosure tag support so they can play with iTunes.

TypePad

TypePad, a Six Apart hosted blogging tool also supports mobile posting and does publish the proper enclosure tags, allowing programs like FireAnt and iTunes to see the enclosures and automatically download them in the background. There is a configuration setting in TypePad where you specify the email address of your mobile device and you're provided with a special email address for sending the posts. The email address is a random look-ing string of letters and numbers so it's a good idea to enter it in the address book on your phone. Getting your phone's email address can be done by simply sending an email from your phone to your normal home email account. The return address should work.

ALERT It's a good idea to reply to that test email to verify it is working in both directions so as to avoid any issues with setting up a moblog. The email address you see when you send a message *from* your phone may not work on a return path (i.e., you can't send messages to it) but it will be the one you need to paste into the configuration pages of any moblogging services you sign up with.

Audioblog.com

Audioblog.com, (which is also covered in Chapter 12, Hosting) offers podcasters a simple and unique tool for hosting audio and video and posting it to their existing blog. On sign-up, you provide Audioblog with the login and password info for your hosted blog. They support most major weblog software and services, including Movable Type, Blogware, TypePad, WordPress, Blogger, pMachine, LiveJournal, and many others. Audioblog lets you upload audio and video posts and will then send it directly over to your blog with the right enclosure information so iTunes and other aggregators can see the nice tags and download the media files properly.

Audioblog also offers a moblog tool where you call into a phone system and can record and post your podcast from anywhere a phone is available. Not only can podcasts be called in, they can be emailed in as can vlogs. Video or audio enabled phones can be used to send the file directly to the Audioblog servers, which in turn post it to your blog. It's not limited to emails from PDAs and cell phones, posts can be emailed from any device than can email an attachment. The service isn't free but the flexibility of the service and growing features makes a great tool to add rich content to your vlog and podcast from anywhere in the world.

Inside the Industry

The coolest thing about audioblog.com is their video format translation. Audioblog automatically translates video from its mobile phone format to Flash video, so that it can be embedded in your blog web page and seen by anyone with flash. But even better, Audioblog automatically translates into the .MP4 format expected by the iPod with Video, as well as the Playstation Portable, and creates the appropriate, enclosure-happy RSS feed for automatic consumption by video blog aggregators like iTunes.

Laptop "Moblog"

A bulkier yet effective way to moblog is to simply use your laptop (see **Figure 7-7**). It's not as slick as the camera phone method but it does have some advantages. Some of the newest laptops are only twice the size of a PDA, and pack all the punch of a conventional desktop system. And getting the video uploaded from your laptop is no big challenge either, because most wireless carriers offer data service through their phones for an added fee.

ALERT Fees vary wildly between carriers so it's a good idea to shop around. The speeds offered by different carriers also vary. But if you use your laptop in "tethered" mode, i.e., accessing the Internet via a cable or Bluetooth, ensure you are on the "all you can eat" wireless data plan, lest you encounter costly overage charges of many dollars per megabyte.

GPRS has been around for a long time and can have you surfing the Internet at dial-up speeds. Sitting in an airport for a few hours with the option of no Internet or slow Internet makes for a simple decision. GPRS/EDGE (60–80 kbps) has given way to EVDO (300–500 kbps), which gives near-broadband (slow DSL) data rates.

Figure 7-7
Dell 700m With T-Mobile EDGE/GPRS card and Intel USB Webcam Moblog setup

There are three ways to get this mobile data access. Using a data cable or Bluetooth to connect to your phone will allow you to use your wireless carriers connection software to get on their network. Most carriers also sell PCMCIA cardbus data cards. There is an added cost for the card but the connection will be somewhat simpler (see **Figure 7-8**). Laptop manufacturers are even putting EVDO and EDGE hardware along with GSM card slots in their newer systems. You simply slide the GSM card into the laptop, run the connection software and you're online.

Figure 7-8
T-Mobile V330 GPRS and Bluetooth-enabled phone, and Sony Ericsson GC83 EDGE and GPRS T-Mobile connection card

If the data connected phone setup is not within your current technology portfolio WiFi does provide a very workable alternative. Hotspots abound with T-Mobile being the largest provider of pay-to-play road warrior connectivity. If you already have T-Mobile phone service, the Hot Spot service can be added to your account giving you WiFi access in a large number of airports, coffee shops and public places. Other vendors do exist and some hotspots are free. Free, always the best price is harder to find but requires no credit cards or pre-existing contracts. Some municipalities are now offering city-wide free Internet service much to the chagrin of carriers that charge for access.

Once connected, creating the podcast or video blog is basically the same as what you would do from a desktop computer. If you have a DV or MiniDV camera, you will need a FireWire connection to connect to your laptop and capture the video (see **Figure 7-9**). More and more laptops are available with FireWire ports on them. If you're FireWire deficient, an add-on card can be had from a local big-box electronics retailer for about $50. The same capture and editing software used on desktops can be used on laptops, although there may be a performance difference with the difference being slower capture and rendering. Non-DV cameras pose a different challenge, capturing composite or S-video. USB-based video capture devices, although not optimal can be used to move analog video into your laptop, but unless you want to become one of those Starbucks Cyborgs who look like they've set-up a home office near the newspaper rack, you're not going to want to carry around too many devices. We're *mobile* blogging, remember?

Figure 7-9
On-board FireWire port. Also known as 1394 or iLink connections

Video blogging on the road can also be done with a USB webcam (see **Figure 7-10**). These devices are not going to provide video anywhere near as nice as a DV cam, and may be very frustrating by outside light conditions with their slow exposure adjustments, but they will capture video. It may be choppy, it may have strange color and bad white balance but depending on your quality goals you may find them perfectly adequate for blogging.

Editing the video will be the same process as it is on a desktop system but will likely take longer for the final video to render and convert to MOV or whatever final movie format you will post. Since you're going with a mobile format, and skipping most post-production, editing should presumably be used here to lightly trim the video save it in a small web-friendly format.

Author's Tip

If this is the video capture route you are going to take, it's a very good idea to shut down all service and applications not needed during the capture. Every little bit of system resource you can make available will help ensure that there are no dropped frames. Don't check email, surf the web, or do anything at all during a capture. Any CPU usage spikes will cause the capture to hiccup.

One benefit of a USB webcam is that it will record that video in a smaller, more compact file format to begin with, which can speed up the encoding to a web format somewhat. Some USB webcams will even record straight to an MOV in software, which eliminates the need for transcoding the file. It will still need some editing but editing the smaller MOV file is straightforward.

Figure 7-10
Intel USB webcam

Author's Tip

Make sure the webcam is saving the file to the aspect ratio, and size you intend to use for the post. Webcams often assume you're not going to post the file somewhere that file sizes matter. If you end up in a situation where the video size is just too large, you may have to re-encode it with QuickTime Pro in order to smash it down to the size you need. The re-encode should be quick since the source type is the same and the file is already somewhat compact.

Mobile audio productions for podcasts are far simpler. Nearly all laptops have a microphone input. Capturing audio is far less processor intensive and can be done with the majority of laptops without closing applications or shutting down services. The key here is to use a high quality microphone. A hand-held or even better, lavalier microphone (see Chapter 10, Audio Production) can be connected to the microphone input directly or through the use of a converter cable. The editing of audio should work in exactly the same way as it does on a desktop. This is a scenario where having a quality set of over-ear headphones is crucial.

The laptop does afford another convenience over the cell phone method of posting, use of a standard web interface to post. Cell phone/PDA podcasting or vlogging is very convenient but offers some limitation in how the post comes out and can be a little tough to use for posts with more than a line or two of text. Laptops are nice in that you are able to post from anywhere yet have the flexibility to post using the full-featured tools of your blog admin and posting pages.

Posting From PDAs

Connected PDAs (Treos, Pocket PCs), share a lot of features with their classic mobile phone counterparts. The Treo 650 and 700w, Audiovox PPC 6700, Samsung I730 can all make phone calls and get on the Internet just like a regular mobile phone (see **Figure 7-11**). They also share the ability to record fairly watchable video and audio. Where they diverge is in the browser department. Connected PDAs sold though wireless providers, particularly newer ones that run the latest Palm OS and Windows Mobile 5, come with powerful and robust browsers that can do almost as much as your desktop browser can. The main difference is the screen size and funny bunching up of web page layouts when a browser can't render the page properly. Other phones that can render HTML do it with many limitations making sites with any code complexity impossible to navigate.

Figure 7-11 Treo 650
PalmOS-based PDA phone

PDAs offer more screen real estate and memory for applications like Internet Explorer Mobile Edition. The ability to go directly to websites like TypePad, Blogger, Movable Type and Audioblog through a browser to make your post makes moblogging a lot simpler. Some blog hosting sites also offer a PDA-sized version of their site, which makes everything fit nicely into the browser. PDAs that have stretchable windows, allowing you to scroll over to the right to see the rest of the page make the browsing experience a little more realistic but require a bit of scooting around to get to everything.

Inside the Industry

Palm and Windows Programs

There are a number of blog posting programs that are installed on Palm and Windows devices. Some have grown to support file uploads and some have not. mo:Blog *http://www.tektonica.com/projects/moblog/* has grown to meet the new needs of podcasters and mobile video bloggers. Currently there are only a small handful of applications built for PalmOS or Windows Mobile specifically to upload files to blogs. The sheer newness of mobile device-based video blogging and podcasting is the main reason for the dearth of products in this niche. Soon it won't be a niche, it will be a very real product category. Fortunately, most blogs support email postings with attachments, which is a nice temporary workaround. Simply capturing video or audio and emailing it from a PDA to a site such as Textamerica or TypePad will get the results you're looking for.

There are many little holes here and there and those holes make it difficult but not impossible to develop a process that includes a mobile device, software and blog service that renders the XML feed or blog page you are looking for. The technology is changing every day so be sure to pester your blog host or be ready to jump ship to another provider.

In order to make sense of the moblogging-podcasting insanity, draw the flow out on a sheet of paper. Starting with the phone, list what file types it creates. Then look at a list of blog hosts and what file types they support as well as how they accept postings. Once that list is narrowed down, narrow it down further by eliminating the ones that do not generate the RSS XML you need. If you want iTunes compatibility, Audioblog might be your choice. If you want it to go directly to a web page instead of your own blog, Textamerica might be the one. If you have all of the pieces on the front end with MOV and MP3 files, TypePad might work better plus it works with iTunes.

Your quest may require you to rethink your wireless provider as well. The ideal video blogging and podcasting phone is one that records QuickTime MOV files and has a voice recorder that creates MP3 files. With those two file types, you're almost guaranteed to be compatible with any enclosure compliant blog, podcast or video blog host.

Conclusion

Mobile devices are quickly developing all the tools needed for multimedia blogging. As more and more people post video and audio to their blogs, they will be looking to their humble PDAs, cell phones and laptops to free them from their desktop tether.

Treo devices record video as 3GP. Sending a Treo recorded 3GP video through their email posting service to Textamerica will render a proper, viewable video within the page when viewed with a browser. It will not come up in iTunes nor is the RSS XML generated enclosure compliant. Recording WMV video on a Treo 700w and sending it through email to TypePad will end up as an enclosure compliant XML feed although iTunes will not give any love to the WMV file type. FireAnt will give it love as will most other readers.

Audioblog.com comes the closest to being a complete solution for moblogging, transcoding the video it receives into both iPod and Flash formats for iTunes and web page compatibility.

Having a solid workflow is critical when podcasting or video moblogging. It may take some time and effort to get your moblogs out to the widest possible audience. Blog hosting services are changing their offerings to meet new multimedia needs. Wireless providers are introducing new and better phones and PDAs every day. Keep an eye out for a device that suits your particular specifications. You'll end up loving the multimedia features of your phone or PDA.

Author's Tip

In order to have a successful completely mobile podcast or video blog:

- Make a list of your phone's file output types
- List all of the blog host providers and what file types they support
- Narrow the list by eliminating the ones you cannot post to through either email or through the PDA/phone interface
- Narrow the list further by eliminating the hosts that do not generate the RSS XML feeds or pages you want. That could be iTunes tags, enclosures, or embedded media in pages

---

CHAPTER 8

In the Studio and On-the-Go

There are a variety of different formats for podcasts and video blogs, from rough, unedited impromptu clips to fully-scripted broadcast quality productions. Whatever format you choose, your video will have to meet minimum standards of quality for your audience to watch it. While we don't know what that threshold is, the information in this chapter should help you surpass it.

The same principles of recording good audio and video apply in the studio or outside. Whether you are producing raw, short clips of content with no post-production, or trying to pilot the next hit TV series on the Internet, the style of your own blogging efforts and the format of your show will determine how much of a studio you need to build.

All that's needed to get good results are good eyes, good ears, some patience and creativity. Money never hurts either.

This chapter covers:

- Spaces and acoustics
- Spaces and video
- Virtual spaces
- Audio and video on-the-go

Spaces and Acoustics

Finding a good spot to record audio is often harder than finding a place for good video. Audio is finicky; there are sound-reflective surfaces and ambient noises to contend with everywhere. Without going into the science of acoustics, the ideal audio recording location will be somewhere relatively small with lots of sound deadening material and no hard and flat surfaces like glass, sheetrock, concrete or wood in the immediate area. The reason for all of this echo/ambient noise phobia is that whatever the microphone picks up is on your recording, sharing noise space with your voice, detracting from the overall quality of the production.

ALERT **Going Pro vs. Going With the Flow**

! This section goes into detail about how to deaden the sound and inexpensively build yourself a home studio where you can record broadcast-quality (i.e., professional radio) sound.

The question is, do you want or need to do that? Indeed, it's a matter of taste, audience, the time you have, and how "real" you want your podcast to sound.

You can simply grab a mic and start recording, and if your content is good, people will tolerate some imperfections and listen to it anyway. As you gain more experience, your technique will improve, and your shows will get better. Unlike radio, you can learn on the job while podcasting.

So don't feel like you have to do everything here; these are simply tools to help you get the sound you want, not to scare you off. The important thing is to get your voice out there, and then use the information in this chapter to make it sound even better.

For the home setup, working on as small a budget possible, while still getting positive results, it only requires raiding all of the beds and linen closets and heading down to the DIY store. Your blankets are well-suited to the task at hand with their built-in baffling, uneven surfaces and dense material. Goose down comforters are ideal, assuming that its blankets or nothing. Goose down muffles sound quite well even in less dense summer quilts.

Another good cheap option are moving blankets. There are two kinds of moving blankets and the difference is significant. The new style that you will see on U-Haul trucks is a matted fabric that does provide some sound deadening but not a great deal. The older style, with the square quilting are heavier, more durable and better at muffling noise. If a local mover is selling old ones that are torn up, you could get a nice pile of them for a song.

With the assumption that you'll be recording somewhere near your computer, there are a couple of options: You can set up more permanent sound dampening or have a setup that can be put up and broken down for storage during the times you're not recording so as not to clutter up the space.

Any professional sound equipment catalog or on-line store will offer some type of acoustic sound treatment, and will often carry a wide variety with a range in price. Wedge style and egg crate style foam are typically the most popular and do very well to knock down echoes and insulate the space from some ambient noise. This type of foam is often secured to the walls of recording spaces but can, with some creativity be put into use in a more mobile setting.

ALERT Egg crate style foam sold as acoustic sound product will often sell for five times the price of a nearly similar freight packing egg crate material that will do the same job.

One way to create an easily broken down sound dampening "room" is to create a few false walls that can be moved and stored easily. Wedge type foam comes in different shapes and sizes. If you choose to record your audio at your desk, check off a few things first:

- Is there a window in this room that lets in street or other outside ambient noise I don't want in my recording such as dogs barking, busses driving by, kids playing?

- Can I turn off or block out interior ambient noise such as heating/air conditioning units, fans, people talking, computer and video equipment cooling fans, neighbors walking around above me?

- Are the ambient sounds something I can reduce significantly with the use of blankets?

If you can secure relative silence, great, if not, consider finding a quieter room on the interior of the building and away from appliances or noise generating equipment. Even your computer may be making too much noise in the room where you are podcasting or filming—either get a quieter computer or a quiet laptop that you can do your recording on. Avoid garages unless you've put wall-to-wall and floor-to-ceiling carpeting; the lack of sound absorbing fabric and surplus of hard flat surfaces will make setting up good sound a much harder task.

Start by getting your hands on some foam. 4' × 2' sections and 12" squares are relatively standard sizes and depending on your implementation you will likely need a little of both. The key to reducing echoes is to cover the areas sound will reflect on hard surfaces and reflect back to hit the microphone. Imagine you're trying to create a dome around your body, focusing on your upper body and more specifically in front of you. For example, if you're sitting at a desk to record, the wall space in front of you to 120 degrees (just a little in from the limits of your peripheral vision) and vertical to about 5 feet above your head should have 90% foam covering.

Having a computer screen directly in front of you will reduce the effectiveness of the process. Having carpet on the floor takes care of that plane and ceiling tile found in most offices does assist somewhat. If at all possible, get some extra foam above you.

To better cover the spaces on your desk and to keep sound issues to a minimum, make some handy baffles. Take a 12" square of foam and attach a triangle of cardboard to the back of it at a perpendicular angle making what almost looks like a photograph frame that would sit on a desk, it now has its own little stand. That baffle can be used to cover up all variety of acoustically reflective objects without having to touch them or cover them directly.

The same trick can be used for the space behind you. Head down to your local *Home Depot* or *Lowes* and pick up a few sheets of home insulation rigid foam board. The thicknesses vary so be sure to get it at least 1' thick. The entire sheet will likely be a 4' × 8' section. While you're there, grab an extending razor knife and a pair of leather palmed cheap work gloves. Since these will be used to make standees, you can cut them to size in the parking lot if the huge sheet will not fit in your vehicle allowing you to cut it later.

ALERT Cutting foam in parking lots is not optimal but if you must, you must. Use caution with razor knives; use gloves in case the foam gives too suddenly and always cut away from yourself and your hands.

The rigid foam will be very useful to create a standing sound break or collection of breaks. The insulation foam itself does work to reduce echo and insulates you from sound as well as make for a perfect backing material for the acoustic foam, which can be secured to the insulation with spray adhesive.

Making the sound break stand can be done in a number of ways, the simplest is to attach TWO lengths of 24 1' × 2' wood strips to the bottom of the sound break which will make it look like an H. Setting the 1' × 2' into the bottom edge of the sound break with a notch so the feet and the edge are flush with the floor allow the feet to be better secured to the break. The feet can be glued in place and if more strength is required, cut right triangles (a triangle with a 90% angle on one side) out of extra insulation foam and glue them vertically between the feet and the body of the break. The triangles will add some rigidity, keeping them from flexing or wobbling as they are moved around (see **Figure 8-1**).

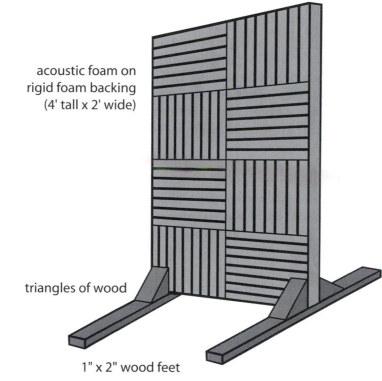

acoustic foam on
rigid foam backing
(4' tall x 2' wide)

triangles of wood

1" x 2" wood feet

Figure 8-1
Movable acoustic foam wall

The insulation and acoustic foam can be used in many different combinations to assist in making each space more conducive to good sound recording. Experiment with placement and test out different recordings until you get the results you are looking for. Always be on the lookout for quiet and well-insulated places and materials that can help improve sound production.

Spaces and Video

Video production adds a new element to the equation but don't forget the importance of the acoustic aspects when looking for places to shoot video and how that space is set up, it only requires a little more creativity.

The Set

Even the talking-head video blog requires a set. The set is comprised of lighting, props and backdrops. The simplest version of this scenario is to simply place the camera on a tripod where it can record you, and you do your show from wherever you see fit. There are four basic elements to deal with:

1. Is the setting right? Is everything that is going to be in frame what I want to see in the final product? What can I add or subtract from the shot to make it look better?

2. Is the lighting going to complement the shot, how do I control the lighting in the shot in order to make it look more professional?

3. Am I getting good audio, are the microphones right for this setting, how do I control the sound so I don't have to re-shoot this again or dub the sound?

4. Are there any trademarks or other materials held by litigious copyright holders in my shot? If so, I take them out of the shot or is it fair use in this?

ALERT You may be surprised what things in your shoot can be infringing. Things like music, product logos, ads, posters, TV in the background may be protected property and require written releases in order to be reproduced, even if they are in the background of a video blog. Read Chapter 14 (Licensing and Copyrights) for more information.

The set is everything that is going to be seen in the video frame so it's important to make sure that it only contains the things you want to be seen. It's all part of the story. If you're video blogging about serious Middle East politics and sitting on the couch next to you is a collection of stuffed animals, the strange juxtaposition of biting political commentary and Raggedy Ann might not help convey the gravity of the message.

Directors have an amazing job; they have to consider what the entire frame of film is saying and not just what the actors are reading, so dress your set according to the message being sent. Car talk video blogs might be well set in a clean garage with a nice car in the background and a big bright red tool chest off to the side. The same show with the same script hosted from the beach just doesn't hit the mark.

Lighting

The basic goal with lighting is to create a natural looking scene that isn't distracting and has no unwanted shadows.

There is no one single right way to light, it's an art form and depending on the very specific scenario of your shoot, different lighting requirements will be required. Lighting a scene properly doesn't have to mean setting up a diesel generator out back or buying a professional lighting kit. You can get started with lights you have on hand.

In most video productions the simple but standard *3-point* lighting system is used to provide good and professional lighting (see **Figure 8-2**).

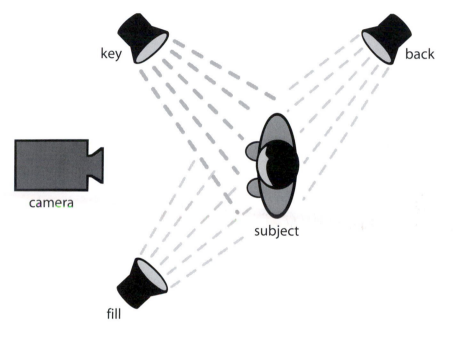

Figure 8-2
3-point lighting

In a 3-point lighting setup, lights are typically set-up on tripods and set-up around the subject. The main *key* light is the brightest light and provides the majority of light. The key light is either to the left or right of the camera aiming at the subject directly from an angle. A *fill* light, placed on the opposite side of the camera gives some light to the shadowed area and brightens up the darker side of the scene. The back light, often behind or above and behind the subject adds depth and more definition to the subject while also reducing shadows. After spending our lives accustomed to professionally lit scenes, bad lighting can be jarring to viewers. The trick is simply to use three light sources, making shadows subtle and pleasant and providing adequate visual depth to the scene.

Author's Tip

There are many subtle details that add up to professional video. While you can use the house lamps you already own, indoor shoots can always benefit from a good, natural looking light source and that will require a trip to the camera store.

The local mall camera shop will be less likely to have a full-suite of production gear so it's good to do a little research. Places like Cinema Supplies *http://store.yahoo.com/cinemasupplies/* and Studio Depot *http://www.studiodepot.com/* can ship all of the best stuff right to your door.

One of the most popular lighting elements is the light and tripod kit. It's simply a tall tripod with a very high power bulb, around 500 watts and a reflector. These look a lot light clip-on shop lights but these reflectors are highly polished and the bulbs put out significantly more light. These kits can be coupled with a number of accessories like reflective umbrellas, translucent umbrellas and soft light boxes (see **Figure 8-3**). As each situation will be different and there are too many possibilities to cover, it's best to take a photo of your set and some of the dimensions down to a good camera and video shop and discuss the set with one of the professionals that work there. They will likely be able to offer you a few different options and some price ranges.

Figure 8-3
Pro lighting gear

It's a good idea to get lighting that is flexible and can be used in a number of situations. Uni-taskers don't get a great return on the investment unless it's used for that single task over and over again. Lighting is also very fragile so having extra bulbs and expendables on hand will make life easier.

Tools

If you've ever seen a movie set, the grips and gaffers, the folks in charge of electrical, lighting and most scene setup have a tool belt that puts both Tim Allen and Batman to shame. None are identical but all are very well thought out. Here are a few things a gaffer or grip might have on his or her belt (see **Figure 8-4**):

- Multitool like a *Leatherman* or even better a Gerber tool (*http://www.gerber-tools.com/*) is a core requirement. Its combination of cutting, poking, scoring, measuring, and prying tools can apply to most tasks.

- Rolls of gaffers tape often hang there waiting to be helpful in securing lose dangling cords, taping over floor running wires to prevent trip-hazards binding panels together or any number of things tape can do.

- Zip ties compliment the tape by allowing heavier things to be secured, more wires tied together while being easy to remove.

- Box cutter/razor knife.

- The Sharpie magic marker can write on nearly any surface, even ice. On any movie set there will be at least as many Sharpies as there are people.

- C47 also known as a clothes pin is perfect for securing lighting gels, holding a sheet in place or propping up a prop.

- Measuring tape.

- Set of basic hand tools, slotted pliers, needle-nose pliers, Philips head screw driver, flat-head or slotted screw driver.

Author's Tip

There's a vast difference between consumer, "prosumer," and professional grade products. It's true that over time consumer gear can exceed the quality level of what was considered professional just a few years earlier. Nonetheless, there is a difference, and when you find yourself battling with bad color, tapes with glitches in them, or hard-to-control picture settings, you'll understand why pro gear costs more. Get started with what you have, but find out what your peers are using for the podcasts and video blogs you like the most. Once you learn what you need, you may save a lot by buying used from another podcaster who is upgrading too.

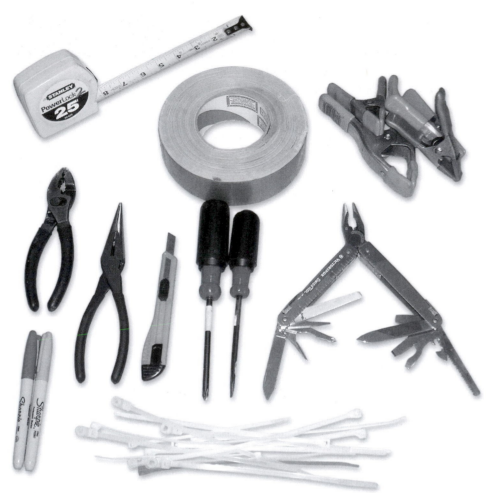

Figure 8-4
Tools of the trade

The list can go on and on but the bare essentials cover things you need to get your set looking like it needs to in short order and without actual construction. Other useful things to have on set are milk crates to carry things as well as to raise object up into view. Sand bags will keep lighting kits and anything that can topple from jiggling or falling over. Small wooden wedges can get furniture and other props to sit at a desired angle or take the wobble out. A Velcro kit with peel-off adhesive is a must have for hiding equipment within the scene or quickly but not permanently attaching something to something else.

A matte dulling spray will take the glare off of shiny surfaces like glass, lenses, headlights or other objects that might cause a *lens flare*, the bright haze or distinctive flaring light caused by a strong light source that goes straight into the lens. These tools and expendables are all easily sourced from a local film/photography production store.

In preparing the set, make use of the acoustic materials to minimize reflected sound and reduce ambient noise. Once again the blankets and baffles come into play. In this setting, the sound deadening materials may not fit well in the shot. One option is to have them as close to the sound source as possible while being out of the frame. They can also be hidden behind a back-drop or in the scene but obscured by a prop. Using a boom microphone or lavalier type microphone (**Figure 8-5**) will allow for far more sound quality control and somewhat lessen the need for a great deal of sound-proofing.

Author's Tip

The local mall camera shop will be less likely to have a full suite of production gear so it's good to do a little research. Places like Cinema Supplies (*http://store.yahoo.com/cinemasupplies/*) and Studio Depot (*http://www.studiodepot.com/*) can ship right all of the best gear right to your door.

Figure 8-5
Lavalier microphone

Virtual Spaces

Today's technology allows audio and video creators to do a lot of virtual "smoke and mirrors." Just as your sound stage can be under a towel, your backlot sets can be figments of your computer's imagination. With modern digital technology, you barely need a set at all. Here are some tricks of the virtual trade.

Double Ending

Double ending is a trick used by podcasters that can be used for video blogging too.

It's often hard to score an interview with someone except over the phone, due to travel or schedule problems. But phone interviews sound very, telephonic.

The trick of double ending is to put a quality recorder on both ends of the interview, as well as talk on the phone. If you're really trying to make it easy for your interviewee, you can purchase a lecture recorder and Fedex it to them. When you call them, ask them to press record and set it on the desk. Record the phone call as a backup, and record your own voice locally with another quality recorder.

Then, when they send you back (or upload) the interview to you, you can splice the two together, and edit to taste. The product will sound like an in-person interview.

A video blogging version of this can be used to simulate a live interview. You've probably watched TV shows (and video blogs) where they break to a local correspondent. They'll even banter with each other, to give it a live feel: "Now, we'll go to Chuck...Chuck, are you there?"/"Yes, I'm here Cindy, and the weather is great."

If you need to remotely interview someone, have them set their webcam or local tripod-mounted video recorder to record. Call them on a cell phone so they can use an unobtrusive earbud for the actual interview. If they don't have a camera, and video would really help the interview, send them a small digital video recorder, with a mini tripod. This setup should cost as low as $300. Have them set it on the desk or a shelf, point it, and ask them if they can see their reflection in the lens. This will give you a double-ended video interview, which you can splice together in the same way.

Skypecasting

Skype is a very very popular *VoIP* (Voice over Internet Protocol) service that is basically an Instant Messenger, which also does phone calls. When used between two computers, the audio quality actually exceeds that of telephones. *Skypecasting* is a fantastic way to do multiparty conference call collaborative blogs and interviews and is very popular among podcasters.

Recording Skype calls is a bit complicated but the results sound good. The simplest way to record such a call is to take a digital recorder, (such as an Iriver 899) and split the speaker output from your PC to the recorder. But if you want a complete in-the-computer approach, there are software programs that can grab the Skype chat and save it directly to the hard drive as a sound file.

The basic technique is the same but uses different programs to record Skype on Mac OSX and Windows platforms. An excellent diagram of the process can be found at *http://log.hugoschotman.com/hugo/2005/04/advanced_podcas.html* (see **Figure 8-6**). If you're doing it on a Mac, you can find a tutorial at *http://www.macdevcenter.com/pub/a/mac/2005/01/25/podcast.html* and on Windows at *http://www.skypejournal.com/blog/archives/2004/12/skype_podcast_r.php*.

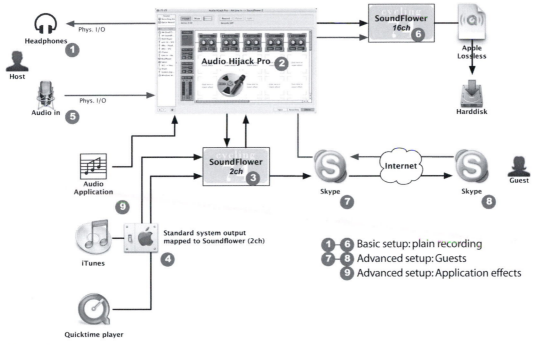

Figure 8-6
Skypecasting system diagram

Inside the Industry

Apple has recently added a similar feature to Skypecasting in their iChat instant messaging product and GarageBand audio editing software. You can easily start a multiparty audio chat in iChat, and it will automatically record each party's voice as a separate track in GarageBand. iChat and GarageBand are both part of Apple's iLife software, which includes a complete start-to-finish podcasting and video blogging tool suite. You can get more info at *http://www.apple.com/ilife/*.

Virtual Backdrops

You've probably heard of *bluescreening* or *greenscreening*, also technically called *chroma keying*. This is a technique of having a distinctly single-colored background behind an actor and then using it to superimpose that actor on other scenery where the color was. If you've ever watched the weather or the Daily Show, you've seen this technique used. You can even shrink your actors and layer them—whatever achieves the visual result you seek.

Chroma keying programs and plug-ins are available in the more professional line of video editing programs, such as Final Cut Pro and Adobe Premiere. Making a suitable green-screen is quite easy—you can purchase green felt from a fabric store and pin it to a wall for decent results. There are many tutorials on chroma key technique online. The Bicycle Sidewalk video blog has a nice tutorial (*http://www.bicycle-sidewalk.com/?p=64*) on how he superimposes himself on the video blogs he makes (**Figure 8-7**).

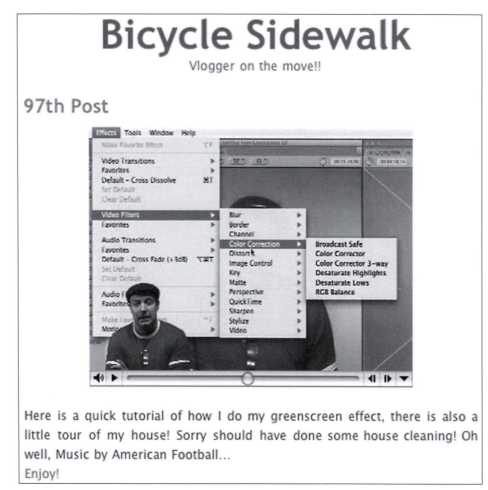

Figure 8-7
Talking torso superimposed with chroma key

Taking the video camera on a walk can be a fun and engaging part of filming but can make the video very shaky. If you've ever gotten a headache watching VHS tapes of old family parties, you know how unwatchable and unstable video can be. Much of this can be alleviated with practice, but there is some technology you can bring to bear on the problem as well.

Audio and Video On-the-Go

Taking the show on the road brings with it some new and interesting challenges. Things to consider are lighting and ambient light control, sound recording outdoors and camera stability. Things we take for granted in an enclosed space can come back and ruin a seemingly simple outdoor shoot.

Daylight can be a good and bad thing. A nice, well-lit outdoor scene can look great on camera as long as the sun isn't wreaking havoc on the video by shining into the lens. The same can be said for shooting indoors where the sun can shine in through an open door or window. The sunlight can mess with the white balance of the camera and make for a poor image. The solution is simply to change the camera angle or partially block the sunlight (with a window shade or a tall building or tree) to get the light down to a manageable level.

Record Redundantly
A great way to guarantee you can get the results you want is to put a mic on everyone. Barring that, you can use portable MP3 recorders to supplement the audio that your video camera records.

A couple years ago I bought a simple recorder for lectures, an EVR-500 from Beat Sounds. This MP3 player/record unit records voice through its built-in microphone into MP3 format. With just 256 MB of memory, it can record hours and hours of audio on a single AAA battery. I use it whenever I deliver a filmed lecture, because I usually can't get a feed from the lavalier mic they rig me up with, and my camera is always at the far back of the room.

You can buy a half dozen cheap lecture or audio recorders (a colleague of mine really likes the iRiver 899) and put them near all the subjects. Some even have lanyards and you can put them around the necks of the people talking.

When you go to mix down the audio or video at the end, you can mix the best audio feeds in with the video you have on your camera.

Audio is harder outdoors too. If you're doing a scripted outdoor scene, you can put lavalier microphones on all the actors. If the subjects are still (as in a wedding) you can use a shotgun mic (which picks up sound in a particular direction). But if it's just informal, documentary style blogging, you're going to have to improvise to get the audio right. The key is to get a microphone as near the subject as possible while not messing up the spontaneity of the scene.

There are several things you can do to mitigate shaky video while filming on the move:

- Practice holding your camera stable and level while moving around.
- Practice moving the camera smoothly and deliberately.
- Combine above techniques with a camera that comes with image stabilization.
- Add a steady-camera type device to your collection of equipment.

Many cameras come with different "fuzzy logic" image steadying technology, it's always best to try it out in the store and see if it works for you. If you're already in position of the camera you like and don't want to buy a new one just for one feature, an external steadying device will make pictures much more still and offer a more stable filming platform.

There are a lot of free "hacks" that you can do to get an image stabilized. The website *http://www.cs.cmu.edu/~johnny/steadycam/* offers a DIY guide that shows you how to build a very capable device for $14 out of simple Home Depot parts (see **Figure 8-8**). They also sell them for $39 if you can't be bothered to make one.

Author's Tip

Improvised Camera Mounts

The bottom line on camera stabilization is simply to keep the camera still. And that doesn't really cost a dime. There are as many ways to keep the camera still as there are nonmoving objects.

If you have a small camera phone, you can set it to record and stuff it into a shoe and use a sock to hold it still. If you're driving and want to get a view of the road, set your video camera on a heavy sweater or towel on the dashboard.

If you're out and filming near your car, you can put the camera on your car hood or roof and aim it appropriately. Again, some clothes can be used to hold it somewhat still and aim it better (and not scratch your paint).

Need a tall shot? Start running your camera, climb a tree and put it in a sweater nest.

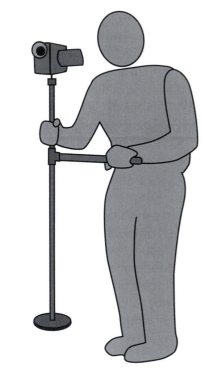

Figure 8-8
Poor man's steady camera mount

Other companies like Studio 1 Productions (*http://www.studio1productions.com/smoothcam.htm*) make more professional looking systems that does the same thing using the same physics.

If part of your video blogging involves road scenes, travelogues or even car chases, you may not want to risk your expensive camera falling off your car when the duct tape comes loose. A company called ChaseCam (*http://chasecam.com/*) makes suction-cup mounting brackets for your camera for the outside of the car.

The minimum set of tools you need to video blog is ultimately:

1. a video camera
2. a computer
3. an Internet connection

Conclusion

Video blogging is a new medium, but video is not. The difference with video blogging is that you can reach an unlimited audience at minimal cost.

Whether you intend to build a dedicated video blogging or podcasting studio or you simply want to point and shoot, there's a minimum level of quality you'll want to have.

You can build a studio cheaply, and creativity will be a big money saving tool. Many of the items needed for setting up a studio may already be close at hand.

Look at what other podcasters and video bloggers are using. There are many people doing the same thing, and even documenting their results, which can help you avoid reinventing the wheel.

CHAPTER 9

Essential Tools

As much as the postage stamp-sized video clips of old were cool, we've moved on. At five frames per second in a 160 × 120 pixel window, Internet video used to be a very substandard experience, a novelty at best. That has all changed. Podcasting and video blogging have removed the majority of the barriers to high-quality Internet video.

Producing online streaming video, even today, requires special filming considerations. Video blogging does not. When you stream, you have to cater to the lowest bandwidth of your audience—as low as 300 kbps—and make your video meet that low standard. That translates to simple, uninteresting sets, narrow camera shots, and little motion.

Podcasting and video blogging have no such limitations, because the audience downloads it as fast as they can. For the most part, you can shoot whatever you want, and the quality will be limited more by your own production skills than any bandwidth or financial considerations.

That brings us to audio and video editing. Since there are no longer limits to what you can produce, you should get familiar with the tools of video editing. There are probably *too* many books already on this subject, so this chapter will focus on listing the tools you'll need for audio and video blogging specifically.

This chapter will cover the tools you should have including:

- A powerful computer
- A/V Editing software
    - Mac editing
    - PC editing
    - A/V format converters and transcoders
    - Audio capture

- A/V hardware
  - Built-in microphones
  - Wireless microphones
  - Headphones
  - Speakers
  - Interview kits
  - Video cameras
  - Tripods

A Powerful Computer

You might have all the computing power you need right now, you might not. Each software package is going to offer some type of minimum and or recommended hardware setup to get optimal results. Depending on their motivation, you may or may not be well served following those recommendations.

Following are a couple of general recommendations that are generalized but should serve as a template for those building their own systems from scratch or ordering one to spec online.

Moderate System (PC)
2.5 Ghz Intel (Non-Celeron/Mobile) or 3200 AMD CPU
1 GB RAM
7200 RPM EIDE Hard drives 200+GB
ATI / Osprey / Winnov video capture board
Creative Audigy sound card with SPDIF / Optical inputs
Windows XP Pro

Moderate System (Mac)
Any desktop iMac or Mac Laptop

A low end, just-scraping-by system will be problematic and cause more headaches than it's worth. The worst problems come up because of a deficiency in RAM. When too little RAM is available in a system, the computer has to go to the disk drive for more room, and the slowness causes a massive backup similar to what happens when a tractor-trailer jack-knifes on a freeway: not only does the tractor trailer stop moving, everything else behind it is affected and suddenly stops moving.

7200 RPM and faster drives are recommended for video, and the faster you get, the more performance you will see. Performance does also equal better quality dubs pulled from the video capture board. If the drive is too slow, the board will not be able to write all of the video data to disk and will drop frames. Western Digital offers a 160 GB 10,000 RPM SATA hard drive with a 5.4 ms average seek time, which is 2,800 RPM faster than most other SATA drives and twice the seek speed. Although SCSI drives are still much more expensive, they are built to higher tolerances and perform much better. The Seagate Cheetah comes in 10K and 15K RPM models and when assembled into a multidisk RAID, disk operations happen at break-neck albeit bank-breaking speeds.

Author's Tip

If you go out and buy the second down from the fastest CPU available on the market (for PC) you don't lose much in the way of power. Don't buy cheap RAM, get Kingston or Corsiar and the fastest FSB (front side bus) speed you can match up to the motherboard and CPU. Slow RAM is a real and irritating bottleneck.

ALERT

!

Drive performance is measured in a number of ways. Overall throughput is important and related to the speed of the bus and the speed of the spinning disk. Another critical number is the seek time. Some drives may spin quickly but have slow seek times. If you are looking at two drives with similar RPM numbers but one has a 5.4 ms seek time and the other has a 9.5 ms seek time, the faster one (the one with the *smallest* seek time) will be able to find data on the disk much faster.

The disk situation can become very complicated in short order. There is a lot of risk mitigation that has to be taken into consideration when important data is living on disk drives. Backing up a terabyte of data can be an expensive task requiring tape libraries that have prices starting in the 10K range and go up sharply from there. Most video editing systems use a combination of disk performance and redundancy setup in order to optimize both performance and redundancy. In order to talk about that, we should cover the basics of RAID and which RAID types matter.

RAID 0	Stripe set	This type of RAID is not redundant at all. It literally stripes a file system across a set of disks in order to use multiple spindles to work at the same time, thereby increasing the overall max input and output. This offers the highest levels of performance while offering the worst level of safety. If one disk fails in the stripe, the entire file system is toast. Period. It's a great system to use if the data on the stripe in not critical but contains large files that push the disk I/O to the limit.

RAID 1	Mirror	Mirror is exactly that, two disks that mirror each other. Used often as a protection method for boot drives on workstations it's effective for keeping systems up even in the event of hardware failure. Many mirrors can be hot-swapped so the system never has to be re-booted for a new drive to be re-installed. Mirrors can also be used for any other system drive but the next version is often more advantageous and adds performance benefits that a mirror does not.
RAID 5	Stripe set with parity	How did we go from 0 to 1 and directly to 5? Raid 2, 3 and 4 are not terribly popular and account for a small minority of implementations. People may argue their reasoning for using a RAID 4 as a video drive array, but when it comes to wide-spread compatibility across RAID controllers, best practices dictate RAID 5. This version of RAID allows for a large number of disks (it only requires three drives as a minimum) to have the benefit of the RAID 0 type striping but adds parity to the mix. Parity writes extra data across each of the disks, enough so that if any one of the drives fail, the RAID set can keep operating without any data loss at all. The huge benefit is that a 4-port SATA raid controller can be purchased for less than $250, and a large SATA hard drive can be found for $100 to $200 each, allowing you to have around 1 terabyte of usable, high performance, protected disk space for less than $1,200.

Although RAID 1 and 5 offer some protection, there is no substitute to backing-up data files and keeping them in a secure location. Mirrors can fail, RAID 5 arrays can suffer multiple disk failures. Don't leave yourself exposed, have a back-up plan.

Strong system PC
Intel Pentium D 3.4 Ghz / AMD Athlon 64 4800
2 GB RAM
6-8 SATA Raid controller
SATA RAID 1 Mirrored boot drives, Raid 5 data drives
ATI / Osprey / Winnov video capture board
Creative E-MU 1820m Pro-audio system with balanced inputs
Windows XP Pro

Strong system MAC
Any dual-processor desktop Mac system without "i" in the name.

The strong system raises the stakes and cost somewhat but puts you firmly into a high performance editing system. The faster processor allows for faster effects and shuttling through video and audio files, the RAM helps keep more data in memory rather than having to go to the disk for access and the RAID is a vast improvement for all disk access and redundancy. The strong system does not have to be a whole upgrade, elements of this configuration cam be added to the moderate system to improve performance in key areas that are more of a concern for your specific production needs. Every set of components has its upgrade path and most systems can be upgraded during their lifecycles. The upgraded Creative E-MU 1820m Pro audio system allows for professional audio recording, bringing up the level of quality for all audio input, processing and output. The addition of balanced inputs allows professional quality microphones to be directly connected to the computer for the highest quality voice and sound recording.

The component levels don't stop here, there are many more, much higher quality components that can offer better video capture, sound recording and system performance but the prices begin to get very high, and there is a level of diminishing returns when it comes to the area of video blogging and podcasting. Its not that the quality won't be noticed; it's more that the medium does not always require broadcast quality production standards.

A/V Editing Software

There are a number of standard, popular applications used on both the Mac and PC platforms and we'll go over some of them here.

If you already have tools you're using for video editing, you may not need anything else. If you're unfamiliar with video editing, you should play around with the software that came with your computer or camera so you can get educated enough to see if you need to upgrade. And if you are already familiar with video editing, chances are you already have an opinion about what you need.

Mac Editing

The iLife suite of applications from Apple cater to the blogger and are actually designed for the budding video podcaster (see **Figure 9-1**). The iLife suite includes a photo editing and sharing program, iMovie HD that allows you to import HD DV video and edit it, and iDVD that lets you make the edited film into a DVD movie, complete with menus. The podcasting part comes in with GarageBand and iWeb, also included in the package. GarageBand lets you create and edit podcasts and iWeb packages up the whole thing and uploads it to your .Mac account (Apple's hosted web service platform) blog, or your own blog.

Apple succeeds in taking complex and disparate processes and turning them into a cohesive workflow that an average user can follow through to the final product. It's the fact that they complete the process that makes it a compelling product.

Figure 9-1
Apple iLife suite with podcasting support

Apple's Final Cut Express is a middle ground between iMovie and Final Cut Pro, their high-end professional offering. At $300, you get the advanced main edit windows features of Pro but not some of the more Pro-oriented features and effects of the $1,000 version. That said, Express does offer HD editing, which can let you publish HD video blogs with the same amount of effort it takes to produce a regular video blog.

GarageBand comes with every Mac as part of their iLife suite, and given that it includes podcasting-specific features in the '06 version probably makes it the best choice if you're on a Mac.

If you come from a music background, the Mac is also host to a number of leading studio applications. If you're creating a radio show with music, fades, effects, and the like, you could use ProTools (*www.digidesign.com*) or any similar audio apps.

If you're doing straightforward podcasts with voice and maybe adding some sound clips, there are very inexpensive apps that would fit the bill. Amadeus (*http://www.hairersoft.com/Amadeus.html*) is a fantastic program for OSX, which supports basic audio conversion and track overlays and costs only $30.

PC Editing

You probably can't buy a decent PC today without a pre-installed video editing application. If your computer didn't come with one, you can download Windows Movie Maker free from their website (*http://www.microsoft.com/windowsxp/downloads/updates/moviemaker2.mspx*). And if you purchase a digital camera, or a FireWire card to hook it up to your computer, you're probably going to get software packaged with it as well. Long story short, you probably can't help but have a free video editing app on your computer. The good news is almost all of these are sufficient for basic moviemaking.

Now, if you're looking for more, Adobe Premiere and Sony's Vegas products are outstanding editors (see **Figure 9-2**). The Vegas Movie Studio Platinum product is a good, HD capable, fully-featured editing tool that shares the same interface as the Pro version, while costing only $129. It's in the same price range as Adobe's Premiere Elements, which has a similar set of features and capabilities, with the exception of HD support in the Adobe product.

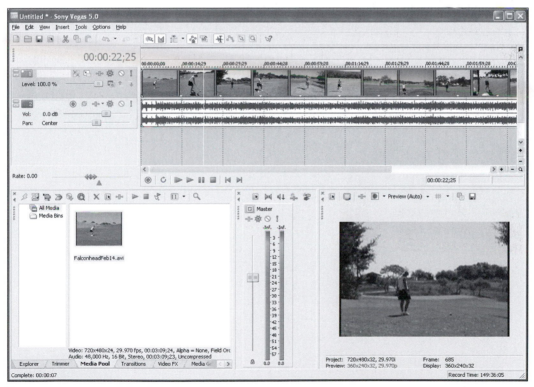

Figure 9-2
Sony Vegas

There are close to 100 sound editing applications on the market, most of which do in essence the same thing, edit audio. Choosing one that does the right job for you is a matter of price point and features.

Sony (through its acquisition of Sonic Foundry) offers two outstanding products for editing audio: Sony Sound Forge Audio Studio $69 and Sound Forge 8 $299 (see **Figure 9-3**). Audio Studio is a somewhat pared down version of the $299 Pro package but still offers a slew of features that should cover all but the most extreme podcasting needs. The Pro version offers many more audio tracks and filters that can come in handy for cleaning up noisy tracks from recorded phone calls or outdoor recording.

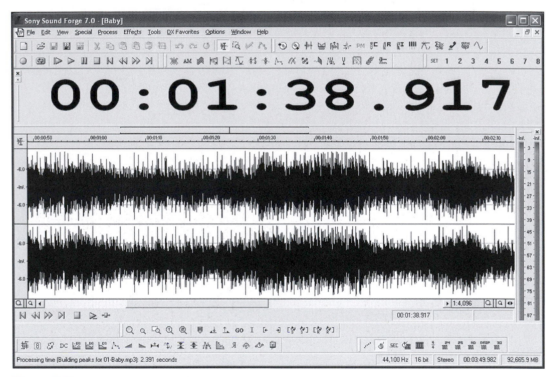

Figure 9-3
Sony Sound Forge

Adobe also offers a nice editing package, Adobe Audition, for $349, which has similar features to Sound Forge. If you're used to Adobe products and like to stay in the family, it would be worth trying out. The nice thing about these products is that they are all available for trial downloads, even the most expensive ones.

Little things like a sound bed can set your video blog or podcast apart from the rest of the field. Sony Acid Music Studio and the Pro 5, $69 and $299, respectively, let you create loops and even create music from scratch. Not having to license original music will save you legal headaches as well as add something very personal to your recording.

A/V Format Converters and Transcoders

So what tools do you need to make a video blog? Because there's no single video standard yet, you'll be doing a lot of *transcoding* (converting from one video format to another).

The QuickTime Pro application (*http://www.apple.com/quicktime/*) is only $30 and provides amazing results (see **Figure 9-4**). Both Windows and Mac versions do the same thing and offer an inexpensive tool to video bloggers. It doesn't hurt that iTunes likes the format and it can offer problems when other media types are used in enclosures.

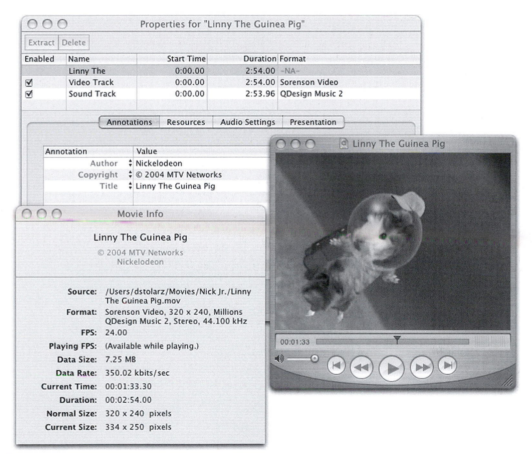

Figure 9-4
Apple QuickTime Pro

Even if you don't buy the pro version of QuickTime, there are a variety of apps that produce iTunes, iPod, and Playstation Portable compatible MPEG-4 MP4 files.

The MPEG-4 file format, in the form of an MP4 file, is the pervasive file type in the video blogosphere for a number of reasons, including widespread player support, cross-platform compatibility and quality, and the fact that MP4 and AVC files are supported by iTunes and the iPod with video.

For the PC, many of the countless video conversion apps that run on XP are adding an "export to iPod" and "export to PSP" option, showing just how prevalent the format has become.

FFMpeg is a set of open-source video conversion tools. There are probably hundreds of free, shareware, and payware tools that simplify the use of these tools. A decent list of such applications can be found at *http://ffmpeg.sourceforge.net/projects.php*. The good thing is, you can convert almost ANYTHING to an iTunes/iPod compatible video blog with these tools.

On a Mac, some tools that use FFMpeg are iSquint (*http://www.isquint.org/*) and FFMpegX (*http://homepage.mac.com/major4/*), which takes nearly any type of file type and converts it to an iPod-sized file (see **Figure 9-5**). The nice feature this adds is the ability to convert files encoded in DivX and XviD. Since it's free, it won't set your budget back any and the more tools like this that you have at your disposal the better. After a while, our archive of random videos we get from various sources becomes a melting pot of different size and format videos.

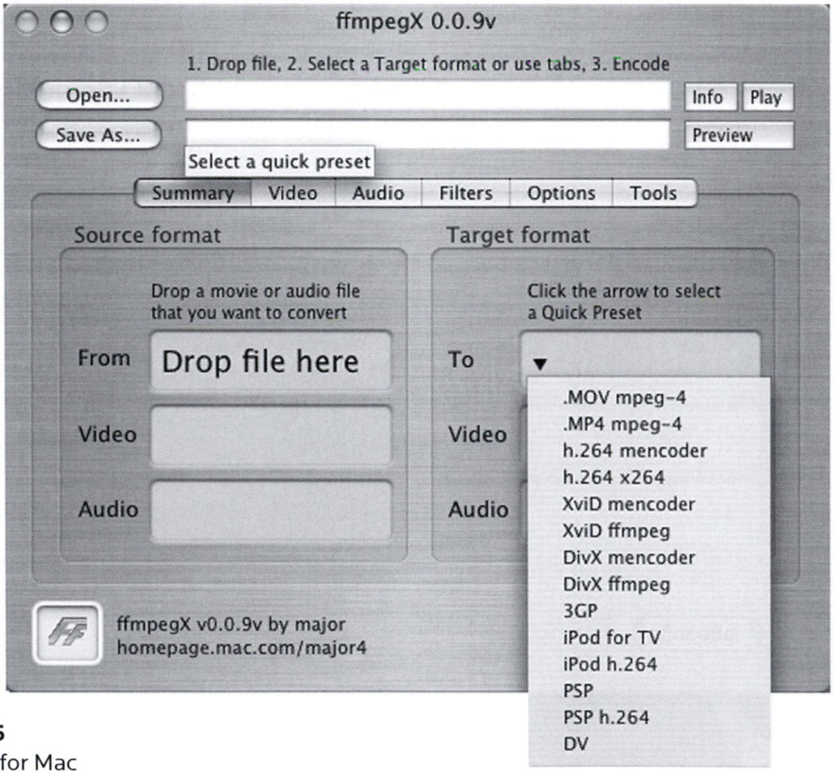

Figure 9-5
FFmpegX for Mac

Canopus, a well-known and long time player in the video conversion space offers a number of tools that can help transcode just about any format into just about any other format. One of the nice things their Pro Coder 2 application has is the ability to convert the proprietary 3GP and 3G2 video files made by Palm Treos into QuickTime or any other kind of format (see **Figure 9-6**).

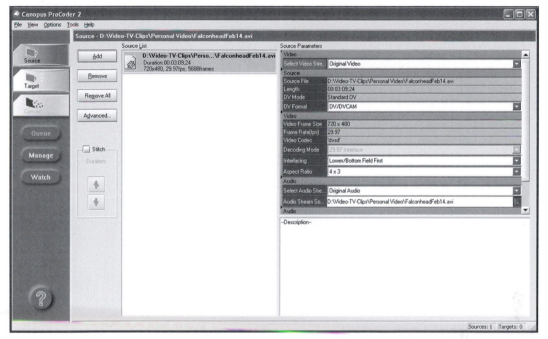

Figure 9-6
Canopus Pro Coder 2

Inside the Industry

Box vs. Contents

A metaphor may help you better understand the alphabet soup of acronyms, file extensions, and codec names that we gloss over in this chapter.

In a nutshell, there are two concepts. There's the *file format*, which is a sort of box that audio and video and text and graphics go into. Then there are *codecs*, compressor-decompressors, which are the way the audio, video, text and graphics are squeezed into the box.

Following are some examples of file formats. These are boxes, mere files into which you can stuff one or more codecs:

- *.MOV, .AVI, .WMF, .RM, .SWF, .WAV*

Then there are *codecs*, the actual guts of these files:

- MPEG-4 (technically, part 2 of the standard), AVC (Advanced Video Codec) aka H.264 aka MPEG-4 part 10), WMV (Windows Media Video), WMA (Windows Media Audio), DivX (a version of MPEG-4 version 2), 3ivX (a better implementation of MPEG-4), MPEG-1 (found on video CDs and video games), MPEG-2 (Found on DVDs and Satellite), Sorenson, FLV (Flash Video), SWF (Flash animation files).

To confuse the issue, some boxes can only hold one or two kinds of guts. In this case, the "Box" contains only one type of codec, but that same codec might be stored in a more generic AVI or MOV box, too:

- MP3, MP4, M4V (MPEG-4 video for iPod), M4A (MPEG-4 audio), MPG (MPEG-1 or MPEG-2), ASF ("Advanced Streaming Format—holds only WMA and WMV data), FLV (Flash Video).

Are you still confused? Well, that's because the one and true codec has yet to emerge. Nonetheless, it may help you, when you get a file, or have to produce one, to differentiate between the name ("I need to make an MOV because it's playing in iTunes") and the guts of the file, be they MPEG-1, MPEG-2, MPEG-4 version 2, or AVC/H.264/MPEG-4 part 10.

It's worth commenting on a couple of other file formats. The application FireAnt (see Chapter 4, Tuning in) supports a variety of downloadable video blog formats, including Windows Media and QuickTime. Realistically, you could encode in any format you want, as long as your audience downloads the appropriate codec. But MPEG-4 (specifically the various Apple/Sony variants) have the edge on Windows Media codecs and DivX's MPEG-4 for video blogs today.

WMV is native to Windows platforms but Mac users have to have the Windows Media Player installed to view those file types and the percentage of OSX systems with the WMP is relatively low.

RealVideo has sort of faded away with QuickTime and Flash in the lead, and is not really relevant to video blogging.

DivX and XviD are very popular for people making large digital movies (i.e., feature length movies) to play on computers on DixV-compliant DVD players. These codecs are standard MPEG-4 codecs, but they are designed for big files, like DVD and HD quality movies. As a result, conventional large-format DivX and XviD files aren't directly compatible with all portable MPEG-4 devices, especially the iPod and Playstation Portable, nor do they play in iTunes (but they do in Firefox with appropriate codecs).

Some video bloggers produce multiple versions of their files: an iTunes, iPod and Playstation Portable-compatible MP4 file, and then a higher resolution HD DivX or Windows media file. This would be something you would do to *increase* your audience at request of viewers and listeners. You'd want to make sure you were compatible with applications like iTunes and FireAnt first.

Offering file types that are not native to your target audience can work very well as long as you offer a direct download of the codec from a prominent place on your blog along with a description of what they are downloading and why it's needed.

The bottom line is, in video blogging, you're best off targeting one MPEG-4 format to satisfy all the iTunes iPod guys, and another format such as Windows Media or H.264 (both HD video capable) if you want to do a higher-res, standard or high-def version of your blog.

ALERT

!

Although files can be made using DivX, XviD, WMV and Real, each one has its issues, and none of them play in iTunes or on a video iPod. Whereas QuickTime has always been a distant third in the online streaming standards race, QuickTime-compatible MPEG-4 and AVC (MP4, and M4V files) are the de facto standard for video blogs today.

If you're producing video blog content, you can certainly use another format to satisfy other niches of users—Flash is popular—but you're severely limiting your audience if you don't offer an iTunes (and iPod) compatible MP4 file.

Audio Capture

Sometimes, you may want to record a track from an old tape, the phone hook-up or some other audio device and make it into a quick MP3. MP3myMP3 (*http://www.mp3mymp3.com/*) is a free and very useful program that can record from any recognized input on your computer (including anything being played back on the sound card) and make an MP3 out if it directly. There are a few useful configurations that allow you to adjust levels and encoding bitrate and quality. As long as you can plan a sound on your computer, including streaming audio, you can convert it to an MP3 (see **Figure 9-7**).

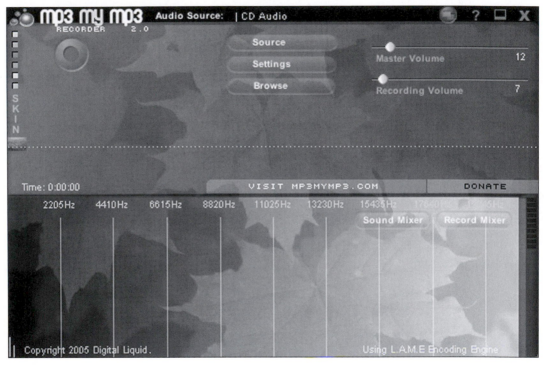

Figure 9-7
MP3myMP3

Author's Tip

You can find a comprehensive list of Mac-based audio capture, editing and manipulation tools here:

http://www.pure-mac.com/audio.html

A similar program for the Mac, Audio Hijack (*http://www.rogueamoeba.com/audiohijack/*) can be used for the Skypecasting (discussed in Chapter 8) as well to record sound from any particular application on your OSX system. It records each sound separately, so beeps from your IM don't get into the audio interview you're recording.

A/V Hardware

A lot of the hard-and-fast rules of professional video production go out the window when it comes to video blogging. The reason is, this emerging media really take all comers. If you want to podcast audio clips by uploading voice mail messages that you email to yourself, that's OK. If you want to do all your video in a fairly dark room using your grainy mobile phone video feature, which may totally do the trick for your subject and audience, that's OK too.

If you look at the range of production value now visible on television—everywhere from prime time, to cable, to infomercials, to reality TV, you realize that the audiences are accustomed to much less spit and polish than was expected in years past. Because of screen sizes, you also get away with a lot more—if your video blog is usually going to be 4" diagonally, you don't have to worry as much.

Built-in Microphones

In pro video, you would normally never want use the built-in microphone in a video camera. It's there as a last resort and will record every little sound in range. The same advice applies to the built-in microphone in most laptops.

The sound pickup of a built-in microphone is so small that Bobby's soccer game gets recorded with all of the sound from down field as well as close range.

If you recorded the same game with a well-calibrated *shotgun microphone* (a directional microphone mounted on a tripod that can be aimed at a distant sound), a few wireless mics on players, a wide pickup for the crowd and an audio mixing board, it would sound like a pro-soccer game and might be fun to watch for someone other than parents of kids in the game.

In a small room with low echo, however, it might do the trick. Purely informational video can be adequately conveyed with that, although the sound will always be better if you can mix in sound you've mic'ed closer to your mouth.

Wireless Microphones

Video blogs tend to focus on people talking, which takes us to the lavalier microphone (see **Figure 9-8**). This type of microphone is wirelessly connected to the audio input of the recorder. It's comprised of two parts, the transmitter and microphone. The microphone portion is actually quite small, but its specific purpose and placement within 18" of the mouth allows for its small size. It's connected through a long wire to the transmitter, which is often worn at the small of the back. The transmitter is about the size of a pager and runs on AA or AAA batteries. The receiver portion looks a lot like the transmitter, but its wire tether plugs directly into the microphone input of the camera.

Lavalier microphones will cover the vast majority of recording needs. Stage and studio style microphones are harder to work with in a video environment. You could use a *boom microphone* (held overhead with a pole), or hand-held microphone, or even a portable lecture recorder if you are interviewing people on the street or if holding a microphone in your hand is part what you want to show on screen.

Figure 9-8
Sennheiser lavalier microphone

Headphones

Editing audio and video means having to have a keen eye and ear tuned for the little pops, hisses, color variations and nuances that you might otherwise overlook when simply watching or listening to content. A good set of over-ear headphones can be purchased from Sony, AKG, Denon, Audio Technica, or Sennheiser (see **Figure 9-9**). Over-ear is important because of its isolating properties. The on-ear headphones can cause ear fatigue and simply don't reproduce sound as well. Whatever you do, do not use any type of noise canceling headphones. Those Bose Quiet Comfort headphones might have been very expensive and sound great on the plane but will not work well for editing.

Figure 9-10
Sony MDR-SA1000 studio monitor headphones (*http://www.sonystyle.com*)

Speakers

It's also important to have a good set of speakers for your computer. Video and audio play-back should be done under the best circumstances possible. A set of powered studio moni-tors from Roland or JBL would provide studio quality sound while being useful for computer audio reproduction. The speakers that come with a computer technically produce sound, but that's being generous. Ditch them right away and head over to the music store to look at what musicians use for their home studios.

Interview Kits

Telephone recording kits are very useful when conducting a phone interview or using a voicemail message as part of your podcast or video blog (see **Figure 9-10**). There may be legal issues associated with recording a phone call, so make sure you check your state laws before putting someone on the air without them knowing or without having them sign a release. Radio Shack is a popular purveyor of such instruments and a decent rig can be had for about $20. The phone-style jack connects to the handset and the other end connects to the line-in input of your computer.

> ## Author's Tip
>
> If phone interviews are a major part of your podcasts, check the previous section (A/V Capture) as well as the section in Chapter 8 on Skypecasting.

Figure 9-10
Radio Shack telephone recording adapter

Video Cameras

A camera is the key component in producing a video blog, and most off-the-shelf DV cameras will do the trick. Many connect via USB (on the PC at least) but you're better off with one that has a FireWire/iLink port for full compatibility.

For audio quality, look for a camera that can plug-in an external microphone (most can) and then turn off the built-in one (or just record on a separate recorder and combine the audio and video in your editing stage).

After that, focus on features such as the ability to set the *white balance* (this helps the camera keep colors true when different light sources are present), extras like image stabilization, and lens quality.

There are so many makes and models of cameras on the market.

The best thing to do is consider your budget and the features you have to have. If buying a new camera, DV is the only way to go. Other formats are on the way out so even a good deal isn't a good deal. You sacrifice image quality and ease of dubbing by using VHS-C or Hi8. Take a list of features you want down to the local big box retailer and look at all of the cameras in your price range.

Author's Tip

Fancy on-camera effects are, at least for video blogging, a waste of money. The quality of the recording and the ability to get the video and audio you want is, at the end of the day all that matters.

- Digital: DV-tape based or solid state (Flash memory) recorder
- Microphone input
- Size—handheld, stealthy, if you're filming on the go, or big, solid if you're tripodding and need a bigger lens
- FireWire/iLink port
- Manual white balance
- Image stabilization

Tripod

Cameras will need a stable platform to sit on and do their recording thing. Tripods are built to do just that. There are huge variations in price for tripods—They can go from $20 to several hundred dollars. As long as the legs can be adjusted to any height and the tripod doesn't wobble, it should be fine. Don't agonize over tripods, get one that works for the size camera you get and move on.

There are also mini-tripods, about 3–5" high designed for digital still cameras. You can also use these to set a video camera anywhere (see Chapter 8), and having one of these is a cheap, useful addition to any video blogger toolbox.

Conclusion

A fairly powerful computer, fast hard drive, and a good amount of RAM is needed if you're going to do anything with video besides trim the ends off and upload it. There are hundreds of audio and video applications and though we can recommend a few, they all do pretty much the same thing. Once you get in the professional range, there's only a handful and there are copious resources online to help you make that decision.

The leading standard for vlogs, video blogs, or video podcasts, depending on what you want to call them, is some form of the MPEG-4 codec. Unfortunately, MPEG-4 has many flavors, and the version your camera records is not the same as DivX, is not the same as Playstation, and won't play in iTunes without conversion. Since many video blog sites are only viewed online, Flash is becoming the standard for online video blogs. If your video blog gets popular, you can add additional formats to satisfy even more niches of your audience and ensure that everyone can watch.

All you really need to do a video blog is a camera, and to podcast, you really only need a way to record a digital sound, which almost any device you have can do. Putting microphones next to the people talking, in a podcast or video blog, is the best way to get their sound right.

Podcasters and video bloggers love to share their knowledge. Find a high quality podcast with a similar format to your own, and ask them what they use.

CHAPTER 10

Audio Production and Post-Production

Recording and producing good audio is an exercise in sweating the details. Each phase of the recording, editing, fixing and rendering builds upon the steps taken before it. You can't take a garbled, windy, low volume recording, hit a few buttons and magically have the background noise scrubbed out and the voice pulled-up clear as day. It might be possible to make some improvements to a bad audio track, but the work involved far exceeds the little effort and consideration it takes to do it right in the first place.

This chapter will cover:

- Microphones, mixers and pre-amplifiers
- Production notes, preparation and voice talent
- Recording
- Editing and mixing
- Mixdown and compression for podcasting

Microphones and Mixers

Just about everything around you have a built-in microphone these days. Your cell phone, PDA, MP3 player, lecture recorder, laptop, and video camera all have the capability of recording sound. While most of these can do an adequate job, there is a lot of technology and technique behind audio recording, and the right microphone for the job takes many forms.

Microphones

The first thing you might notice about a decent microphone is the price tag. There are many products in this life that are more expensive than other products, which are exactly the same save for a designer label. Both products were made by the same people in a factory in a far off land but one person sewed a Prada tag on one and another other person sewed a Target tag on the other. Their respective prices are in no way related to the actual quality of the components, build, or overall usefulness; they are directly related to the price people are willing to pay for a brand.

Microphones are not like that. When you pay more, you're usually buying better technology. When you plunk down $200 on a good microphone, it's money well spent. $200, by the way is not expensive for a decent mic, in fact, it's on the lower end of the scale in the big universe of professional quality mics. That said, most podcasts will gain a huge benefit from that $200 mic.

What's the difference? Well let's cover the two most popular microphone types: dynamic and condenser.

Dynamic Microphone

A *dynamic microphone* uses a wire coil over a magnet with a diaphragm attached to the coil. When sound waves hit the diaphragm the coil moves, which creates an electrical current by moving across the magnet. These microphones are sturdy, general-purpose mics that don't need a power source and have few moving parts.

Condenser Microphone

The *condenser microphone* makes an audio signal through a diaphragm that vibrates two plates within a capacitor. The condenser mic is a much more sensitive microphone that produces a stronger signal. Its only drawback is that it's not very hardy and shouldn't be used in situations where it can be banged around such as audioblogging in Pamplona or interviewing Sean Penn.

Microphone Pickup Patterns

Microphones come in a number of pickup patterns that determine which direction the mic will pick up the most sound. There are a number of patterns including omnidirectional, cardioid, hypercardioid and bidirectional. You'll run into the first three at most music stores. Bidirectional is an oddball and is rarely used, which is your cue to pretend it doesn't exist (see **Figure 10-1**).

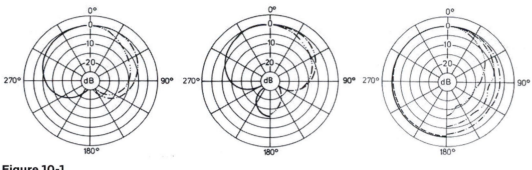

Figure 10-1
Microphone pickup patterns

Omnidirectional

On the other hand, the first three are worthy of note. *Omnidirectional microphones* record everything in all 360 degrees around it. Sounds great? It's not. Not really, at least. Recording in a studio likely means you know where you are going to be in relation to the microphone during recording, rendering about 270 degrees of the omnidirectional mic useless. But the omnidirectional microphone doesn't care that you only want the sound coming from your mouth recorded, it's more than happy to pick up everything. Background noise becomes part of the show with the omni. These are great for poking into a crowd for a big noisy sound clip, and terrible if control and direction matter.

Hypercardioid

The *hypercardioid microphone*, also known as a "shotgun mic" has a far more directional pickup pattern. As nice and pretty as they are, they tend to be quite expensive and better suited to soundstages and professional voice-over studios. In effect, you have to keep your head and more specifically, your mouth in the perfect spot to get the right sound out of it.

Cardioid

The *cardioid* microphone is the all-around favorite. Its pickup patters is shaped to pickup the sound from an area that allows for some head bobbing and rejects sound from the outer areas where ambient noise might come from. This type of mic also has a well represented pickup pattern, leaving you with a lot of brand and price options.

With all of that data well digested, what's the "right" microphone? In the video blogging production chapter, we mentioned the lavalier microphone. An advantage to using this microphone is that it keeps a somewhat constant distance and can be used on the move, and wirelessly. These types of microphones are a little more expensive than a regular microphone of the same quality due to its wireless ability and form factor. In the end, the size, shape and pickup pattern will be based on your particular production needs.

Microphone Budget

For around $100 you can find a decent microphone that will do your podcast or video blog proud. In fact there are many options in this area so pick one that has the connection type you are going to use, either XLR balanced (see **Figure 10-2**) if you have a pro sound card or a 1/4" jack which can be easily and without degradation turned in to an 1/8" jack that plugs right into your computer. The Audio-Technica AT2020 large diaphragm condenser microphone hits the price point and has a great sound. Another very popular podcasting microphone is the Marshall MXL-990. It's going to run about $70.

Figure 10-2
XLR connector

Figure 10-3
Audio-Technica AT2020 condenser microphone

Are you podcasting on the run, on the road or just wanting something cool? Some pod-casters are hailing the Samson Audio C01U USB Studio Condenser as perfect for the task. Rather than needing audio input which might be absent on a laptop, the Sampson needs a USB port and can be found online for about $80 (see **Figure 10-3**).

Figure 10-4
Audio C01U USB studio condenser

In the $200 to $300 range, you don't get much in the way of features so you're buying quality. Microphones are simple devices that do one thing and one thing only. For the added price, the condensers will be better engineered and produce a fuller and brighter sound. Audiotechnica, Shure, AKG, and Sennheiser all make great microphones and will have a wide variety of prices through their ranges.

Mixers and Amplifiers

Since condenser type microphones needs *phantom power* to operate, an external power source is needed. This power is most often provided by a microphone pre-amp or a mixer that has phantom power. Dynamic microphones don't require power and can just be plugged right into your sound card's microphone input. Microphone amplifiers and mixers come in a wide range or prices from basic $50 models to fancy ones that use tubes and cost hundreds.

Some podcasters come from an audio background and are happy to have an offboard (hard-ware, external, not software) mixer in their studio setup. They're great for multiple inputs and more complicated setups but a single person podcast just doesn't require one. A video blog where an interview is going on and people are wearing microphones will necessitate the use of a mixer. It's all about the application.

There are many mixers on the market and it's easy to get confused with all of the options. Basic level settings, phantom power and two microphone inputs and some stereo line should suffice, but make your decision based on your current and possible future input needs. Having a mixer between the input devices and your recording device will let you set all of the levels on the board and tweak them just right so the audio recorded is perfect.

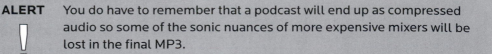

ALERT You do have to remember that a podcast will end up as compressed audio so some of the sonic nuances of more expensive mixers will be lost in the final MP3.

Most people are happy to use a software-based mixer such as what's included with sound card hardware from Creative Labs and similar products, so it essentially boils down to your preference and budget. The Behringer UB802, a stand-alone mixer, has two mono channels, two stereo channels, and two microphone pre-amplifiers (see **Figure 10-5**). Behringer makes microphone pre-amplifiers as well that only have microphone inputs. The Behringer MIC200 is a good option if you don't want to mess with a full-size mixer.

Author's Tip

What is XLR and why do I care about balanced audio?

Good question. XLR connections (see **Figure 10-2**) go hand-in-hand with balanced audio. Long runs of cable are more susceptible to radio interference from computers, microwaves, cell phones, or anything that gives off RF signals, which is just about anything electric.

In an unbalanced cable, there are only two wires; hot and ground. In a short run they're fine but with any length over 6' you can run into interference that comes out as noise in your recording. Since microphones have very low signal strength, any noise will be a lot of noise.

Balanced audio uses two wires for signal and one wire for ground. In a balanced XLR connection the two wires that carry signal carry opposite sides of the signal and are twisted together (but not connected to each other) and the audio is the difference between the two voltages. Without going into the gory details, balanced microphone connections offer a superior connection, particularly around other wires or going over distances, and you'll find that the higher quality microphones don't offer anything but XLR.

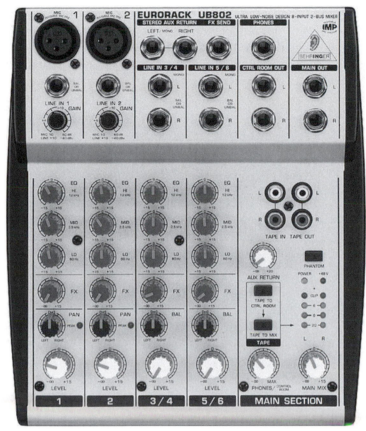

Figure 10-5
Behringer UB802 mixer

Audio Tools

There are a few universal tools you'll want for your podcasting kit. A pop filter, which is a loop of metal or plastic with a thin material stretched across it. The pop filter is mounted so the filter part is between your mouth and the microphone. It's a genius little rig that reduces the P and T sounds that tend to spike the audio levels and cause clipping. The other must have is a microphone stand. The stand might seem like a boring holder that simply props up a mic but it's a bit more than that.

A good microphone stand will help isolate vibration and can be adjusted, silently, while recording. A squeaky cheap stand will make noise if you have to adjust it. Unwanted noise is bad. Some stands are very simple and just sit on a desk while other, more expensive ones have articulated arms that let you move the mic around and hold the microphone in a web of elastic further protecting it from vibration.

There is no one setup that works for everyone. Each podcaster and video blogger is going to have their own setup, requirements, price points and preferences. Audio folks might like to have a mixer, computer folks might like the USB microphone, trust-fund kids might want a $500 Shure studio microphone. Most often, price and application will dictate the setup. When that is the case, spend the most on the microphone and with whatever is left, get the other gear you need.

Production Preparation and Voice Talent

Podcasting and video blogging can be used for an infinite number of show types but they will all share one thing: format. Not that they will have the same format, they'll all have a format, something that takes the show from beginning to end.

Production Notes

Movies and TV shows use scripts to cover specific dialogue but that's a little too structured for this medium. An easy way to keep the show flowing is to make a bulleted list of talking points. There is no particular format because everyone process information differently. A sheet of paper with a list of topics/talking points that can act as a quick-peek guide will help keep you on track through the recording without having to stop and start again and again.

You can go so far as to break down the whole show into segments and add notes on where you'll insert pre-recorded sound-bites or music clips. The depth is up to you, but make it clear enough to walk you through the show from beginning to end. Here is a quick example of show notes:

Show Notes—Show 05 – April 26

- Roll show intro music

- General ID and intro piece

- Show topics overview

- Upcoming podcasting and video blogging book

- News items

  – Clip intro

  – Audio clip—Interview with Bob Smith S-05-NC01

  – Comments

  – Clip intro

  – Audio clip S-05-NC02

  – Comments

- Opinion piece

- Wrap up

- Outro

Some people will just wing it, fly right into an angry rant, recite poetry, have an introspective conversation or just talk until they're done. The more professional it is, the more people will recognize the pattern we're all used to. It's like a phone call that typically goes like this:

Phone rings, hello, negotiating if both parties are the ones that should be talking, greetings, the obligatory 'How's the family?' conversation points from most to least importance, lull in conversation, thinly veiled excuse to get off phone, some OKs and agreements and goodbye.

That's what we're used to. When we stick to some semblance of established media paradigms, we make it easier for the audience to focus on the content. In other words, audiences need a familiar structure like the three-act play.

The Power of the Voice

We all have an expectation of how media is presented. It's programmed into us from the first time mom plopped us in front of the TV so she could talk to her friends, and we could learn the nature of our culture through produced media and advertising. As we get older and have seen and consumed thousands of hours of produced media, we develop a framework of expectations around the look, feel and sound.

For example, Don LaFontaine's voice is as familiar to you as that of some family members, yet you probably don't know his name and wouldn't recognize him if you saw him. Don is the voice you hear when you see a movie trailer. He's done more than 4000 of them as well as a number of other voice performances that permeate our existences without much notice, but he's in there, in our heads. His voice is what we, at a subliminal level, expect to hear for a movie trailer.

We're so programmed to hear his voice during movie trailers, producers have found that audiences who hear a trailer voice over with his voice will be more likely to see the movie than an audience who saw the same trailer but had a different voice-over actor. That's the power of subliminal expectation.

Learn How to Speak

It's important to make a reference to the simple act of talking. Podcasts are often a spoken work experience so talking is going to be a part of the process. In conversational chatter, we can be lazy, it's expected. In a production seeking to be somewhat professional it's a good idea to get your radio voice going.

People listening to media are processing information from many levels. They are listening to the content of what is being said, the quality of the recording and the

> **Author's Tip**
>
> Podcasting and video blogging are new, but the medium of radio is not. Video and audio productions are firmly rooted in the media we all grew up with and see and hear every day. When producing your magnum opus, remember that if you want people to listen and focus on the content it's important to present it in a way that they understand and are used to. Just leave out the laugh track.

quality and nature of the words being used. Words are important things. Word and phrase selection tells people about the person speaking. Someone from Texas might be speaking and they'll drop in a "fixin to" and a "ya'll" and you'll know where they're from. Is it important? Possibly. It depends on the content and the nature of the show.

Ditch Lazy Terms

We don't often notice our lazy language skills and can even be affronted when told about them. Throat clearing and body noises are distracting and detract from the recording. Radio stations have a little gadget called a cough switch right near the microphone that lets the speaker clear their throat while the mic is momentarily silenced.

Audio recording undesirables:

- Throat clearing, coughing and other noisy body functions (assuming those elements are not part of the show).

- Ums, uhs, ers, and nonword noises emanating from the mouth or throat.

- Like, you know, yeah, its-like, and he was like, and we were all.

We're so used to seeing and hearing professional interviews that when we hear someone making "um," "uh" and "er" sounds, we make a judgment about the person speaking when we hear people using the lazy language we might use ourselves.

Recording

Audio recording is a topic worthy of a volume of books. In 1877 Thomas Edison invented the first audio recording device, a simple phonograph. Once the phonograph let the world know sound could be recorded, a whole industry started that has been producing improvements and new technologies that show no signs of tapering off.

In this digital age we've gone in a funny direction with regards to sound quality. On the one hand, we want crystal clear, realistic sonic reproduction when we watch DVDs, but are happy to listen to the compressed and somewhat inaccurate sound reproduction of MP3 files. Dichotomy is part of life, and both of those concepts can be embraced by the same people, and in most cases is. That said, in the case of lower quality recordings, there is still the expectation of a certain level of quality which exists somewhere between CD quality and the Stephen Hawking-ish voice of the National Weather Service.

When recording for a podcast or video blog, it's still important to maintain high quality sound for as long as possible even though the final product will be in a lossy digital file format. The oft-used term "garbage-in garbage-out" comes to mind. A bad phone recording is going to be near impossible to fix. Even if it is fixable it will take a lot of work, which is counter to the basic premise of podcasting.

When recording audio, you'll have lots of setting options presented to you and the numbers and terms can be dizzying and could take a few classes at the local community college to explain properly. When recording, you're looking to get the most out of it while not compromising the quality or wasting space. "CD quality" is achieved at the magic combination of 44.1 khz/16 bit. The files will be quite a bit bigger than MP3s but you'll have the best quality recording to work with.

Other sample formats and sampling rates might be touted as sufficient, but any higher and it's a lot of space used and any lower and you'll sound much more FM than CD. There are a number of great books on audio engineering that can explain the specifics of sampling rates and formats if the subject matter is of interest.

File Formats
On the Windows platform, the main file format used for uncompressed audio files is WAV; it is a lossless format that holds up and edits well. Recording directly to MP3 is done often, but when mixed with other tracks in the editing process, gets compressed again which can lead to sound quality degradation.

Try, if at all possible to compress audio from a lossless format to a lossy format and stay away from compressing compressed audio. Each time a compressed audio track is mixed and compressed, it loses data and the sound suffers. The Mac standard high-quality but big file size format is AIFF. Recording in AIFF and WAV will ensure you're working at the highest quality.

Mobile Recording Studio
We covered a number of studio setups but there are some great options for working on the go. Some popular MP3 players support recording as a feature that is sometimes overlooked. Not only are there portable MP3 players that can record, there are professional digital recorders that, while not cheap, are designed and built for the job of recording high quality audio.

In the MP3 player cum-digital recorder, the iRiver 700 and 800 series players can record your audio as MP3 files (see **Figure 10-6**). They're smaller than a pager and will give you a decent recording, nothing like the studio but still somewhat acceptable. The fact that they are also MP3 players lets you use them for fun stuff when not working as a recorder.

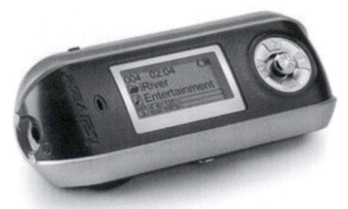

Figure 10-6
iRiver iFP-895 MP3 player and recorder

If your podcasting keeps you on the road more than in the studio, the Marantz PMD660 is everything plus the kitchen sink, while being small enough to fit in an inside jacket pocket (see **Figure 10-7**). Running on two AA batteries it can record for hours while providing phantom power to XLR connected condenser microphones that need it, or dynamic microphones that don't. Its $400–$500 street price makes an investment, but you do get 90 minutes of uncompressed 16-bit PCM audio recorded to a CF card or 36 hours of 128 kbps **.mp3** audio on the same card. It's outfitted with an on-board USB connector, which makes it very computer friendly.

Figure 10-7
Marantz PMD660 professional digital audio recorder

Roland Edirol's new R-09 records 24-bit/48 khz uncompressed WAV files and has a built-in mic as well as min and line-in inputs and records to SD cards (see **Figure 10-8**). It will record MP3s as well, but unless space is an issue with the SD card, it's best to record at the best quality possible. It's a little cheaper than the Marantz and is even a little smaller. No phantom power but its built-in mic is nothing to sniff at. If James Bond were an audiophile, he'd own one. Their R-1 model is also very respectable and should be considered in the mix of portable recorders.

Figure 10-8
Roland Edirol R-09 professional digital recorder

Levels

Without going into gory detail that would get audio engineers excited, we'll talk a little, and we do mean a little, about sound levels. Recording good sound takes a little practice. Distance from the microphone might make for low sound levels, getting too close and not keeping a constant volume might cause clipping. Clipping is bad. Clipping is when too much sound enters the audio device and reaches 1.0 on the meter. Once the level gets to 1.0 it can take no more, and what ends up being recorded is a terrible noise that clips out what was supposed to be there, never to return.

ALERT If you clip during a recording you might have to go back and re-record that segment and splice it back in.

!
□

It's better to record at a little bit lower level than up high near the clipping range. You can always boost the level up later and if you're using a good balanced microphone in a very quiet space, there will be little noise or hiss boosted up with the rest of the track. Just watch the level meters while recording and try not to clip.

An audio compressor can help take a little pain out of the recording equation. A compressor/gate helps keep the overall recording level, level. It can keep you from clipping and when the sound goes too low, it boosts it back up so the overall recording doesn't have highs that are too high and lows that are too low. Portable compressors from dbx, and Alesis and are found at your local music store starting at around $50, and can get as expensive as a small car. Staying at or around $50 should suffice for podcasting.

Editing and Mixing

Not all podcasts or video blogs are edited. Simply recording sound, encoding it into an MP3 and posting constitutes a podcast. The same goes for video, there are no rules saying you can't shoot some footage, turn it into an MOV and attach it to a blog post.

If you're looking for more of a professional feel, editing is going to come into the picture. Sound will always benefit from some editing. A sneeze, loud spot or long pause will find a way into a recording, particularly in your early work.

Snipping coughs and "ums" out of the sound tracks of video can be a little more challenging and might require some ingenuity. In audio there is no face to make the expression of coughing but in a video seeing someone cough and not hearing it might be odd. This is a good place to either cut the part out, use a cut-away, reverse angle or insert some stock footage. Or, leave it in and just lower the audio track for the moments you're making the undesirable sound. This is where a good *music bed* (background, instrumental music to set mood) can cover up problems.

When working with multiple sources, the likelihood is that each one will have different volume levels. Tying them all together might be jarring when a soft voice cuts over to a loud music track. Most editors will come with sound processor tools; the most basic but also most useful is the normalizer. The normalizer can be used on individual tracks, the whole project or just selections of tracks.

Most sound processor plug-ins will be able to be applied to small selections all the way through entire projects. Equalization, noise gate, compression and limiting can all be used to improve the quality of less-than perfect clips and tracks.

Software

Cleaning up recorded track in an editor is as simple as opening the file and working a few basic functions you're already very familiar with. Copy, cut, paste and select will be able to cleanse your recording of a multitude of sins. Most editors work with a very similar toolset and have the basic functions. For as many sound editors there are, they all do fundamentally the same thing. What sets them apart from each other are sound processing features and the user interface. The interfaces although not too dissimilar differ in tool placement and layout.

The software you use is a critical element in the podcasting process. It's where the sound will come in, be edited and mixed, mastered and compressed. Like many other aspects of production there are cheap tools and expensive ones. In the case of software, you'll be making your selection based on features and ease of use.

Two-Track Editors

Sony's Sound Forge product line has been a digital recording mainstay for years due to its flexibility and ease of use. Recording with Sound Forge is as simple as selecting the recorder function button from the toolbar, setting the recording attributes and pressing record. When finished, pressing stop ends the recording and a new track is opened up in the main edit window (see **Figure 10-9**).

Author's Tip

The silent parts during pauses and the like are useful snippets that you could keep, perhaps in a mute track where you can drag copies of the silence over the ums and coughs. Silence can also be used to add a little time in between talking. If you got a little quick on something you might need to paste in a little silence. Make sure it blends well with the sound on each side; you might use a transition effect to smooth out the sound.

Author's Tip

There are two flavors of audio editing software, two-track and multi-track. Two-track editors like Sound Forge and BIAS Peak are perfect for two-track recording, editing and mixing but don't allow for adding more tracks such as a music backgrounds and external sound clips.

Author's Tip

With a simple two-track editor, your original master recording and the delete button, you're ready to clean up the track. The beauty of digital editing is Undo. The seldom honored undo function should be lauded for the millions of hours it's saved humanity from having to re-do stuff.

Pre-recorded files from other sessions, devices and sources can also be opened up in the editor for mixing. Sound forge is a great tool for video bloggers, allowing for a video track to be displayed. The powerful Sound Forge tools can be applied to the audio for video blogging if the audio tools in your video editor can't do what you need them to.

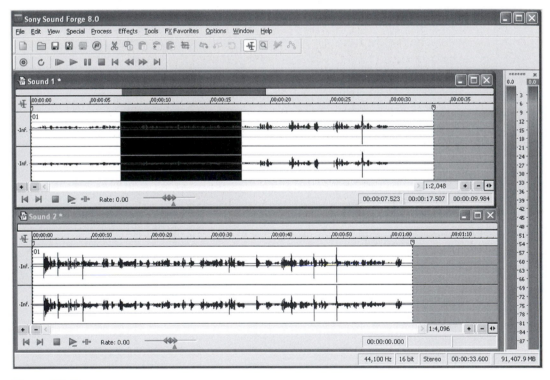

Figure 10-9
Sony Sound Forge 8 main edit window

BIAS Peak for Mac users is a powerful two-track editor that also allows you to edit sound alongside a video track (see **Figure 10-10**). It's filled with professional grade real-time effects, custom fades and more. It supports many third-party plug-ins and is one of the tools of choice for Mac-based podcasters who are producing pro-quality podcasts.

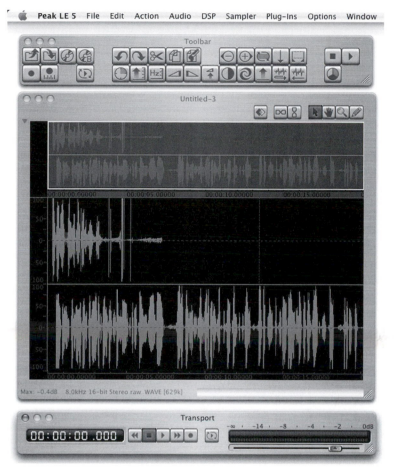

Figure 10-10
BIAS Peak two-track editor for Macintosh

The cursor in the waveform workspace of most audio editors lets you make selections. While playing through the track you can snip out the "uhs," "ums," dead air and other undesirables. The same rules apply to multitrack editors, but these tend to be a little more fun and also offer more interesting and power effect tools. The same selecting can be done but with the extra tracks you can use them as place-holders for little clips, lay two soundtracks down and try each one by making it live or muting it. It might seem a little intimidating, but the multitrack editors are great and give you more latitude in editing, particularly when editing video.

Multitrack Editors

Multitrack editors do essentially the same things two-track editors do but focus more on track mixing. Some podcasts are simple stereo linear spoken word productions that need a little trimming here and there to clean-up the recording and are sent right to MP3. More involved podcasts might have a soundtrack, external interview clips, sound snippets and other audio elements that need to be arranged. Two-track editors just don't do that. Your audio editor needs will be defined by the type of video blog, or podcast you're producing. A multitrack editor might not be necessary when you're cleaning up an interview but will be needed if that interview will be part of a collection of other elements.

Programs for the Mac such as Audacity, GarageBand, Adobe Audition, and Sony Vegas for Windows have enough tracks to make anyone happy (see **Figure 10-11**). Drag and drop clips, music and voice all over the project, record a new voice track, mix it down to two tracks and compress it to MP3 all from one program. If you're torn between the two, a multitrack editor might be for you.

You might have noticed that we mentioned a video editor in the list of multitrack audio editors. Multitrack editors that can handle video and audio don't actually care what the final product is. Vegas will not be offended if your project has no video track. If you already have a video multitrack editor, there is no rule saying you have to buy an audio specific tool. More and more, media is just media and the applications don't have strong opinions either way.

Figure 10-11
Adobe Audition 1.5 Multi-track editor

Mixdown and Compressing for Podcasting

The process of mixing the multitrack file to two channels happens when you export your master file to an uncompressed, lossless master. A master should be portable so it can be worked on other editors so esoteric lossless file formats that might be great on your particular editor might not work in another editor. The output file is the result of all of the channels being mashed together, nicely mind you, into just two tracks. Once mastered, it's ready to be compressed for podcast.

Modern audio editors will have the capacity to export or save your project as an MP3 file. With the master opened in your editor, select Export or Save As from the File menu. This is a similar process to mixing down and mastering. Save the file as an MP3 in either 22K 16-bit for high-quality voice or 44.1K 16-bit for CD quality sound. That's it, your podcast is ready!

Author's Tip

Save the uncompressed master file. Burn it to CD or otherwise archive it, it might come in handy later if it ends up being used for radio or TV and needs to be exported at a higher sampling rate.

The whole process breaks down into basic steps. Your hardware and software may be different from the next podcaster, but the overall process will follow these basic steps:

1. Connect audio source equipment to your sound card
2. Open the audio editor/recorder
3. Create a new file and set the sampling rate
4. Play a recording sample, adjust levels if needed
5. Cue the source material from the beginning
6. Hit record in the recording software then play on the source
7. Stop recording when the sample you wanted is recorded
8. Edit the file
9. Mix down channels into one for mono or two for stereo
10. Perform any required sound processing
11. Save master as WAV or AIFF uncompressed audio at 44.1 16-bit as a master recording of the session
12. Encode to MP3 at either 22K 16-bit for high quality voice or 44.1K 16-bit for CD quality audio
13. Upload podcast
14. Enjoy fame and public adulation

Conclusion

A good microphone is something worth investing in. If you have experience on camera or on the radio, great; but if you don't, you'll want to listen a bit to make sure you have good "mic presence" and don't stammer, um, and colloquialize excessively.

There are a number of types of microphones depending on what you're trying to capture. You'll want them all eventually, so understand which one is the right tool for the job.

It's not even necessary to edit a podcast, but most people do so they can polish it and make it sound its best.

The process of editing and mixing can be a little intimidating at first. Editors have a lot of buttons and settings many of which may be utterly unfamiliar. There is a lot to be said for going through the tutorials and manuals of your software, you're bound to learn a lot more about its functionality that way.

Video Production and Post-Production

A video blog can be as simple or complex as you want it to be. The upside of the medium is that there is no automatic expectation from the viewing audience for special effects and fancy transitions. That's not to say you shouldn't have effects or transitions, it just makes your job a little easier. The real focus here is on content, a concept that should not be forgotten while in post. A short but tight video without wandering shots, long pauses or distracting cuts is going to keep the viewer locked in. Focus on the rhythm of the video, keep it moving, keep it interesting and you'll keep the viewer.

This chapter covers:

- Planning ahead
- Encoding video
- Editing

Think Post-Production While in Pre-Production

The little things done before a camera is even powered on can make editing your blog much simpler. Having good audio production does directly relate to video post production. If you have to dub anything in post because a microphone was not set up correctly or the volume was set to low, it will end up as more work on the back end.

Think about how the lighting will come out on the tape. If you have a set stage or have the ability to use the same space and lighting for all recording, shoot 5 minutes of test roll and digitize it. Look for bright and dark spots, sound quality, echoes, vibrations, flaring, focus, color reproduction, depth of field or anything that can be remedied before committing to a production shoot.

Any debugging you can do before a shoot will prevent unnecessary interruptions re-takes or worse, having to fix it in post.

Doing test-takes during the day when stores are open will let you make quick fixes that require new parts or supplies on the spot rather than having to wait until the stores are open again.

As part of most professional productions there are a whole host of people on the set to make sure everything that needs to be done actually gets done. There is nothing more irritating that digitizing a lot of media only to remember that you needed to go back out and shoot missing b-roll shots of traffic, people walking, the dog chewing something or reverse angles of an interview.

Author's Tip

B-roll or "stock footage" is a great tool for productions. When you see a movie or TV show and there is footage of people on the street, news footage, a plane landing or some shots where speaking cast is not involved in a shot, that's an example of stock footage. Most of this footage is either sourced from companies that specialize in stock footage or the production sends a crew out to get these shots while the director focuses on the scenes that require direction.

Footage Sources and Acquisition

Making good video is an art. People go to film school and work for years on technique. Good photographers know how to frame a shot. There is a lot to be said about taking one good frame of film. The one frame has to speak for itself.

Video was long viewed as a tepid, soulless medium best suited for news gathering and talk shows. Some art was lost for a while in the early years of TV. Film continued to evolve but video was the ugly step-child. Within the last decade or so, cinematographers and directors who once swore they would never stand behind a digital camera have found a way to use their cinematic skills to make video look good.

This rebirth was not just the product of film folks looking for off-time income, TV directors became more creative with their craft. Covering the art of cinematography and direction is out of the scope of the book but there are a few basic things to remember when shooting video for video blogs.

When shooting an interview, use the reverse angle. This is a great technique when you have one camera and want a little shot variety. In a face-to-face interview single-camera shoot, you get the two-shot. The frame has both people in the shot and it's static. No movement. That's not terribly interesting. News reporters who only had one camera in the field did a little trick. They would record the interview with the camera only pointing at the interviewee. During the time the host was talking the camera man might adjust the shot, zooming in or out but making sure not to make adjustments while the subject was talking.

When the interview was over, the cameraperson would turn the lights and camera on the host. The host would then go through the whole interview again, one sided, without the interviewee, asking all the same questions, adding some clips of a thoughtful "hmmmmm," or "of course" and useful clips.

In the edit bay, the two recordings would be interspersed, making it look like there were two cameras on the shoot. When the shot cuts to the interviewer asking a question, it's footage from after the interview but looks like it's just part of a seamless, live shoot with multiple cameras and a switcher. When two cameras are used, the second camera can shoot wide two-shots, close ups, and other fill footage.

A lot of production value can be had from just one camera, it just takes a little ingenuity.

Stock Footage
Stock footage can come from a number of sources. Archive.org is a great, mostly royalty-free source for digitally encoded video b-roll. Stock footage can come in a number of formats from 35mm film, which unless you have a telecine will be useless, to video tape, encoded MPEG video and DVD. When sourcing stock footage, make sure it comes in a format you can use or convert easily, in this case encoded video files are best. If pre-digitized media is not available, DVD video or DV tape is the next best option. A search on Google for "Stock Footage" will offer up hundreds of sites that offer many different kinds of stock footage.

File Conversion
Converting a DVD to MOV or MPEG files can be a little tricky. Many movie studios have worked very hard to vilify DVD ripping software as it could be used to infringe on copyrighted material although it does have many legitimate uses.

There are tools available to pull the VOB (MPEG-2 Video OBject) files from a DVD to your computer's hard drive but with the DCMA and all of the lawsuits closing down these software makers, the applications may be hard to find. DVD Decrypter was the most popular application for

Author's Tip

Companies that provide stock footage don't exactly give the stuff away. There are some compilations of royalty-free stock footage that can be had but most of the good stuff has to be bought al-la-carte. This is where being resourceful comes in handy. The Library of Congress has a massive video archive, some of which is royalty free.

stripping the files out of the DVD to your hard drive. MacTheRipper is a similar program for the Macintosh. *www.videohelp.com* is a good source for tutorials and other programs that are available for the task. Just make sure you are within your rights (see Chapter 14, Licensing and Copyrights) before you attempt to pull files off of a DVD.

Once the VOB files are ripped to your computer they can be converted to the format you're editing in with a number of available applications.

Applications such as Canopus Pro Coder (*www.canopus.com*) will handle VOB files as well as many other file types but weighs in at $499. If you're going to be getting footage from a lot of different sources, it's $499 well spent. Their ProCoder Express product sticks to basics and will only set you back $59. Both products should be able to convert unencrypted VOB files as well as DVR-MS and 3GP. The last two formats mentioned are quite interesting and very useful. DVR-MS is the file type created by Microsoft Windows Media Center PC DVRs. Pro Coder can convert that proprietary file into just about any other file type you want allowing you to make use of anything recorded on that DVR. Make sure you read the section on fair use before using captured video from a DVR. 3GP on the other hand is the file type many phones use when encoding video. The format is great for sending via MMS from phone to phone but in order to edit it, it has to be transcoded into an editable format.

There are many different free and not-free transcoding applications available from retail stores and the web. Before shelling out hard earned money, poke around *www.videohelp.com* and see if there are any programs that fit the bill for the encode/transcode you're looking to do. A free tool like VirtualDubMod can turn many file formats into AVI. While AVI may not be your end result format, you can still edit it and once finished, encode into the final format. There will be a loss of quality but it's good to see if it's an acceptable one. Tsunami MPEG Video Encoder XPress covers a lot of formats and won't put a huge dent in your wallet. QuickTime Pro makes converting many formats into QuickTime for only $30. This is one of those tools that is just about required if you work with digital video for the Internet.

Sources

The Windows Media Center PCs are not the only DVRs you can use as sources. In reality, anything with a video-out connection can be used as a source. DVRs from many cable companies such as Comcast, Time Warner, and even TiVos from DirecTV or stand-alone models are outstanding source devices because the video can be queued, paused and jogged back and forth, letting you record as much or as little as you need. They can also record things while you're gone, which is a nice feature. Has anyone figured out how to program a VCR yet?

Recording from DVD using analog cables can be problematic because many content makers add features to their media to make it difficult to record from device to device. Macrovision, without going into its technical details effectively makes the image just unstable enough that when trying to dub it the destination recorder gets a bad image.

You may not experience the effect of Macrovision while dubbing from your DVD to the encoder card on your computer. If that's the case, great! If not, and you just have to do it that way, rather than ripping the DVD and transcoding it, you'll need a TBC, also known as a Time Base Corrector. TBCs help to stabilize video moving from one machine to another and can be useful for encoding old VHS tapes that have degraded with time. TBCs are not something found at your local big box store and tend to be classified as pro gear which makes them a little more expensive. An inexpensive model, the DataVision TBC-1000 can be had for around $300 new or somewhat cheaper on eBay.

It's also important to mention that VHS players and video cameras can be sources as well but older tape formats and equipment may produce poor video on transfer. The TBC can help stabilize but putting old media in the newest, best equipment you can borrow or buy on the cheap will improve the base video quality more than trying to correct for an old tape reading head (see **Figure 11-1**). If you're going to dip into a large old tape archive, have your tape player serviced and cleaned or knuckle down and buy a new player with a high quality head. The investment will save countless hours of trying to improve poor encodes. Remember, fixing it in post is no fun and will not always yield desirable results.

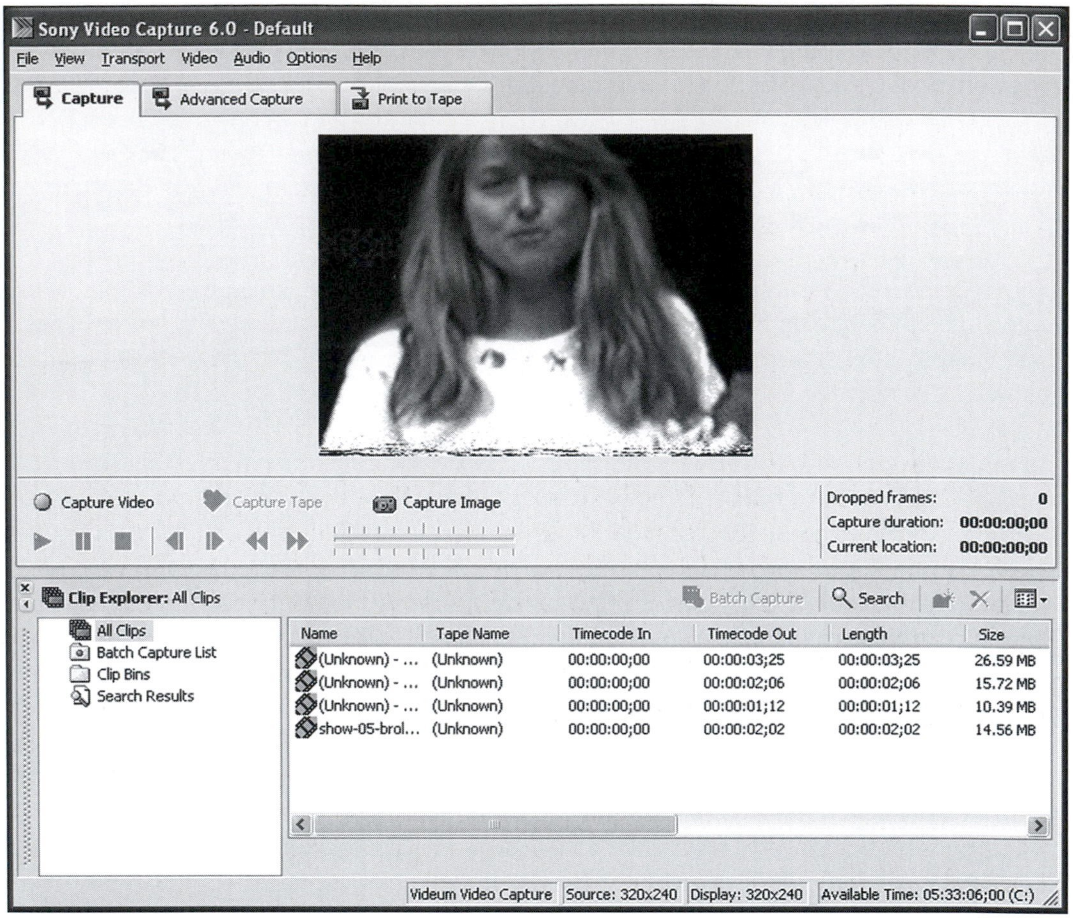

Figure 11-1
Poor video quality capture

Author's Tip

The key to good, usable footage is to maintain high quality production from start to finish. Use the best source possible and process it as few times as possible. It's the same rule that applies to photo copies and tape duplication. While making a "copy" of a digital file is making an exact, bit for bit duplicate, taping a tape is not an exact copy. Copying copied copies of analog material creates video and audio degradation.

Interpretations occur when going from one file type to another. Some file types manage a conversion well, but others may visibly suffer. Keeping the number of processing, converting, rendering steps to a minimum will ensure that the clips you end up editing together are of the highest quality possible.

Digital Asset Collecting and Assembly

Have you ever looked at a directory of files wondering which one has the clip you wanted but the names didn't relate to the content in any way, leaving you to preview dozens of files in search of the right one?

Setting up a simple naming convention of just committing to giving files descriptive names and defined directories does two things; allows you to find things more quickly and makes your library into a better footage resource for future projects. There is also another benefit; work files, if named well can be discarded, freeing up valuable storage space.

Naming can be taken to the Nth degree by following a strict regimen or kept simple by simply using descriptive names.

> **ALERT**
>
> ! There are no spaces on the Internet. File names, even on your computer should be cleansed of spaces. That's a little harsh, but a space in a file name will not work in any URL. Use the dash "-" or underscore "_" where a space would go. Abstaining from the use of capitalization will also simplify file management and URL creation. It's also important to point out that webservers care about caps. They think Rubble.mov is completely different from rubble.MOV. Keep life simple and get used to being a space-free file namer.

Using simple words in your file names will help identify them and make your post production process much faster.

Keywords to use: Show#, master, dub, workfile, dv-conversion, to-encode, final, no-audio, hd-dv-source, vhs-source.

A few examples of file naming that can help describe files to the editor:

    show-05_dv-master.mov

    show-05_b-roll_street-int-03(bob-r).mov

    show-05_test-letterbox01.mov

    show-06_dvd-pull_j-davis-speech_6min-32sec_letterbox.mov

    show-06_host_talking-head_reverse-angle.mov

    show-06_final-product.mov

The more you can describe the clip, the more value you get out of the media in it. The order can make a difference if you're sorting your footage by show numbers but can be prefixed by types such as master, work, dub and final.

Breaking out files into directories based on qualities like test files, work, loops, backgrounds, final edits, stock footage master files and video imports can keep things you need for every show separate from files you will only use once or for a specific subject.

Things tend to pile up after a while. Knowing what goes where and what files are will help you clean out directories of massive DV and analog video captures that are no longer needed. Burning files to DVD can help keep your local system unclogged.

ALERT When moving very large files to DVD, it's a good idea to make at least two copies and keep the DVDs in perfect condition. Larger files tend to have more problems when being copied back to the computer than smaller files. Finger prints and scratches can render a DVD-R useless by obscuring just one little section of a track where a large file resides.

Encoding Video

Video editing programs such as Sony Movie Studio, Adobe Premiere Elements, Microsoft Movie Maker and iMovie know that before editing anything, video and audio has to travel from the original source into a digital file on your computer first. Each program will have its own terminology for the process. Look out for tools within the application called "import," "acquire," or "capture." In Windows Movie Maker, the process is "Capture from video device" (see **Figure 11-2**).

Author's Tip

Some DV camcorders will come with their own software packages and requirements for connecting to your computer. DV is best imported via FireWire but footage can be captured using the S-Video or composite output connections on the camera. Doing so will severely degrade the video and should be avoided. If a $40 FireWire card is the difference between capturing native DV and having to use an analog connection, spend the $40.

Capturing video on a Windows-based computer comes with a little requirement that if not understood and taken care of, will leave you scratching your head, frustrated. Windows file systems have evolved over the years. Only a few years ago, a 4 GB disk drive was considered quite large. The older file systems such as FAT16 were designed in such a way that they could not recognize a partition larger than 4 GB. FAT16 could see a 4 GB file but the volume size was limited to 4 GB which didn't help matters much. FAT32 was a large improvement with partition sizes up to 32 GB but still maintained a 4 GB maximum file size. NTFS on the other hand can handle a volume size of 256 terabytes, a substantial improvement. NTFS can handle a maximum file size of 16 terabytes. A terabyte is 1,000 gigabytes. Trying to edit 16 GB video files in not recommended.

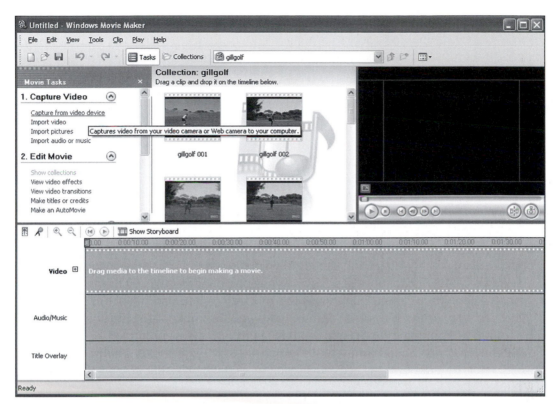

Figure 11-2
Windows Movie Maker capture video selection highlight

What does all this file and volume size stuff mean in terms of video capture? If you have a volume formatted in FAT32, 4 GB will be the file size limit the system can support. With DV video capture working out to roughly 13 GB per hour, it's not a lot to work with. On NTFS file systems, your DV tape will end long before the file gets anywhere near a fraction of the limit.

If you're not sure how your disk volumes are formatted, go into your system properties in Windows XP by right-clicking on "my computer" and selecting "manage". Under the storage icon in the navigation pane select "disk management" (see **Figure 11-3**). You'll see all of the recognized partitions in your system and how they are formatted.

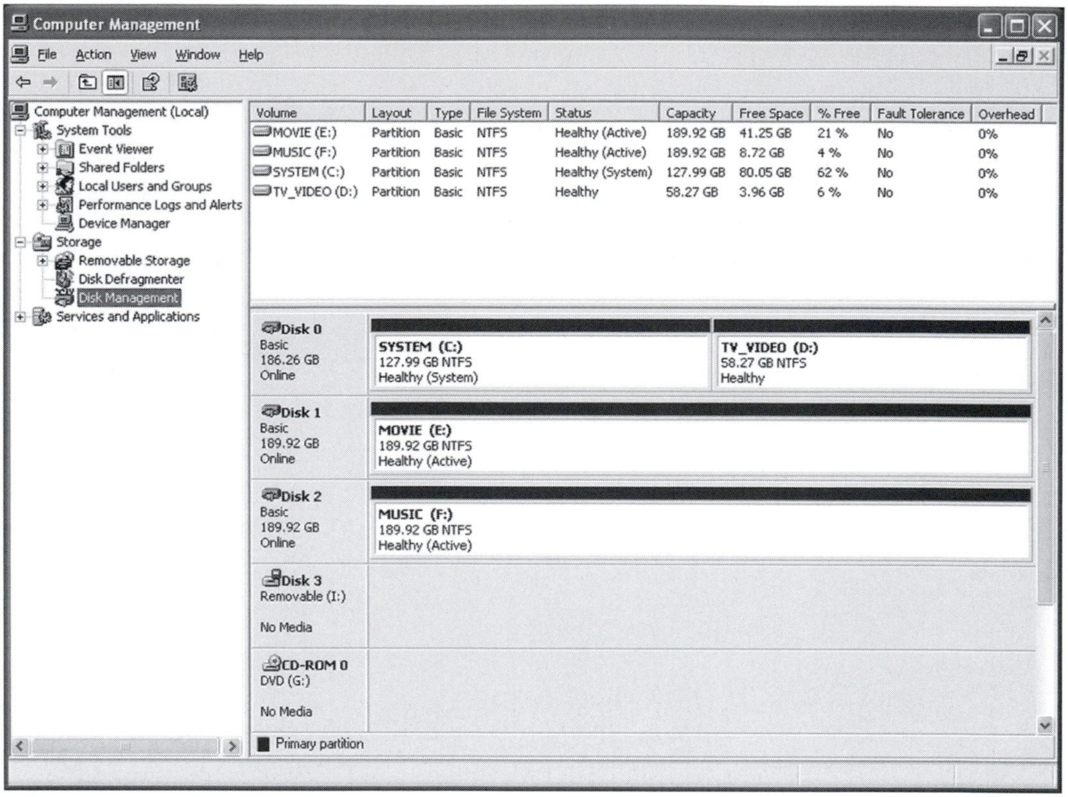

Figure 11-3
Windows XP Disk Manager showing volume information

Author's Tip

Formatting the partition or drive that contains your system files is bad for obvious reasons. Only format disks or volumes that do not contain system files or application files needed by programs to run. Most video editing systems use multiple disk drives both internal and external. Video is space intensive and drives are cheap. When in doubt or in need of space, buy more disk and format it properly.

If the disk you're using for media capture and storage is NTFS, you're in great shape. If not, there is work to do. *The volume will need to be re-formatted as NTFS which is a completely destructive process.* Back up any files you want to ever see again. Once you're sure you want to format the drive, right click on it, select "format" and chose NTFS.

Mac users may be wondering if there are any concerns regarding OSX file size limitations. HFS, the Mac file system is happy to accommodate files up to 16 terabytes. Apple-based systems have long been used for video applications so the issue was resolved long ago by simply breaking long captures into several-gigabyte chunks.

Capturing Video in Sony Movie Studio Platinum

The majority of video editing applications come with a capture utility included. The utility works hand-in-hand with the application where after the video is captured the clip is added to the current project's media bucket making it easier to add to the project.

Sony's Vegas Movie Studio Platinum is a lightly pared down version of their larger professional video application, Vegas 6. Both programs share the same look and feel so moving between them is quite simple. The capture utility is also very much the same between the two. Found under the File menu, Capture Video opens up the capture window. Vegas will show the default video capture device first but can be instructed to look to an alternate video capture device through the Video menu at the top of the window. Some video capture boards have multiple inputs which can also be selected through the same menu (see **Figure 11-4**).

Further down the Video menu there will be a Properties command that lets you configure the way the video is presented to the capture utility. Since most vlogs will be captured and presented at 320X240, setting it to that size before the capture will do two things; save disk space over capturing at the maximum resolution and make the final rendering go faster because resizing the video doesn't have to occur during the render.

Before capturing the video, set the capture utility to save the files in the directory you will use for scratch capture space. In Options/Preferences you'll find the Disk Management tab. The capture folders you add to this box will be where the program saves raw capture files. When a folder is full the capture application moves to the next open folder down the line. This is a good scenario when you have multiple disks and a lot of media to capture and don't want to go in and change the setting each time a disk gets full.

Once the video device is ready and queued up, hit the Capture Video button and press play on the VCR/Camcorder/External video device. When you're done capturing, hit the stop button. You can continue to capture clips in the capture utility. When you're done close the window and the new clips will be found in the Project Media tab at the bottom of the editing window. The clips are now ready to be edited.

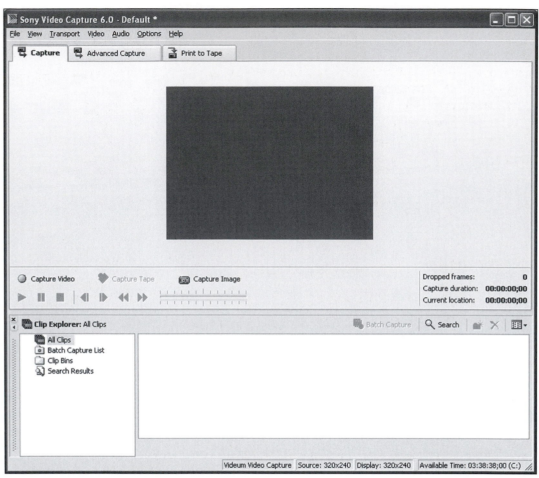

Figure 11-4
Vegas Video Capture window ready to start capturing

Capturing Video in Windows Movie Maker and iMovie

The Vegas Video example used above might have some command sequences specific to the application but the process is the same across all video editing applications that have capture. The basic setup requires a video source connected to a video input device on your computer. The device will have its own configuration utility dialog which can be accessed through its own application or through the capture tool.

Capturing video for vlogging is only a little different than capturing video for output to DVD or other large format media. Vlogs tend to have smaller frames which makes capturing easier on hard disk space. Set your device to capture at 320 × 240 and you'll be able to put hours of video in a relatively small space. If you capture at 640 × 480 or higher you'll eat up hard disk space like its going out of style. iMovie and Vegas both support HD DV editing which as you would expect, has a huge disk footprint.

Author's Tip

Some vlogs are being presented in HD, and if Moore's Law extends to other areas of technology, it won't be long before the expectation for online video will be HD.

Each editor's capture tool will have similar settings, stop and start buttons and dialog boxes where you can tell it where you want the raw capture video to be stored.

More important than the tool is the compatibility of the video capture card. If you've downloaded a demo version of an editor that you like, see what they recommend for video cards. It's better to get a supported card than spending hours to make a bargain-basement card work only to find that it crashes your computer. Sadly, this is one area where unsupported devices can wreak havoc on a project. The unsupported card might come up in the editor but something makes it or the software mad and you're looking at the BSOD or a Sad Mac. When a Mac makes a sad face, we all make a sad face.

Editing

Editing is about prep work. Like a chef, having everything you need right in front of you will things go well and in the case of video, the edit session goes by quickly. Having to go back and re-capture, re-shoot, find footage and so on will make an edit session take much longer than it needs to. If you don't have all of the elements you need and can wait, do.

Even with the powerful tools available in software editors, the mouse and keyboard are sorry tools for the job. From the beginning of video editing with tape, the jog control was used to move around at varying speeds to find frames quickly and set in and out points.

Bella *www.bella-usa.com* makes keyboards with built-in jog dials and application specific keys that make it simple to move around the application without navigating through menus half the time. The $189 spent on the keyboard is cheap considering how much time can be saved by having hot keys laid out and an included jog dial that works natively with the major editing applications (see **Figure 11-5**).

Figure 11-5
Bella Professional video editing keyboard

Contour Designs *http://www.contourdesign.com* focuses on just the jog device. Their $60
ShuttleXpress and $110 ShuttlePRO don't offer the integrated keyboards but will have
you rocking through your project like a madman, or madwoman. The shuttles work with a
surprising number of editing programs including Windows Movie Maker and of course, all of
the Adobe and Sony applications (see **Figure 11-6**).

Figure 11-6
ShuttleXpress jog dial from Contour Designs

Buying a specialized editing tool for a single video editing session might not be money well spent but spending money of a tool that will make repetitive work go by a lot faster over multiple projects is a wise move.

Editing in Sony Vegas Movie Studio Platinum

The workspace in Sony Vegas Movie Studio is broken up into three main areas with some tools interspersed in between. The top half of the window is devoted to tracks. There are tracks for audio, video, text, overlays, music and sound effects. More tracks can be added through the Insert menu at the top of the screen. The time display at the top tells you where you are in the timeline of the video and will be very useful. It can be undocked by dragging it out of its default spot. It can be stretched to any size you want or anywhere on your desktop where it will be easy to see while you're making edit notes (see **Figure 11-7**).

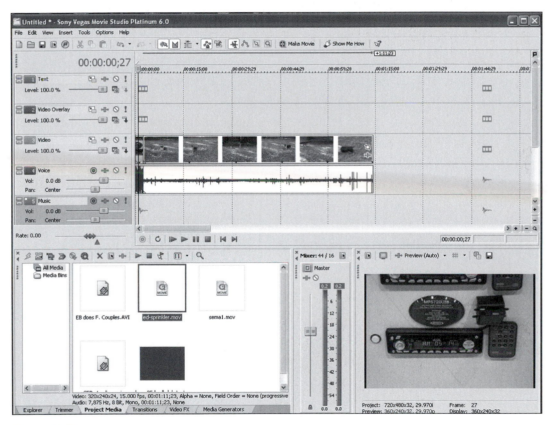

Figure 11-7
Sony Vegas Movie Studio main window

Author's Tip

The Movie Studio edition of Vegas limits the number of extra tracks you can work with in a given project. The big version allows for many more tracks. This is the case with applications like iMovie and Premiere Elements and their larger, more expensive counterparts.

The lower half of the program window focuses on media elements, sound levels and a preview window. The lower left hand window docking area has tabs for Explorer which lets you browse your local system or networked machines for content as well as a Project Media tab that lists the media you've recently encoded and a clip trimmer which is very useful. The other tools in the window don't directly relate to straight forward vlog editing but should be played with to see what they do and how they might be used.

The preview window is just that, it shows how the video will play in its current state. Most of the windows can be undocked and dragged around your desktop. The preview window is useful to undock if you have multiple monitors. Drag it over to another screen and get a much larger preview so small details you might miss are easier to see.

One of the strong points of the Vegas Movie Studio application is the relative ease at which you can move clips through the editing environment. Elements can be dragged in from outside windows or through the included explorer. Editing your captured or existing clips is as simple as dragging them into the video track. Audio included in the clip will fall into place right below the video track and follows the clip wherever it's dragged. Each track can be disconnected from one another or if one is not needed it can be deleted without affecting the other track.

The trimming function can be used through the Project Media or Explorer tabs. Right click on a media element and select "Open In Trimmer." The media is loaded into the trimmer and can be trimmer by using the top slider to mark in and out points. This is useful for pulling selected clips from a large capture. Once a selection is marked in the trimmer select one of the two insert buttons in the trimmer window. The buttons allow you to insert the selection before or after the cursor in the main project timeline.

Trimming can also be done by dragging the head or tail end of a clip in the main window back onto itself. On the other hand you can extend the clip beyond its length in either direction which fills in the new space with looped video from the clip. The trim function of that action is often more useful than creating a loop but the ability to do so is there if you need it.

You can keep adding clips, drag them around the time line and trim them until you get the desired clip sequence. Dragging a clip across another clip will create a transition effect moving from one clip to another rather than a straight cut. Transitions can be made long or short depending on how much you overlap the clips across themselves. If you don't like a clip you've inserted, select it and delete it. Make sure to delete its associated audio track as well.

MP3s can be pulled into the Music track to add a nice sound bed. If you don't have any music you particularly like lack licenses for some interesting instrumentals, you might look into a looping program like Sony Acid Pro ($299) or Acid Music Studio ($70). No actual musical skill is required to create some impressive soundbeds. The software comes with a healthy library of sound loops that can be stitched together to make a unique musical score for your vlog (see **Figure 11-8**).

What makes these tools truly compelling for vloggers wanting a professional sound is that the video can be opened in Acid as a track and scored like a movie or TV show. The learning curve is not terribly steep so trying a downloadable demo of the software will cost you nothing to see if you like it.

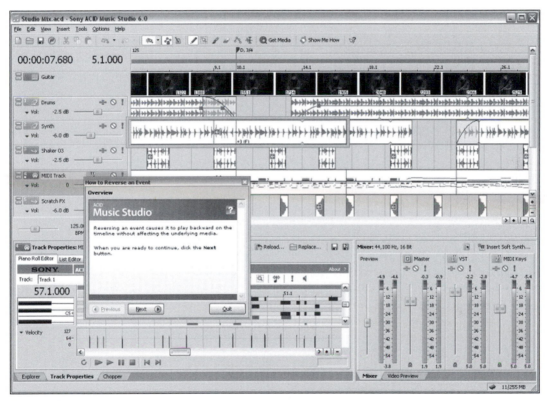

Figure 11-8
Sony Acid Studio main window with video track

Vegas comes with a quick start manual that covers most of the program features but getting up to speed takes less than 30 minutes for someone with editing experience. Those who have never touched a video editing program before would be well advised to go through the tutorials and get a feel for the program. The interface isn't mysterious and every button has a roll-over explanation in case an icon doesn't make immediate sense to you.

When you're "done" editing there are two elements that should be saved; the project file and the video. The project file is the framework of what you've done. All of the video/audio/soundtrack/effects are saved so you can shut down the program and start up again later and your work is not lost. Up to this point, no video has been generated or rendered. The program has not rendered anything; it's just showing you what it *will* look like *when* it's rendered. Rendering is the act of taking all of those edit points and clips and fusing them into a final video file. As you edit, save the project file at regular intervals in case "something" happens. Power outages, reboots, crashes, toddler havoc, etc.

The rendering of the video, which typically only happens when you're done editing, is another command altogether. In fact there are two commands but they are essentially the same. **File / Make Movie** and **File / Render As** both set up the rendering process. **Make Movie** offers rendering options in a wizard type menu system that is suited to output files that don't need special processing. **Render As** gives you access to detailed file rendering options to a much deeper granular level. The benefit to using **Render As** is that you can specify higher quality renders which don't take much longer for short format video files (see **Figure 11-9**).

Most video blogs tend to be rendered as 320 X 240. In the rendering options the options for rendering are presented bandwidth measured streams which is a little less intuitive but the description below each rendering template describes the video size and frame rate. In Vegas 256 kbps video equals 320 X 240 for MOV QuickTime files. Within the Render As window there is a function to customize the rendering properties which is a gateway to very specific settings. For the purposes of vlogging, the standard settings are likely to be fine but don't let that dissuade you from tinkering.

Rendering takes time. How long depends on a number of factors including the length of the edited product, the format, the desired render quality and most importantly, the speed of your computer. Vegas 6 comes with a render farm function that allows you to employ other computers in the rendering process. You may be familiar with computer animated movies that use massive rendering farms. This is the same concept; use multiple machines to shorten the work. This is only a good idea if you intend to produce a lot of long videos.

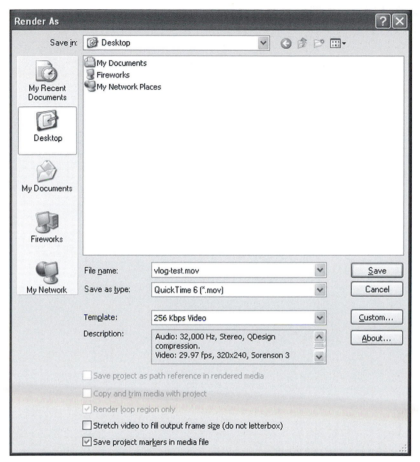

Figure 11-9
Vegas Render dialog

Editing in Windows Movie Maker

The video capture and editing program included with Windows XP is a decent and free tool that makes the process of editing video very simple but has one drawback, it only renders in WMV. If your vlog is going to be distributed as a WMV, you're in great shape, if not, it's not the end of the world. A WMV file can be converted to QuickTime with the Canopus tool but sadly, QuickTime isn't interested in fussing with WMV so that tool will not be useful for the task. With the cost of the Canopus being only half that of Premiere Elements or Vegas Movie Studio, there is a decision to be made about what you can spend and what work you are willing to do to move files from one format to another. As mentioned earlier, each format change means some degradation of video and audio quality (see **Figure 11-10**).

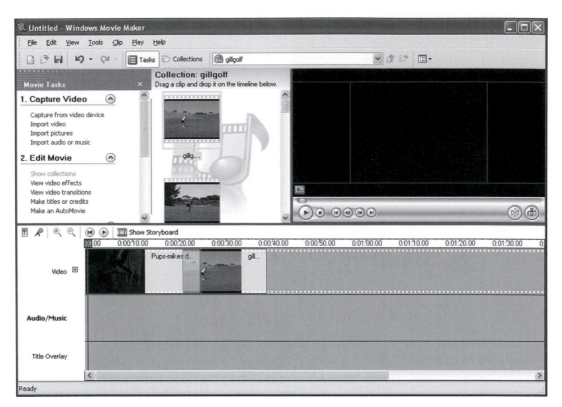

Figure 11-10
Windows Movie Maker edit window

Windows Movie Maker has a solid and easy to use interface and offers a number of good trimming and transition tools but you do get what you pay for. The combination of the free tool and a video transcoder might be cheap but what's your vlog worth?

Editing in QuickTime Pro

One of the best down-and-dirty combinations for the video blogger who wants to keep it cheap and easy is a digital camera and QuickTime Pro. Sure, DV cameras shoot better video and full editing suites offer precise frame-by-frame editing but for the no-frills approach that gets it done with what you've got, it's a good option. That's assuming you've been sold on the idea that QuickTime Pro is a must have utility to any and all vloggers and somewhere, not too far, is a digital camera that takes video.

Most digital cameras that take video do two things that work with vlogging quite well; They shoot in 320X240, the "standard" size for vlogs and they capture to QuickTime right off the bat. After a few quick trims here and there, it's ready to post, going with that fast-and-loose theme here.

Before shooting the video, make sure you've got enough room on the memory card. Each camera will vary somewhat but a general rule is about 15MB for each minute of video at 320 X 240.

There may be settings for the camera's video capture mode, then again there may not be. It depends on the camera. If so, 320 X 240 is the best way to go so no further conversion is needed later on. If there are no options. The likely default is 320X240 so you're still ok. You just lose the ability to tweak it yourself. Control freaks may wince at this but can over come it with a little encouragement.

Author's Tip

Some cameras may limit the recording time which is an arbitrary limitation having nothing to do with space or camera ability.

Once the video is shot, move the file from the camera to your computer. Cameras often have two ways to get to the media; through a USB cable or by removing the memory card and putting it into a media reader slot in the computer. Having the media card in the computer is a faster transfer than through USB. Move the file off of the card before doing anything with it in a editor. Media cards are great for storage but access speed is often slower than disk so it's better off in a fast internal hard drive.

Using QuickTime Pro, open the file and play it from start to finish. In most cases you'll want to trim the head and the tail of the clip unless having footage of you reach around for the power button at the end of the clip is somehow part of the vlog.

Once the file is opened, it looks just like any file opened in quicktime except for a few little details. There are a number of new options in the menus as well as little trim markers along the timeline at the bottom of the window. The markers act as a simple in and out place holder. Don't worry about destroying the video, the original is still on the media card unless you deleted it. If this is the only copy, go to File/Save As and make this version a work copy.

Set the left marker where you want the clip to start and the right where it should end. Use the time slider to make sure the marker is in the right place. Once you're happy with the trim go to **Edit/Trim To** Selection and voila, it's trimmed (see **Figures 11-11** and **11-12**). Save the file with a new name and its ready to upload. QuickTime Pro is not the most powerful video editor around but it's a great tool to trim and render QuickTime files without the fuss of going into a big editing application.

Figure 11-11
QuickTime edit/trim function

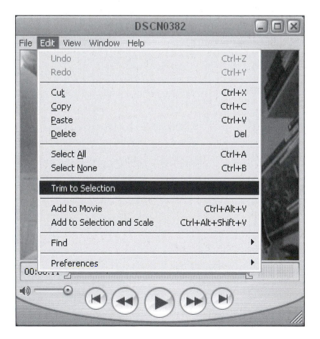

Figure 11-12
QuickTime edit/trim function

The last step is rendering the video file. QuickTime doesn't call its rendering process rendering it's called exporting. Semantics. It's the same thing and found in the same place most other editing programs keep rendering menu items, under File. The export function allows you to render as a number of different file types but only two matter for vlogging; **Quick-Time Movie/Broadband Medium** and **iPod**. Broadband Medium translates to 320X240, another example of a rendering application that does not offer the information you're looking for but can ferret out if you know where to look. QuickTime Movie is, of course, MOV.

Exporting to iPod is a special feature new to QuickTime Pro, it offers a 320X240 video render in m4v, the preferred video format of iPods. If the iPod is your main end user target, this setting is for you. As always, tinker with settings and see what works for you. Most rendering utilities have a myriad of setting that can be messed with. Try them out, it's unlikely you'll break something.

Editing in iMovie & Final Cut

Mac users have it a little easier than Windows users in that Macs are old hat at the video editing game. iMovie is an example of sublime form and function. The edit window is very simple and powerful allowing you to copy, paste and trim clips with ease (see **Figure 11-13**).

Figure 11-13
Apple iMovie main edit window

Video editors tend to stick to what works; audio tracks, video tracks, transitions, trimming, preview windows, sound levels and so on. iMovie is no different. Add in its counterparts, GarageBand and iWeb and the iLife suite works together seamlessly to create a cohesive workflow for video blogging and podcasting all the way to posting and rendering iTunes friendly RSS code. The iLife end-to-end solution is a sort of one stop shop for Mac video bloggers and podcasters.

Apple and QuickTime are tied together tightly so rendering a QuickTime MOV file once the video editing is done is just another step in the vlog workflow that moves from one step to the next.

The mechanics of video editing don't change from application to application or platform to platform. In its most basic and essential form, video editing is taking video clips, cutting them down to size and arranging them into a linear sequence to tell a story. The actual mouse moves and menu items might differ somewhat but in essence all video editing tools do the same thing. The most important thing is to find the one that you're productive with. Then buy the cheaper version that doesn't include all the fancy widgets you don't need.

Conclusion

Although the process of editing is to create a final product, there is a lot of room for creativity. The preparation of video files, sourcing and recording good b-roll and sound video capture process will make editing your video blog a fun process that results in a high quality final product. Each step can be done in a number of ways, rendering different results depending on software, hardware and settings. If you take the time to test out different methods and products, you'll ensure that money spent on tools and time spent working will produce the results you want.

The nuts and bolts of editing video don't change much but the tools used change often. Always be on the lookout for new tools, software upgrades, capture cards or tips and tricks that can improve elements of the process.

CHAPTER 12

Hosting and Bandwidth

This chapter is about hosting and bandwidth, the process of putting your blogs, podcasts and video blogs up on the Internet and paying for the bandwidth used when people see them.

Hosting video blogs and podcasts is much easier than older streaming media, because blogs are served up just like web pages, and do not require their own dedicated streaming server. However, audio and video files are big, and costs can get severely out of hand quickly if not managed correctly.

There are as many options in blog hosting as there are web hosting companies and ISPs. This chapter will highlight some of the key differences between web hosting and multimedia blog hosting, and point out the options, cheap and expensive.

This chapter covers:

- Pricing
- Content hosting
- Basic web hosts
- Web hosts with blogging services
- Feed converters
- Torrents and alternative content delivery
- Free video blog and podcast hosting services
- High-volume hosting services
- In-house and co-located hosting
- Negotiating large hosting deals

Bandwidth Refresher

- *Connection* speeds are usually in *bits per second (bps)*—so your modem is 56 Kbps (56 thousand bits per second); your T1 is 1544 Kbps which is 1.5 Mbps; and your DSL connection could be 5,000 Kbps (5 Mbps).

- Transfer speeds are usually in *bytes* per second—so when you're downloading a 3 mega-*byte* (about 3000 kilo-*bytes*) file, your computer will tell you you're getting "150 kilobyte (KB)/second" transfer.

- There are 8 bits in a byte.

- As a rule of thumb, you can divide the connection speed by ten to get the maximum transfer speed you can expect. So a T1, at about 1,500 Kbps (1.5 Mbps), should get about 150 kilo*bytes* per second transfer. A 5 Mbps cable modem connection could sustain 5000/10 = about 500 kilo*bytes* per second.

Bandwidth Pricing

The most important part of hosting, and why it requires attention, is simple: cost. Video and audio are big files. To put the entire chapter in context, we'll cut right to the chase: Bandwidth can cost a lot, unless it is bought in bulk, subsidized, amortized or shared with others.

There are several traditional of pricing for bandwidth. For simplicity, we'll generalize them into four categories:

1. **Bucket**: Pay us $10 a month and we'll give you 10 gigabytes (GB) of transfer. You'll be connected to the Internet at 100 Mbps, but once you use it up, we'll charge you $1 for each additional gigabyte transferred. Or, pay us $500 a month and we'll provide you up to 3000 gigabytes of transfer.

2. **Pipe**: Pay us $400 a month. We'll give you a T1 worth of bandwidth (1.544 Kbps). Use it all you want. You'll never exceed about 150 kilobytes per second download, for all your users.

3. **Percentile**: Pay us $150 a month. We'll give you all you can eat below 256 Kbps. You'll be connected to the Internet at 100Mbps. If you spike over 256 Kbps for over 5 minutes, we'll bump you to the next tier—512 Kbps—and charge you $300 for the month. If you sustain into our next tier we'll charge you even more—$600 for the month, and so on.

4. **Storage**: Pay us a $49 a month. We'll give you 5 gigabytes (GB) of disk space. Your bandwidth is essentially unlimited (up to the amount of bandwidth we have) in that 5 gigabytes of space. But you can only have up to 5 gigabytes of your media available at any time.

The bucket system is the most common for most personal and small business web hosting situations. This allows the hosting service to cap all their bandwidth, make sure that people don't abuse the service. In this configuration, the server can be the customer's server, or a server provided by the ISP. These prices range from around $1 a gigabyte for light web hosting to perhaps $0.10 a gigabyte for a year commitment of thousands of gigabytes per month.

The pipe system is the most common pricing for office connections, where an office gets a T1 or T3 connection. They pay a flat fee monthly for all they can eat. This can be advantageous for media hosting, because if the pipe is near saturation constantly, then the effective price per gigabyte can be very low. If the pipe is only lightly used, the effective price per gigabyte is high. For instance, if a 100Mbps pipe cost $3,000 a month, and ran at saturation for the whole month would, it would deliver approximately 32,000 gigabytes of data, for a price of about $0.09 per gigabyte. If the pipe cost only $1,000 a month, it would be 3 cents per gigabyte.

Under the percentile system, fairly common for collocation, where you bring your own server into a facility, it's sort of like a cell phone bill—if you stay within your plan, great; if you go over, the bill will give you a heart attack. This is probably the worst kind of plan for a growing podcast.

The storage pricing system is a recent innovation, pioneered by companies such as Liberated Syndication (*http://www.libsyn.com*). With their basic $10/month plan, you can keep 250 megabytes of data on their network (their plans go up to 800 megabytes ,about 0.8 gigabytes, of active content storage), and get all the bandwidth you want. The concept is that the $10 that the majority of people pay for bandwidth that isn't used makes up for the few very popular ones.

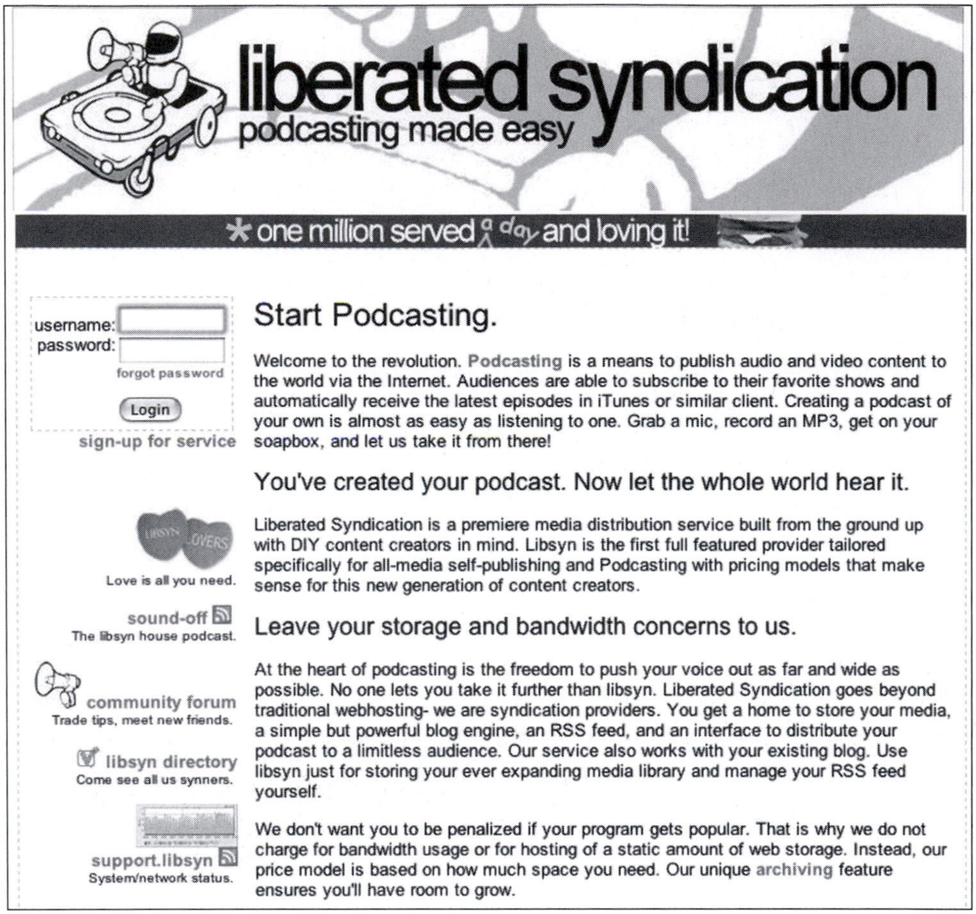

Figure 12-1
Liberated Syndication

Content Hosting

Video blogs and podcasts have common enemies, space and bandwidth. As both get cheaper every day, content seems to rise to occasion and get bigger. Digital video on the Web was once acceptable as a 10 frames-per-second thumbnail. We huddled around it like cavemen did in front of their first camp fires. Ooohing and ahhing, delighting in our new found powers. Creating digital video and audio may seem less mystical now and with that we've come to want more out of it.

Where once a MIDI remake of *Every Little Thing She Does Is Magic* would suffice, the consumer is now demanding MP3s that tip the scales at nearly 2–3 megabytes per minute of audio (at 128 Kbps encoding). Where the blocky thumbnail low frame-rate video was acceptable people want full frame rate, full screen video. Fortunately for us, the video blogs and podcasts don't require such top-notch production. A good 320 × 240 30 fps video clip will suffice in most cases. If encoded well it should handle enlarging elegantly, to a degree. Spoken word podcasts don't need to be at 128 Kbps or 192 Kbps—an 80 Kbps MP3 will more than do.

Bandwidth Amount

How much does a megabyte or two really matter at the end of the day? If you're going to be making a daily video blog or podcast, it will matter a whole lot. Each broadcast will, in most cases remain available, on-line indefinitely. With that in mind, people may be watching the newest offering each time it comes out but there will also be a significant number of people who will be downloading older content. As the library grows, so will bandwidth associated with the back-catalog.

Table 10-1
Hypothetical Content Sizing Estimates

Media	Bandwidth Size
MP3s @ 128K	1 megabyte per minute
iPod AVC Video download 320 x 240 resolution	10 megabytes per minute
30 minute podcast with 1,000 downloads	30 gigabytes transferred
3 minute video blog with 1,000 downloads	30 gigabytes transferred
3 minute video blog with 10,000 viewers	300 gigabytes
30 minute podcast with 100,000 listeners	3000 gigabytes (3 terabytes)

So, at $1 a gigabyte, you'd pay $30 just for 1000 viewers of just one video post. If you got the price down to ten cents per gigabyte, you'd pay $3.00 every time your podcast or video blog aired. If it's a weekly show, that's only $12 a month.

If your content becomes very popular, bandwidth will, of course, increase. A 10 megabyte file downloaded by 1,000 people works out to roughly 10 gigabytes of throughput. But if the audience increases to 10,000 or even 100,000 views for a particularly popular video blog post, the bandwidth for that post alone could exceed 300 or 3,000 gigabytes.

ALERT   **The Paradox of Popularity**

Unlike most pricing models, the more bandwidth you use, the higher the price. Bandwidth is like a cell phone; fine when you stay within your plan, and then outrageously expensive when you exceed it—or it just stops working and gives your audience the "bandwidth exceeded" message.

You have to plan ahead.

Scalability

Hosting content can happen in a number of places. Most content hosting starts in the same facility and often the same servers as the rest of a hosted site. For many companies, that scenario works quite well. When an organization makes their money from their content, the hosting of that content begins to have more attention paid to it when it comes to uptime, speed, storage and management.

As traffic goes up so does the cost and the need to reliably deliver media. The public is fickle when it comes to media delivery. Even a short episode of slow downloads can send people away, never to come back.

Although many podcasters may never grow enough to necessitate the next levels of service, larger implementations will, and may do so quickly. It's important to know where your site is in the scale. The "scale" is not a simple sliding scale that you can hold against your site and know what the "right thing to do" is. To make it simpler, we'll cover some of the content hosting options and what they offer.

Basic Web Hosts

A simple web hosting service where content is served directly from the Apache/MS IIS web farm that is likely shared with other sites is the starting block. It's the cheapest service and with that cheapness you get little else. All content will be treated the same. That's all fine and nice for low-traffic sites. The trouble is in their inherent inability to scale well. As soon as the site gets a spike by something like a mention on Fark.com or a popular news article, the web server may not be able to deal with the load.

In light of the fact that it's difficult to predict traffic spikes and their magnitudes, it's important to consider the risks involved if a sudden spike renders your podcast unreachable. Not-for-profit sites might not lose revenue but un-negotiated overage pricing could render a spectacular bill.

The pain may not end there. Hosting shops may take umbrage with a shared-hosting site that caused other customers on the same service to experience an outage. That incident might also earn a call from the host demanding that you immediately upgrade your service. That may leave you in a position where you have to make a quick decision and likely don't have enough time to migrate to a hosting service with the expanded services you need. If the current provider does have the services, it puts you in a position where bargaining is difficult.

Author's Tip

The incredibly fortunate thing about the many discount hosting services is that they are so cheap to try. You can test the waters and spend $7 to try out a "250 gigabytes of transfer" service and see if their throughput is any good. Post a single podcast or video clip on it and link to it in your blog. If several people complain that they couldn't get the clip, you know the score on that discount service.

Plus, you can do your own poor-man's round robin by using several such services and manually disabling links before you exceed your limit. Since you'll pay a steep $0.50/gigabyte fee for all bandwidth over the 250 gigabytes, that still means that you could serve a 2.5 minute clip to 100,000 people before you were out of bandwidth, all for just $7. Just make sure you keep an eye on it before it fills up.

Podcasters that are trying to generate revenue have the same issues and a few more. Generating revenue depends on an audience that gets what it wants. A slow site that suddenly goes off-air with no warning or details will, not might, will lose a portion of their audience. Less audience, less money. What's more, if the XML feed is syndicated to iTunes and other popular aggregators, the downtime may cause them to drop your feed. Since the site is not only made up of HTML, one must consider the other ways people consume the content. The RSS feeds that get syndicated, the mobile users, the subscribers will all see the outage in different ways.

The key is to avoid the scenario altogether. Before you start adding audio or video to a website, make sure they're equipped to handle the bandwidth.

Web Hosts with Blogging Services

Most blogging software has some basic ability to upload and host images, video, and audio. For a lightly trafficked podcast or video blog, this will be sufficient.

The easiest way to get up and running is to employ the services of an all-inclusive hosting shop. This strategy is best for operations that do not have their own production colocation facility or don't want to deal with the nuts and bolts of setting up server applications. Even those with their own co-located systems could benefit from the service provider model. These multimedia blogging *ASPs* (Application Service Providers) bear the burden of maintaining their own IT infrastructure, application installation, upgrades and performance as well as being able to offer new programs without making the client purchase the entire retail product.

Author's Tip

For corporations new to hosting multimedia but under the gun to start podcasting, ASPs can help them side-step a possible internal IT quagmire. Some IT organizations require a structured security and performance testing. Some even go so far as to require dedicated equipment for new applications.

The ASP model allows the entire service to be handled off-site where the only interaction with the hasted site would be through web-based configuration and posting pages. On the other hand some IT organizations may be enthusiastic to take on new projects but cannot give them all the attention they need. Whatever the case may be it's important to weigh all of the options and find the solution that works for you.

The ASP differs from standard hosting companies in that the hosting is a given but it's not their core business. They support applications and charge for their use. A blog application may be one of dozens that they have to offer. They may offer a content management program, traffic statistics (although most offer it for free) message boards, list-serve, domain name registration, shopping carts, Wiki, site design, and in-house web application development.

For example, Nexcess (*http://nexcess.net/movabletype/*), **Figure 12-2**) and Media Temple (*http://www.mediatemple.net/*) are two of the endorsed Movable Type partners that offer a wide range of services. Bluehost (*http://www.bluehost.com*, **Figure 12-3**) and AN Hosting (*http://www.anhosting.com/*) both offer WordPress hosting. And, Yahoo! Small Business hosting offers both blogging packages.

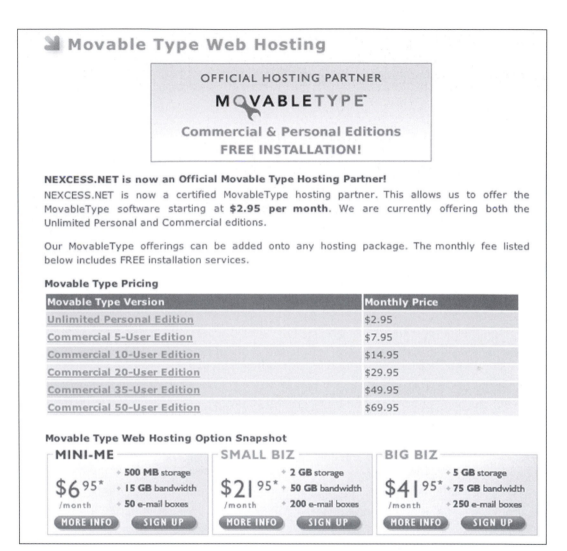

Movable Type Web Hosting

OFFICIAL HOSTING PARTNER
MOVABLETYPE
Commercial & Personal Editions
FREE INSTALLATION!

NEXCESS.NET is now an Official Movable Type Hosting Partner!
NEXCESS.NET is now a certified MovableType hosting partner. This allows us to offer the MovableType software starting at **$2.95 per month**. We are currently offering both the Unlimited Personal and Commercial editions.

Our MovableType offerings can be added onto any hosting package. The monthly fee listed below includes FREE installation services.

Movable Type Pricing

Movable Type Version	Monthly Price
Unlimited Personal Edition	$2.95
Commercial 5-User Edition	$7.95
Commercial 10-User Edition	$14.95
Commercial 20-User Edition	$29.95
Commercial 35-User Edition	$49.95
Commercial 50-User Edition	$69.95

Movable Type Web Hosting Option Snapshot

MINI-ME
$6⁹⁵* /month
- 500 MB storage
- 15 GB bandwidth
- 50 e-mail boxes

MORE INFO | SIGN UP

SMALL BIZ
$21⁹⁵* /month
- 2 GB storage
- 50 GB bandwidth
- 200 e-mail boxes

MORE INFO | SIGN UP

BIG BIZ
$41⁹⁵* /month
- 5 GB storage
- 75 GB bandwidth
- 250 e-mail boxes

MORE INFO | SIGN UP

Figure 12-2

Nexcess

All of these services offer a simple solution: log in, register a domain name, set up the blog site through a set of forms and wait. The waiting is for the domain name to go through the registration process. You may also be transferring the name from another facility, which takes a few days. Once the name has taken hold and all of the global DNS servers are happy and shiny about resolving the name and sending people to the blog site, you're nearly good to go.

Figure 12-3
Bluehost

As is the case with many things Internet, there are more than a few choices. If WordPress or Movable Type don't seem to fit your needs, there are many other, smaller products. All blog programs can support some form of RSS syndication but it's important that the one you pick supports the one that counts RSS 2.0 in addition to a broad range of other RSS standards.

Feed Converters

What happens if you're already using Blogger.com and people love you, you love them, the URL is known but now it's time to add enclosures? Now is not the time to panic. FeedBurner.com can turn your nonconforming text-blog feed into a highly compatible RSS 2.0 feed with multimedia enclosures.

FeedBurner simply processes the feed and offers you a URL that can be offered up to people to enter in their client for the feed. Once you've gone through a simple setup process the feeds start to get processed in almost-real-time. Your audience can come to your website where you posted a permanent FeedBurner syndication link and use that to pull down feeds with enclosures from their compliant reader. Even if your blog already produces compliant RSS, FeedBurner can be used to consolidate tracking for your blog, like a hit counter for your website.

Torrents and Alternative Content Delivery

There has been much talk about the use of Torrents (the name for a file using the BitTorrent P2P download system) to distribute legitimate media files for free.

Prodigem (*http://www.prodigem.com/*) is an example of this type of service. In order to use it, you have to have your media file hosted elsewhere, but then Prodigem can automatically create Torrent files for it. Each viewer who downloads the file will potentially keep serving it to other peers (**Figure 12-4**).

Liberated Syndication also offers automatic BitTorrent sharing of all files in addition to their conventional hosting.

If your audience is of a demographic that uses and appreciates BitTorrent, their use of the Torrent will save you bandwidth for your other audience members.

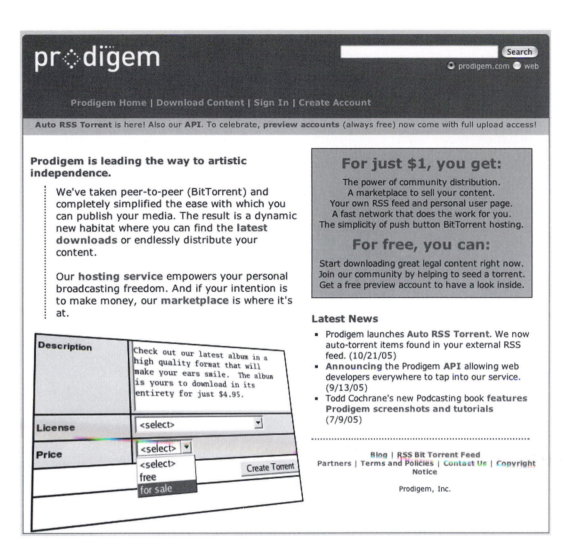

Figure 12-4
Prodigem.com

Free Video Blog and Podcast Hosts

Although this book focuses on semi-commercial and commercial efforts, there are actually a number of essentially free hosting environments.

Some of pioneers of the video blogging or "vlogging" movement have emphasized the critical role of the medium for non-profit, documentary, citizen journalist, and educational use. In most of these models, there is essentially no budget for bandwidth, but the content is potentially more important than commercial content.

There are several services that cater to these socially beneficial goals. An excellent site called FreeVlog (*freevlog.org*) by the enthusiastic vloggers Ryanne Hodson and Michael Verdi shows a step-by-step process for getting a vlog cheaply made and freely hosted.

OurMedia

OurMedia (*http://www.ourmedia.org*), a non-profit organization, has created a "Global home for grassroots media". In conjunction with the Internet Archive (*http://www.archive.org*), they will host, and store audio, video, text, and software for free, forever, no catches. The only requirement is that the content is licensed under a Creative Commons license (see the chapter on Copyrights and Licensing), which explicitly describes what others can do with the material (**Figure 12-5**).

Figure 12-5
Ourmedia.org

Blip.tv

Another free video blog hosting service is blip.tv. This service has a variety of excellent features, allowing you to not only upload video to their service but post the full blog on their site. They give you a URL of <yourname>.blip.tv and can automatically cross-post the same blog entry into your existing Blogger, Movable Type or other blog (**Figure 12-6**).

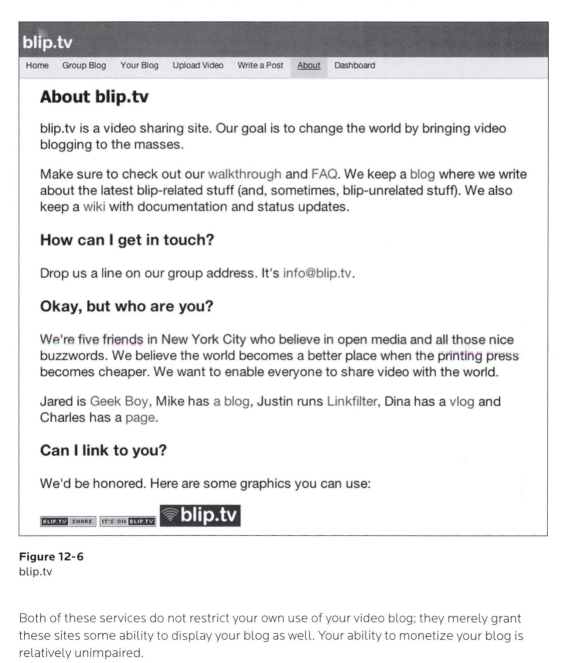

Figure 12-6
blip.tv

Both of these services do not restrict your own use of your video blog; they merely grant these sites some ability to display your blog as well. Your ability to monetize your blog is relatively unimpaired.

The only potential drawback is that a blog that depended on high-availability and uptime for their video blogs could not expect a service level agreement from a free service.

Google

There is one other free hosting option that deserves mention. Google (*http://www.google.com*), the reigning king of search engines, recently debuted their own, essentially free video hosting service and marketplace. You can upload videos in a variety of formats, all of which are automatically transcoded to a Flash-based player format viewable on their site. They also transcode it for the iPod and provide a link to the original version as well.

While not activated yet, Google's faq states that if large videos (like a 500 megabyte movie) get too popular, they will put a price on the video to cover their hosting costs. But their example seems to imply that smaller videos that don't become the next JibJab will be hosted for free.

The videos go through a several day process of inspection to spot check for objectionable content (the list is very standard, such as illegal content, pornographic, etc.) After the video is OK'ed, it is uploaded, and a link is sent to you.

Just like the other services mentioned, Google asks you to designate a license (such as the Creative Commons licenses) for your content so that it is clear to viewers what they may do with it. Through Google can even put a price on video, and restrictions for how often people can watch it, whether it is a one-day rental or a download of the content.

The day-or-more delay in uploaded video becoming available for linking makes Google non-ideal for daily, instantaneous blogging. But for those with a back catalog of video that they would like to provide or even potentially monetize, Google's offering is remarkable.

Based on Google's entering the space, it is probable that Google's search and portal competitors will follow suit with similar offerings.

Podcast Specific Services

Podbus.com is one instance of a web hosting service dedicated for podcasting. Their fees are around $5/month for 300 metabytes of storage and 10 gigabytes of bandwidth, but they charge $0.66 per gigabyte over the 10 gigs.

There are in fact more "podcast" hosts than can be rounded up, all charging similar rates to conventional web hosts.

As mentioned earlier, however, *storage*-based pricing is the newest model, and a model more compatible with potentially popular podcasts. Liberated Syndication (*www.libsyn.com*) was the pioneer in this. An interesting aspect of their service, and part of how they keep this "free" bandwidth under control, is the throttling of earlier posts. After 30 days, posts on their network are automatically archived onto slower servers (bandwidth, not CPU power). Thus, podcasts in active circulation are on the high-speed network, and archived shows, while still available, download at slower speeds.

Audioblog (*http://www.audioblog.com*) is service for podcasting and despite the name, video blogging. They offer between 500 megabytes ($10/month) and 5 gigabytes ($50/month) of *storage*, with *unlimited* bandwidth. Audioblog has even more features such automatically transcoding video blogs into Flash (for web page embedding) and MP4 (for download to iTunes/iPod).

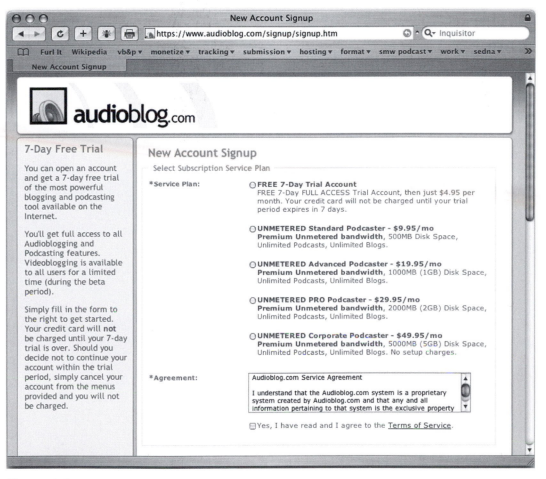

Figure 12-7
audioblog.com

High Volume Hosting Services

Some providers offer scalable solutions where once you hit a threshold your site is seamlessly moved to faster systems with better burstability. That ability to handle a sudden load will not come without an increase in price. How does that compare to the price of having to re-acquire the audience?

Some hosting providers will offer a more robust setup for those that anticipate rapid growth and spikey traffic. The high-volume shared servers can often host hundreds of sites, each with a trickle of traffic. Once moved over to something akin to "business class" your site will get more legroom. Keeping in mind that the XML and HTML account of a tiny fraction of traffic, this should be about the ability to serve media. Conventional websites make this move to advanced web applications or processor intensive database operations.

On the bulk, cheap end of the scale is a very popular hosting company called Cogent (*http://www.cogentco.com*). For years, they have offered a $1000/month 100 Mbps pipe and a $10,000/month Gigabit Ethernet (1000 Mbps, or 1 Gbps) pipe. (See **Figure 12-8**).

With Cogent, you co-locate your own servers at one of their data centers (or they can manage these for you) and these servers serve up all your data. Although this location becomes a single point of failure, the potential bandwidth savings is beyond compare.

ALERT

!

It's important to remember that the media content is not streamed content. Some providers may not completely grasp that and will try to sell you streaming content services. Fortunately, those services do not apply to this technology. Podcast and video blog content is simply a collection of downloadable files. Traditional high-availability web hosting services are all that are needed.

This also means that podcasts and video blogs are comparatively insensitive to streaming media killers such as packet loss and congestion. A podcast download may stall for a moment, then continue, and users of podcast media are accustomed to waiting until the file successfully downloads before they try to play it.

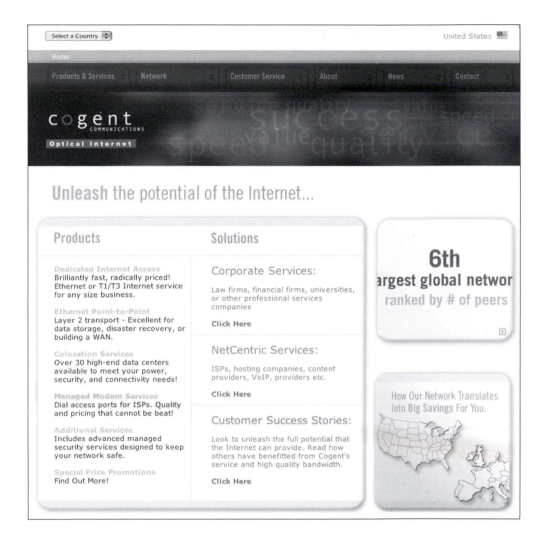

Figure 12-8
Cogent

CDNs (content delivery networks) exist to handle the needs of companies who want to distribute files of any type anywhere in the world at the highest speed and availability possible. Akamai.com is the leading CDN. CDNs, rather than charging the client for spikes, charge for overall throughput. That means if you get a spike where 10,000 people are trying to download a video at the same time, you're charged for how many bytes are handed out, not the amplitude of the demand. These services are used by the largest companies and media organizations,—Apple, Microsoft, Audi, NBC, Fujitsu, etc. The prices are steep—monthly fees can start in the tens of thousands of dollars.

Typically, the blog application itself will not be hosted by the CDN, only the files. A separate, existing web add content management infrastructure would remain in place to handle the text-based requests as well as RSS feeds. Each part of inserting files into a CDN, distributing to the edge nodes, and then storing them has a cost. The usage model with CDNs then is to only use them for static HTML and multimedia files, and cache the files on the network only so long as globally or nationally burstable access is desired.

There are a number of CDNs that have different offerings. Some hosting facilities claim to offer CDN service as well. It's important to vet those offerings and make sure they keep your content "at the edge" rather than holed up in some backwater server somewhere off Guam where download speeds are going to be painful for your users. Akamai and others that play at that tier offer their content at speeds so fast most cable modems can't take advantage of the full deluge and the provider has to throttle down, even under high demand.

When leveraging a CDN for media files and even for image elements and other static content the blog can suddenly handle a great deal more traffic as it's not having to simultaneously hand out massive video / audio files as well as respond to HTTP requests and run the blog application.

In-House and Co-Located Hosting

If your company has in in-house IT organization with existing outward-facing web services or co-located systems you may consider bringing the entire project in-house. I mention this option last because of the cost, labor, SLA and headcount implications. The basic model of blog applications is the ASP so taking this internal requires treating this more like an IT project with ongoing monitoring and support.

One of the advantages to bringing the application into the enterprise is the ability to manage your own people rather than phoning a call center if your have support questions. This model also allows you to leverage existing bandwidth and CDN contracts you may already have in place. If there is excess that is already being paid for, why not use it. You can also leverage existing IT infrastructure including servers, networking hardware and monitoring systems. The marketing and sales folks may also have a vested interest in detailed statistics which can be derived from a number of tracking and CRM packages.

The challenges lie in scoping the project and implementation. An ASP based solution can be up and running in hours where a bureaucratic enterprise could drag out the requirement, budgeting, and deployment for weeks or even months. Smaller, more nimble operations may be able to deploy quickly so knowing the bureaucratic reality of your corporate environment will give you an indication of what to expect and what direction to go in. The portability of these applications is such that if one way doesn't fit your needs, moving them can be done with relative ease.

Negotiating Large Hosting Deals

There are two kinds of purchases, set price and unset price. People often get confused so it's good to outline a few of them to make sure we're all on the same page. Nothing in 7-11 is up for negotiation except, perhaps, the day-old donuts. Gum, Coke and a copy of Low Rider magazine cost what they cost. Bulk never comes into the equation nor does making deals.

Does that mean all brick and mortar corporate retail stores are price-locked? Not at all. Take Best Buy, prices on their higher-end stuff is a little flexible. Each business has, in effect, a deal scale of 1–10. Where Macys is a one, a car dealership is closer to a nine.

Businesses like car dealerships almost require you to deal. Nothing is fixed. Very few people walk into a dealership and cut a check for the sticker price. Due to demand for certain cars, some people end up paying OVER sticker. As strange as it sounds, we do the same in business. We pay more than we have to by purchasing unnecessary extras, more bandwidth than we need, contracts that are too long. We get sucked into the pitch and end up with waste and a bill of goods.

All too often in business people take what they're given, pay what they're told to and never look back. Most businesses fail to effectively negotiate their contracts. Sometimes it's a matter of not knowing what the market is like, not knowing of existing corporate deals, being scared of negotiating or worse of all, not even thinking to negotiate at all. If the person about to negotiate the next hosting or bandwidth deal is the same one that complains about the hassle of buying a new car, they should be quickly whisked out of the deal process.

It sounds simple enough, but factors come into play that causes the process to take ugly turns. Projects are sometimes more like an ambush than anything else. Here is the scenario. The CEO reads an article on video blogging in the *Wall Street Journal*, or perhaps *Highlights*. She gets very excited and bursts into the office telling the senior team that if they don't get a video blog up and running in two weeks their competitor will have a jump on them and the world might just stop on its axis. Gravity stops, the atmosphere sloughs off into space and life as we know it ceases to exist.

Author's Tip

Skill negotiating is considered by some to be an innate skill: You're either born with it or not. That said, anyone within the business who purchases anything at all should be taught how to negotiate. Content and blog hosting deals should be cut only after you're completely satisfied that you're evaluated the entire playing field, eliminated players that don't suit your needs and found the providers that meet your service, customer service and price needs in the contract length that works for you.

Now it's up to you and your team to develop the video blog project. Budgeting, timelines, project management, design, production, hosting, software, hardware, headcount, the whole thing. It's easy to get caught up in trying to cross thing off the list in order to hit a deadline but when it comes to the bigger ticket items and services that will end up as a monthly cost you have to be sure you got the best deal possible.

Before meeting with vendors it's good to have a mantra. Something like "I will not sign a deal today, I will not agree to the first offer, I will not pay list price, I will not buy the first product I see without having seen everything else first."

Vendors want to get you into the longest deal possible and sell as many services as they can. That's the nature of sales. When dealing with vendors you have to walk into the negotiation with two things, a firm understanding of what you need and the ability to walk away if the deal isn't good for you.

ALERT
!
Bandwidth prices have been, and continue to be, notoriously variable. The same connection could be sold for 10 times the price or a tenth the price to another customer. This is partially because bandwidth is bundled with so many other services and service level agreements— guaranteed uptime, hosting, managed services, etc.

Most businesses get into bad contracts because simple legwork wasn't done. Forecasting growth, understanding the needs of your various business units, building a well defined set of requirements and asking a lot of what-if questions. It's also critical to know who you're getting involved with.

Researching the provider through a business information firm like Hoovers.com is a good step. Finding out a little more about the company financials through press clippings and releases is another strategy. This might sound a little like Sun Tzu, and for good reason, the strategy works. Know yourself, know your opponent and you will be assured victory.

What to Look for

Since you have a well defined set of requirements and a firm budget and a list of players it's time to venture forth and find the sweet deal waiting for you. The requirements will allow you to compare apples to apples. If one vendor has a different pricing model, try to get them to put it in terms of how other competitors are pricing their products. If they can't or refuse or even worse, talk around it, be wary.

The end result of these initial vendor meetings is to get a feeling for their offering and to create comparable deals. Little things like what the penalty or charges for bandwidth overages, emergency support, 24 hour customer service, remote-hands and terminating contracts early are critical and should be looked over by your legal people before signing anything. Know what you're up against, have a contingency plan.

Once you've put together three to five deal offerings, look at them side by side with a group of stakeholders. Beat them up, pull the numbers apart. Weigh the pros and cons. Consider things like what it means that a certain vendor has offices three time zones away. What does it mean to your brand image if they cannot guarantee any more than 99% uptime.

Competitive Bidding

Once a short list boils up to the top its time to take them to task and pit them against each other. This is where some people find the whole process rather distasteful. Those people should not be involved in the process as this is where emotions and squeamishness translates directly into unnecessary spending. It might be good to drag a grizzled sales road warrior out if their cave to sit in and help get the best offer out of the vendor. It is common to go back and forth four or five times to get to an agreeable number all the while going through the same process with other vendors.

It can get confusing and frustrating but in the end the few dollars saved here and there, the decisions about service over cost will serve your business best in the end. If your front-runner is a little more expensive than the next one in line, tell them that. Say that the numbers are close and see what they can do.

Author's Tip

In the midst of this it's important to remember a few important things:

- Honesty is key. There is no need to show all of your cards, that's part of the process but it's important to be a straight shooter.
- You'll be working WITH the company you pick. If you squeezed them too hard in the deal they might not be as inclined to give you a hand if you're in need.
- Finally, we are all humans and as much as it's important to get a good deal, it's more important to operate in a dignified way and treat people in a way that you would want to be treated.

It's a bit of a dichotomy but a fine balance can be kept where everyone comes out a winner.

It is a small world and not only might you need to talk with one of the losing vendors down the road, people move around from business to business and they remember things. Be a strong, firm and fair negotiator and not a chiseler that people warn each other about.

As is the case in most businesses it's not a democracy, it's a benevolent dictatorship. The deal decision making should work that way. Everyone has a voice but at the end of the day someone is actually responsible for it to make sense and work. That person makes the decision.

Conclusion

Bandwidth prices are wildly variable in today's market. Even though bandwidth is sometimes viewed as a commodity, the quality of service, uptime, and level of support are significantly different from offering to offering.

A spike in your podcast or video blog's popularity can set you back hundreds and even thousands of dollars with a poorly planned hosting arrangement.

Video blogging services range from completely free (in exchange for light re-distribution rights on their portal) to flat-fee hundreds of dollars a year for unlimited bandwidth, all the way up to tens of thousands a month for a full, world-class content delivery network.

Because of this tremendous disparity of prices, it pays to negotiate.

CHAPTER 13

Assembling Blog Entries

Once the video and audio files have been captured, edited and compressed into their final posting-ready formats, they are ready to be attached to a blog entry. Each blog application will have its own workflow but the popular ones mentioned here are not only feature-rich, they don't leave you guessing. A few of them might need some feed post-processing by FeedBurner in order to make the RSS XML iTunes friendly.

We're also going to discuss some of the more popular free media hosting sites which will help keep the green stuff in your wallet while other people pay the bandwidth bill.

This chapter covers:

- Posting to blogging applications
- Enclosure generating with FeedBurner
- Hosted media services

Blogging Applications

Some of the blog services and applications may not currently offer all of the features you want so be sure to check in with different services on a regular basis to see if one of them offers new services that enhance your podcast or video blog. The chapters on backing up and exporting and administration will prepare you and your content for simple blog migration if you decide to move to another provider sometime down the road.

TypePad

Creating a post with TypePad is very straightforward. One of its strengths is that it creates the correct iTunes friendly XML without any intervention on your part. TypePad also allows you to keep media files on their site which keeps you from having to maintain media files elsewhere. There are size and space limitations which may necessitate alternative hosting.

Creating the podcast or video blog post is the same process as creating post that includes a photo (see **Figure 13-1**).

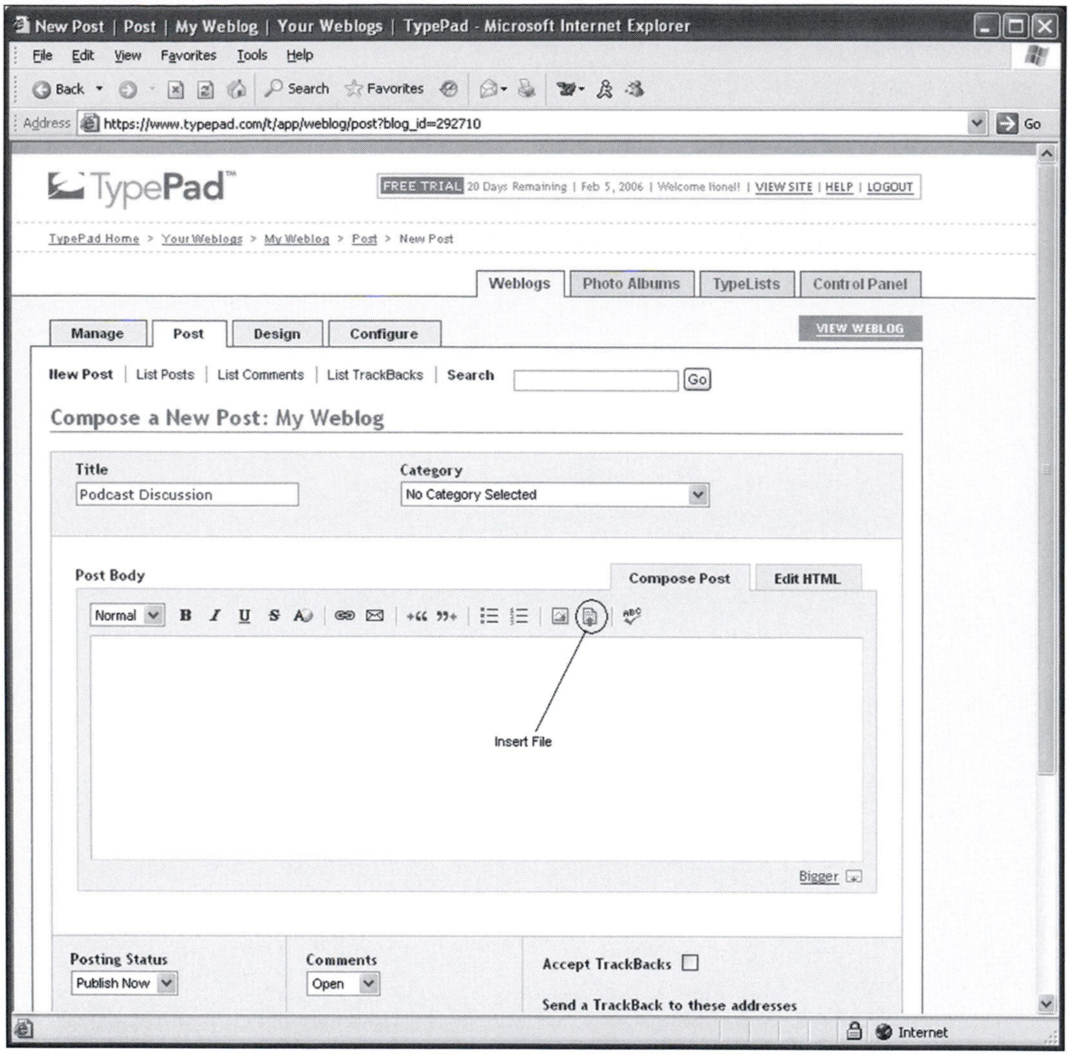

Figure 13-1
TypePad blog post edit window with "Insert File" icon highlighted

Clicking on the Insert File icon in the post creation toolbar will bring up a file upload dialog. Using the browse button, navigate to the file on your computer and click Upload File. If you're referencing a file already hosted, use the "Edit HTML" tag and insert an "A" reference:

```
<p>

<a href="http://www.myhost.com/site-audio/review-podcasting-01.mp3">Download
Podcast</a>

</p>
```

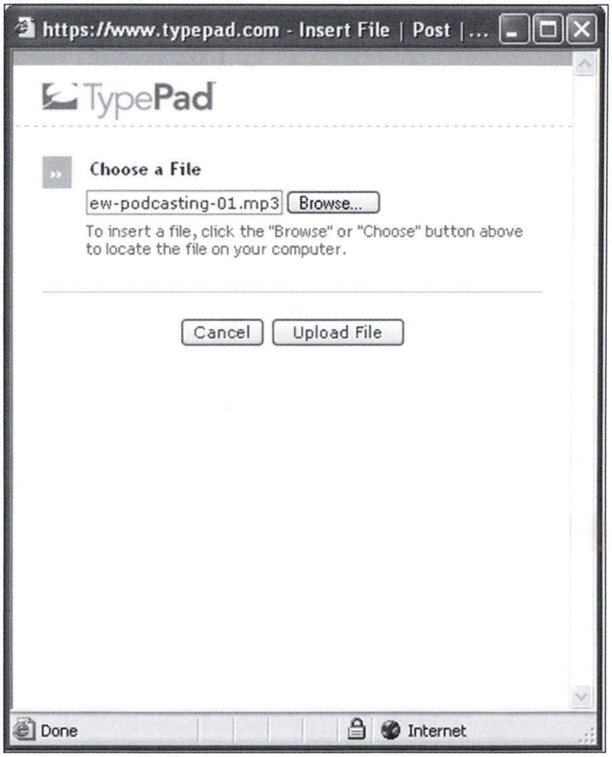

Figure 13-2
TypePad file upload dialogue window

Once the text of the post is in place, the file is uploaded or code is written in to reference the hosted file, click "Preview" to see how the post will look (see **Figure 13-3**). Click on the link to the referenced file and see if it works. If not, go back and edit the HTML link.

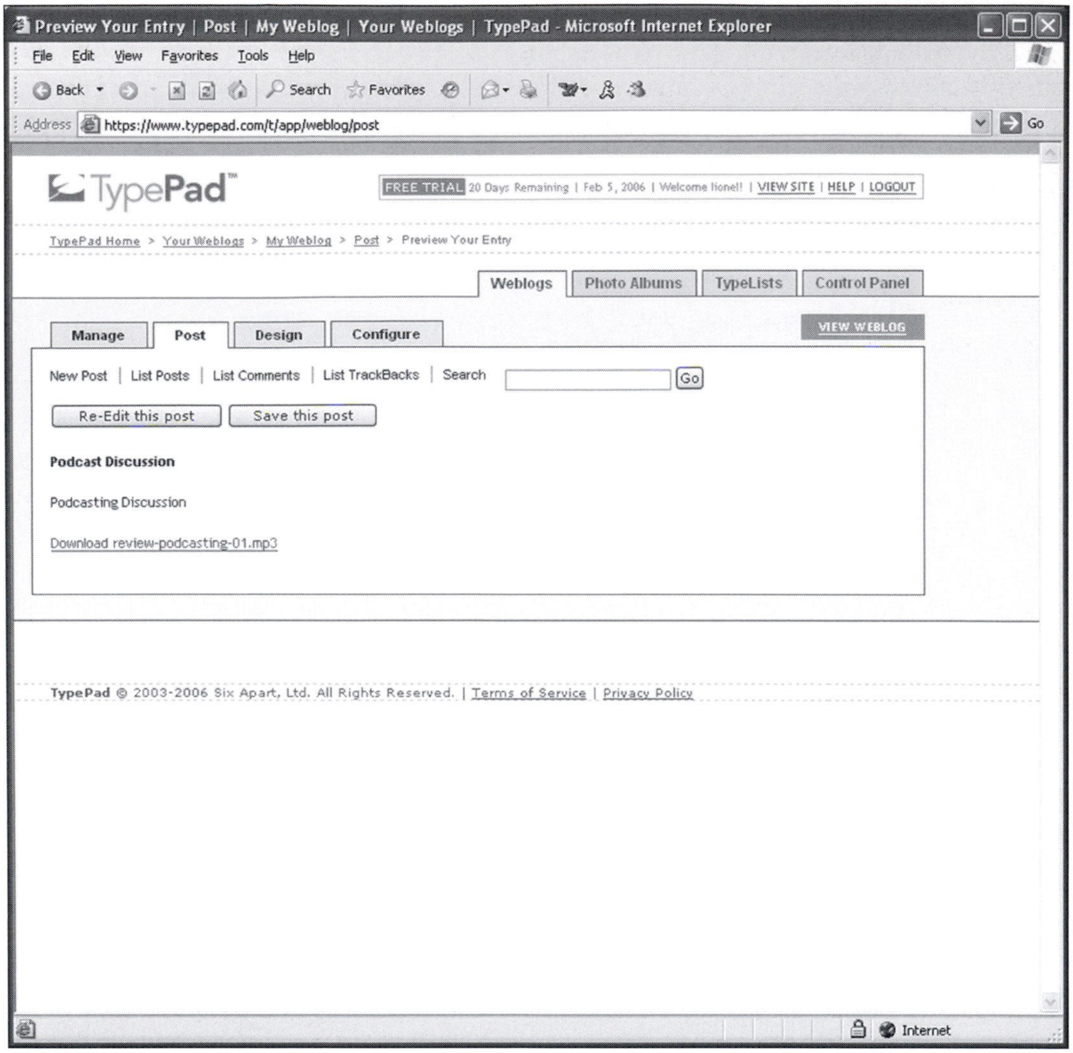

Figure 13-3
TypePad post preview

If everything looks good and the link work, click "Save This Post". TypePad will render the RSS XML and publish the post. If it was successful, the posting and file should come up in iTunes (see **Figure 13-4**).

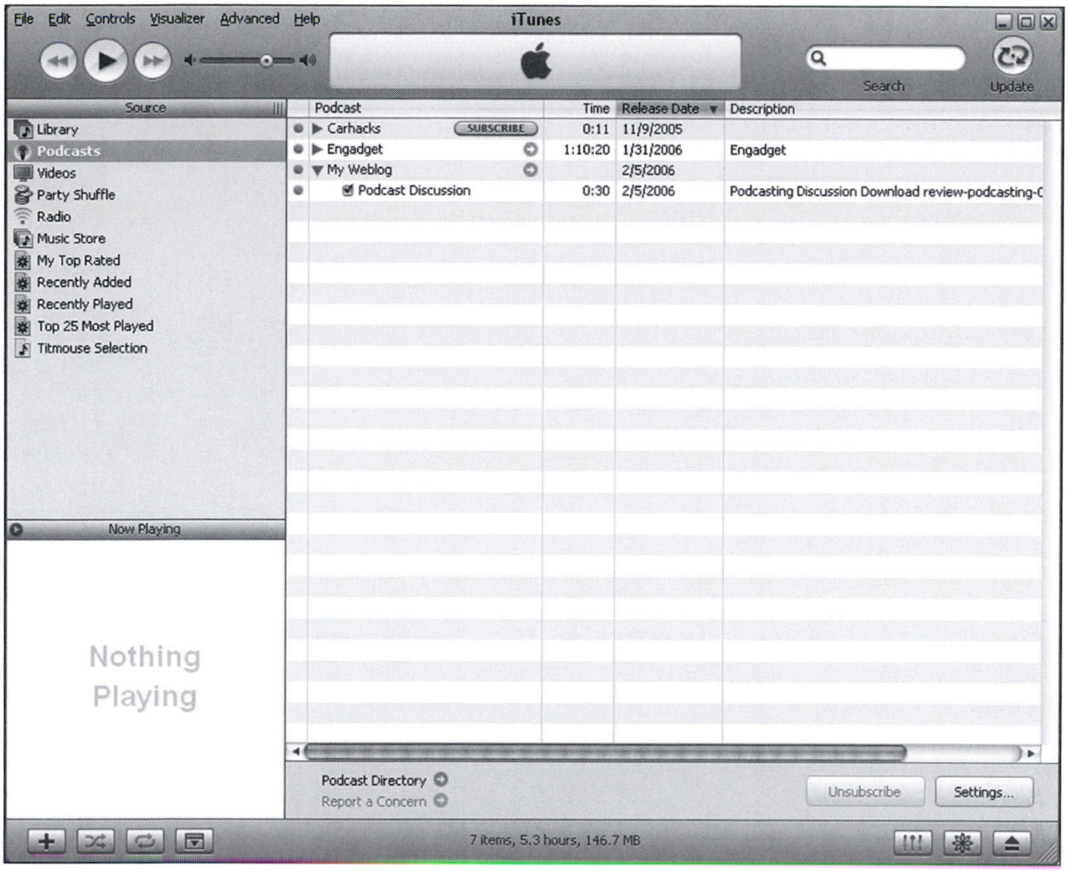

Figure 13-4
iTunes Podcast / Video Blog Subscription Window

Blogger, Movable Type and WordPress

Podcasting and video blogging is still a new phenomenon. So new that developers are scrambling to catch up with all of the new technology needed to support the quickly growing trend. Sites like blogger and applications such as Movable Type and WordPress are not quite up to speed with support for podcasting and video blogging.

For the time being there are only a few options for bloggers using those services. They can call up support every day and pester them to support enclosures and post iTunes friendly XML, move to a provider that gives them what they need or a service like FeedBurner.

Author's Tip

iTunes and some other programs are finicky about the RSS subscription URL they are given. It's always best to enter an explicit RSS URL to guarantee the client application will pull the feed you want. In TypePad sites there is a link in the sidebar "Subscribe to This Blog's Feed" which will link directly to the correct XML. Copy that link and paste it into iTunes, FireAnt or other RSS reader.

Movable Type users have another alternative. There are template plug-ins that can be installed that will make Movable Type publish iTunes compliant XML feeds. The template hack is detailed in the RSS chapter and can be installed in about 20 minutes. Once installed, posting with podcasts and video enclosures is very similar to the Type Pad process.

Until Blogger and WordPress upgrade their RSS rendering engines and templates, the feeds will have to be processed. The downside to processing is having another moving part in your workflow and one more thing to manage.

Creating the podcast post in Blogger and WordPress is also similar to the TypePad process. Create the post in the editor, upload or reference the media file, preview the post to make sure the link works and publish. If it publishes correctly it's time to set up FeedBurner and make the posts enclosure friendly.

Audioblog

Being able to publish correctly coded enclosure compliant posts is important to the success of a podcast or video blog. Audioblog gives you a whole new toolkit for posting, publishing and managing your podcasts. One of its innovative features is their phone-in podcast publisher. You call into their system, enter your PIN and talk until you're blue in the face. When you're done you press a few keys and the podcast is live. No computer involved, in fact the only thing needed is a touch tone phone.

Another thing they do is provide hosting space and publishing. By uploading the media file to Audioblog, you can create and publish your post without having to log into your blog admin interface (see **Figure 13-5**).

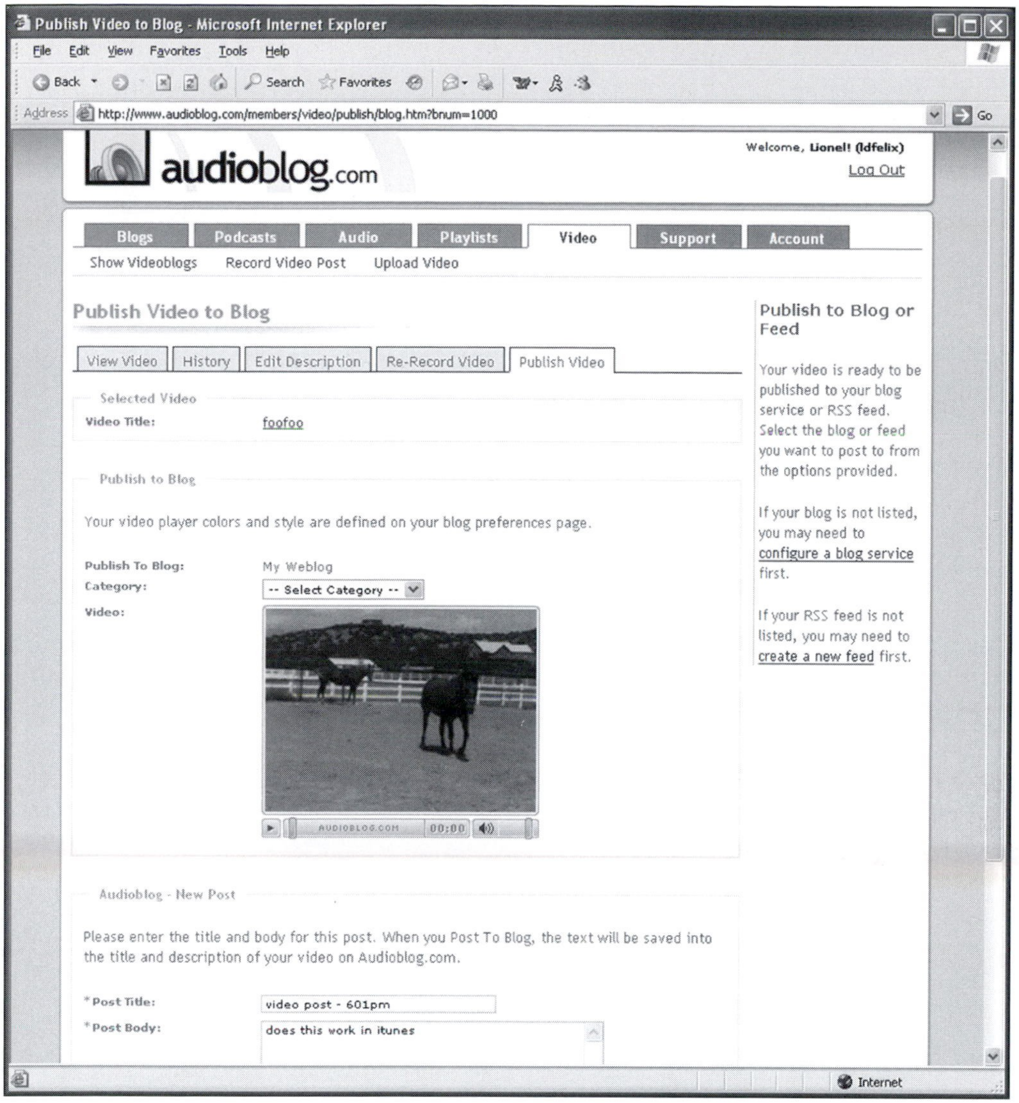

Figure 13-5
Audioblog publishing control

The completed post shows up on your main blog page with an embedded file and a branded Audioblog player. The whole process of uploading and posting is very straight forward and provides nice touches like the embedded media and a selection of player controls to match the theme of your site.

FeedBurner

While WordPress, Movable Type, Blogger and others are working to make their RSS enclosure compliant, FeedBurner offers a free and simple way to turn an enclosure unfriendly blog into one that's loved by all feed readers (see **Figure 13-6**).

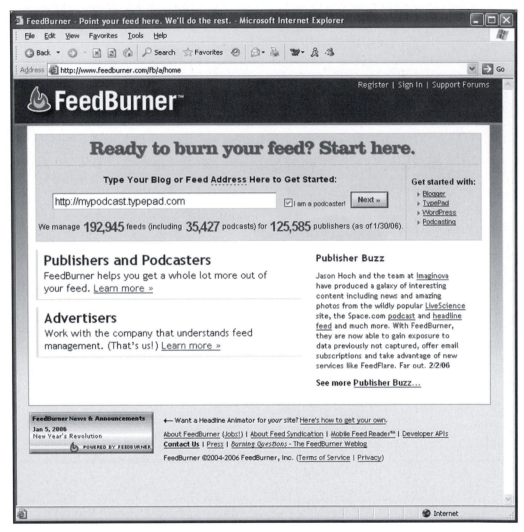

Figure 13-6
FeedBurner sign-up

The sign-up page needs two data points; the URL to your blog and a check box asking if you're a podcaster. If you're including and audio or video, you're a podcaster as far as the checkbox is concerned.

The next page will show you what RSS feeds FeedBurner has found within the URL you gave it (see **Figure 13-7**). It might find only one, it might find 5. Start at the top one and work your way down. If the first one doesn't work you can always go back later and change the feed selection.

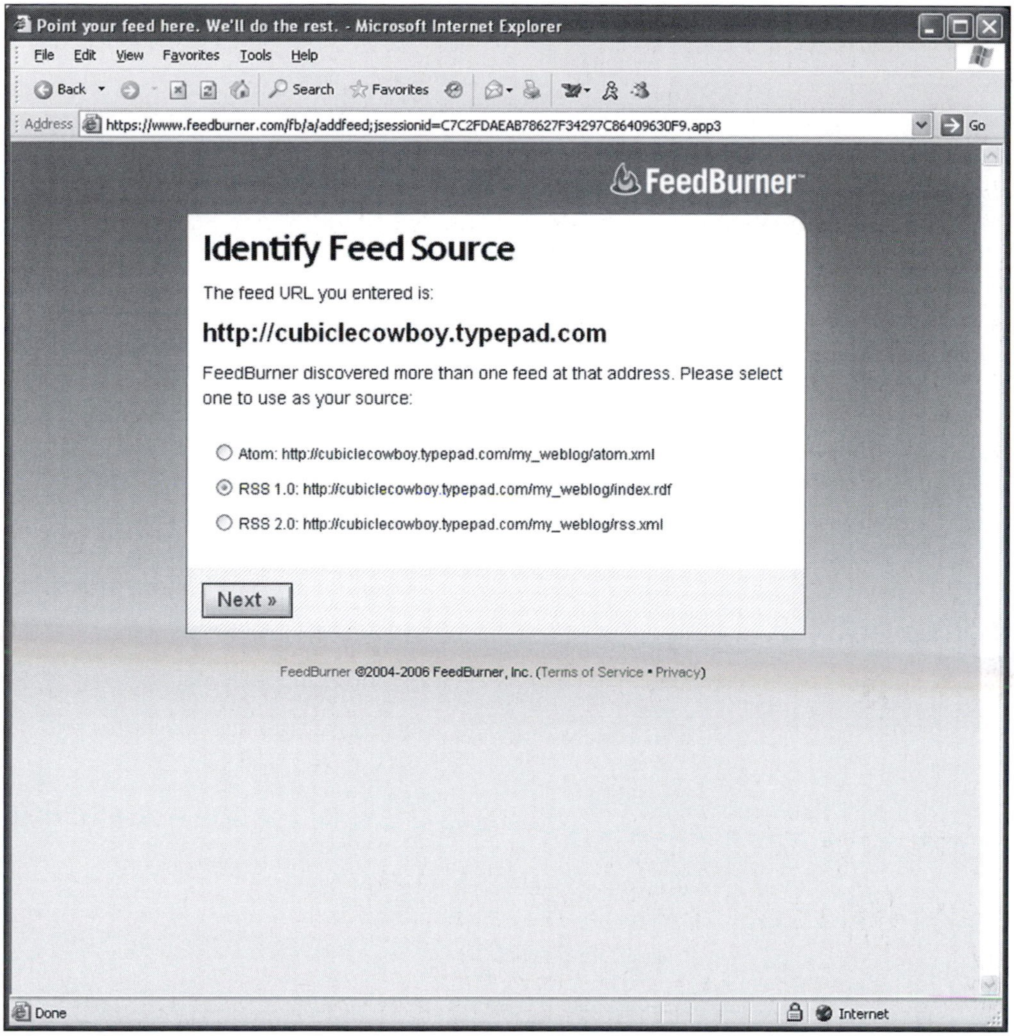

Figure 13-7
FeedBurner blog RSS feed selection

Since FeedBurner is going to be providing the feed, it needs some extra information that will be displayed in the feed reader's fields (see **Figure 13-8**). The title entry is captured by iTunes and other readers as the podcast/vlog description.

FeedBurner will also provide the new RSS XML feed URL that you will offer as a subscription link to readers. In order to make sure people know which feed to use, add the link to the FeedBurner feed in the blog's sidebar close to the top so anyone visiting the site can see it.

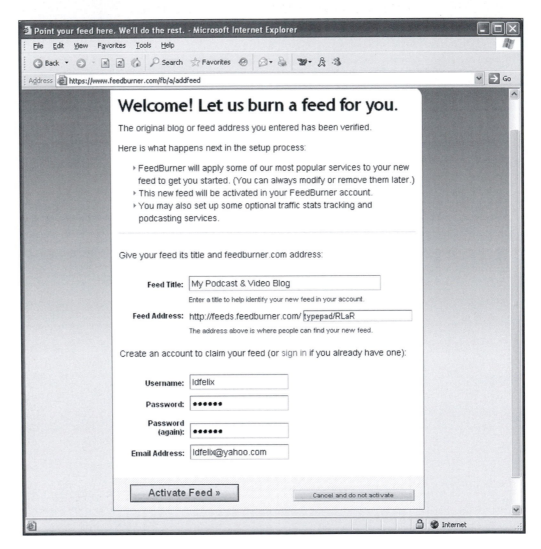

Figure 13-8
FeedBurner title and address

More blog specific information can be added to provide better detail to prospective sub-scribers as well as filling out more fields in their readers (see **Figure 13-9**). The more detail you provide, the more people will know about the podcast and the more likely they will be to subscribe.

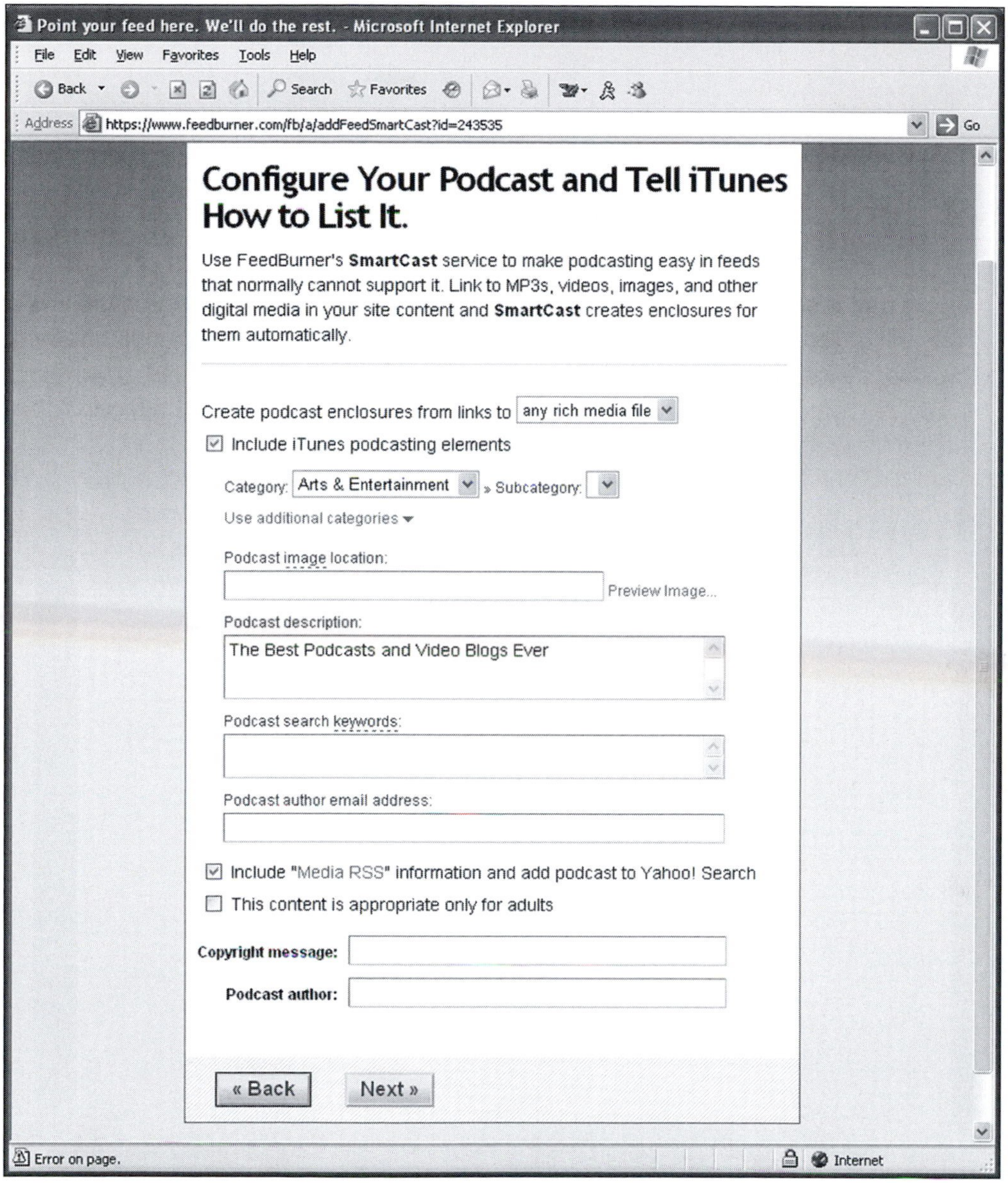

Figure 13-9
FeedBurner title and address

After filling out details on the blog, the feed setup will complete. Enter the feed URL into your web browser's address bar and see if the feed comes up (see **Figure 13-10**). You'll see a version of your blog that's been *Feedburned* in your browser along with a number of links allowing people who got to that URL to directly subscribe using a number of web-based feed readers. You'll also see if FeedBurner handled your media files correctly. The link provided can be entered directly into any RSS reader. Test out the link in at least two different readers such as JPodder, iTunes, FireAnt and Newsgator. If the feeds come up with the rich content and applications like FireAnt and iTunes download the media properly, the feed is set up correctly.

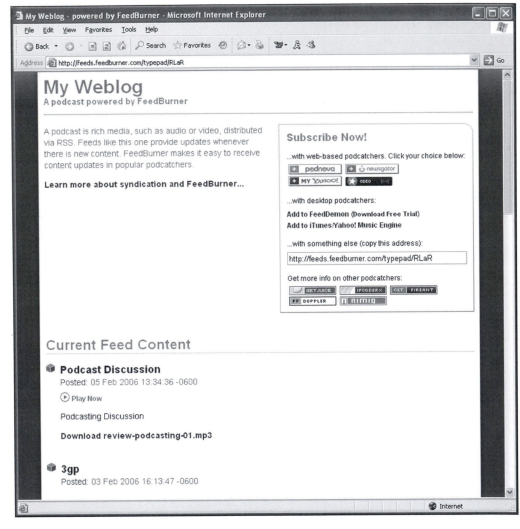

Figure 13-10
Your Site FeedBurned

Hosted Media Services

Blog services like Blogger.com can offer free accounts because blogs have been extremely lightweight. Podcasters and video bloggers on the other hand have massive storage footprints that grow at an alarming rate. There are a number of free and pay services that can play host to your content without causing you to hit the storage ceiling on your blog. Ourmedia.com (which uses Archive.org as a backend) is a free and very simple to use media file storage utility.

Signing up for Ourmedia is similar to the process of creating an account with a webmail provider. They require a username, password and ask nicely for a little personal information. The advantage to using the Ourmedia over Archive.org directly is that Ourmedia streamlines the process to a few simple steps and once the file is uploaded and some data is provided, a URL to your audio or video file is provided and can be pasted into your blog entry (see **Figure 13-11**).

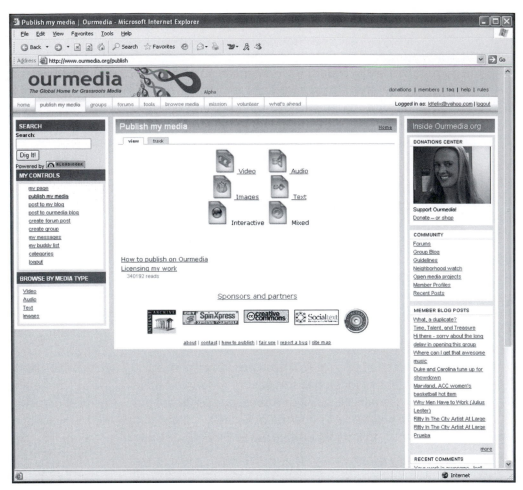

Figure 13-11
Ourmedia media upload selection page

You'll be asked to provide detailed information about the file to be uploaded (see **Figure 13-12**). The reasoning is that the data provided will be used as metadata and the media uploaded will be part of the searchable archive.org repository.

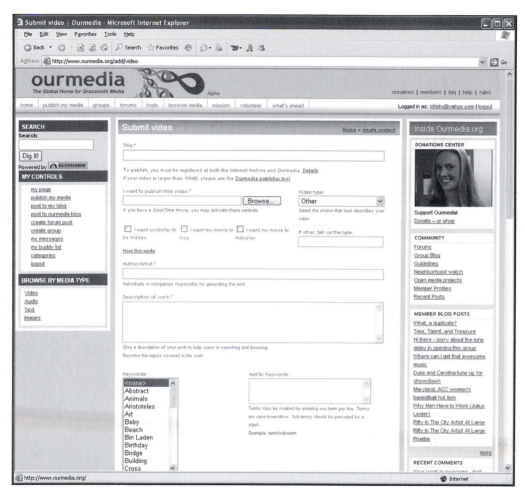

Figure 13-12
Ourmedia media metadata form

The file upload could take a few minutes depending on the size of the file. Once uploaded, you will be presented with a page that shows the uploaded file, the metadata associated with it and a direct link to the file placed directly below the preview pane (see **Figure 13-13**).

The link can be pasted directly into your blog posting and should be parsed properly by the XML generator or FeedBurner.

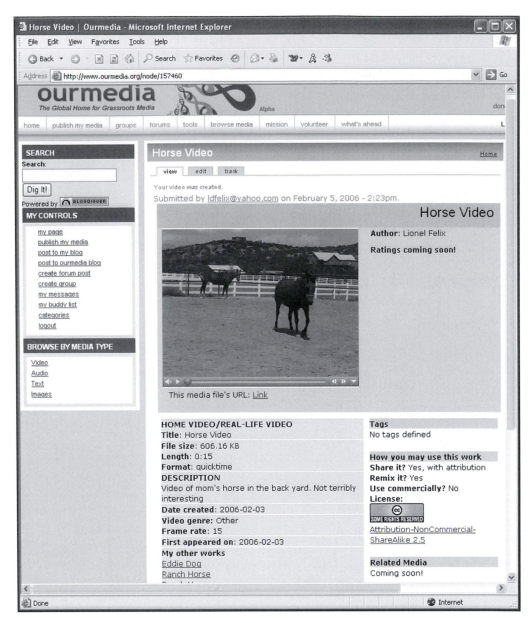

Figure 13-13
Ourmedia success page

Ourmedia is one of a growing number of sites that are happy to host your media files. Akamai, VitalStream and other CDNs (Content Delivery Networks) do the same thing but on a much larger scale and for considerably more money. A CDN will provide scalability that free, single site media distribution portals cannot match.

If your podcast or video blog becomes popular, you'll likely find yourself either cut off or forced to upgrade your service. Some CDNs do offer smaller versions of their services for those left in the middle between trickles of lightly viewed podcasts and major media distribution syndicates.

Conclusion

Picking the right pieces can be an interesting process. Knowing what kind of XML you want generated and the readers you want to target will shape your choices. Each blog application will have its pros and cons which should be weighed before committing to service, administrative domain name work and publicity. Some are free, some charge for their services, your budget will also have a say in the matter.

Features and ease of use are important features but there are a number of data points to consider. Do you want to post from your phone through MMS? Does having to post-process your post through FeedBurner work with your overall blog concept? Does a pay service offer a few features that can compress your production cycle by removing complex posting steps? Make a list of what features are important to you and sort it by priority, must haves and nice-to-haves. Features, budget, ease of use and a good list of requirements will render a few good choices if not a single one that truly shines.

CHAPTER 14

Licensing and Copyrights

This chapter is covers some of the more complex and annoying parts of putting together video blogs and podcasts: Copyrights, permissions, and licensing. While the authors are not lawyers, our goal is to give a good tutorial introduction to copyright laws and issues from a podcasting perspective. We will err in the direction of oversimplification and comprehensibility. Although none of the information in this chapter can be taken as a substitute for professional and competent legal advice, it should increase your understanding of the issues involved.

This chapter will cover:

- Copyrights and other rights
  - Music
  - Film
  - Pictures
  - Trademarks
  - Privacy and publicity
- Podsafe source material
  - Podsafe licensing
  - Creative commons
  - Public domain
  - Fair use
  - Best practices
  - Licensing and rights clearance

Copyrights and Other Rights

We've all heard of *copyright*. Copyright is a set of laws and policies intended to allow the creator of an intellectual work to control how it is copied.

What is a *work*? Well, for our purposes we're talking about *intellectual* (from the mind) creations: music, art, writing, speech, designs, drawings, and so forth. Under the laws of many countries, a creator automatically owns specific rights to the products of their intellect: their *intellectual property*. Intellectual property rights can be sold and transferred to a corporation or another person, but until they are, the creator is the copyright holder and thus the only one with the *right* to *copy* the work.

Now, in order to *exploit* the work, i.e., make money with it, it is necessary for the copyright holder to get the work reproduced without losing ownership of it. This is done through *licensing*. A *license* is a temporary or limited permission to use copyrighted works, often in a very specific and narrow way. The way it works out in practice is that a copyright holder controls most (but not all) rights to publicly present their work. That means, whether the work is reproduced in part or in whole, or used as part of another work, sold, or given away, the rights to do this have to be negotiated from the holder.

The process of getting written permission from each of the necessary rights holders so that a new artistic work containing these elements can be legally distributed is called *clearing* the rights.

In the following sections, we'll take up the most contentious area of the copyright law related to digital downloads today: music. Many of the concepts and rights relating to music apply similarly to video clips and still images that could also be included in video blogs.

Music Rights

Because of all the different ways a work can be exploited, a variety of highly granular *rights* have been delineated by licensing organizations and copyright laws for music. The owner of these rights (the *rights holder*) can essentially "rent out," individually, each of these rights and receive *royalty* payments. Some of the rights are licensed under a *compulsory* licensing structure, so that anyone who pays the appropriate fees can use the music in certain conditions. Most of the rights are completely under the control of the rights holder, who can name their own price and conditions for use of the right.

> **ALERT**
>
> Due to the complex music business, the rights holders of music are usually a combination of record labels, songwriter licensing organizations, and individual artists. In the case of songs composed by one artist and performed by another, different individuals and organizations own different rights, and all of them must be contacted to get permission to use a song in a new way.

Some of the main licensable music rights applicable to podcasting and are listed below.

Mechanical Rights (CDs, digital downloads)

Mechanical rights provide for royalties on sales of a CD, tape, record, or digital download of a piece of music (i.e., a copy of the song that is played back through some mechanical device). These royalties are collected by the record company (the "label"), usually via the Harry Fox Agency, and some small fraction is then paid out, eventually, hopefully, to the songwriter/composer, and performer of the music. There is actually a US government-mandated *compulsory* rate of approximately 9.1 cents per song (2006) owed to the rights holders. This compulsory rate allows anyone to produce and sell a compilation CD of cover songs without getting the explicit permission from the songwriter or rights holder, as long as they pay the appropriate fees. That rate also means that a 10-song CD will generate at most about 80 cents for the rights holder, despite its $12–18 retail price.

Performance Rights (radio airplay)

Performance rights provide for the collection of licensing fees for public performances of live or pre-recorded music almost anywhere. An army of agents working for organizations such as ASCAP, SESAC, and BMI attempt to track every performance of songs in their respective catalogs, whether played on the radio, on a jukebox, in an elevator, in a bar, on satellite radio, television, airplane, Internet, nightclub, concert hall, school, church, orbiting space station, and so on. Each of these potential public-music-playing locations pays ASCAP, SESAC, or BMI either on an a la carte basis or a blanket license for the right to play these songs. And when all the money is collected, these companies use proprietary formulae to pay out the several billion dollars of collected royalties to the writers, composers, and other rights holders on a fair and proportionate basis. This system was originally evolved long before the singer/songwriter model of today, to pay songwriters and composers whenever and wherever their songs were performed.

Publishing Rights (sheet music, lyrics)

Publishing rights, not as relevant here, involve the right to publish sheet music and lyrics to songs. These are protected by copyright as well. Printing lyrics in the show notes of a podcast might require the acquisition of a publishing right and payment of appropriate fees.

Synchronization Rights (film, TV, videos)

Synchronization rights are necessary for any use of music *synchronized* with other multimedia elements as in movies, television, video games, and so on. Because of the effects that a movie can have on the meaning of a song, changing its meaning for the public, the rights to allow a song to be used in part or in whole in a TV show, video, movie, or other production are reserved by the song's rights holder. Generally, the fees for use of a song in a movie can range to nominal sums (hundreds for an independent documentary film using an obscure unsigned artist's song) to thousands of dollars (several seconds of a recognizable song in an independent film) to hundreds of thousands or even millions of dollars (a Rolling Stones song used in a national TV commercial).

Another related right is the theatrical performance right, the right to actually show a movie after the synchronization rights have been obtained. This is why movies and TV shows sometimes change the songs when they come out on DVD; they secured the synchronization and theatrical rights but not the other rights needed to make permanent, nonbroadcast versions including those songs. On top of all this, *soundtrack* rights will be required to produce and sell a record album of the music used in a video production.

Master Use Right (for use of the actual recording, not the song)

Master use rights are an important subtlety to understand. Copyright law was changed in the early 1970s so that the actual *master* recording of a song could be copyrighted, independently of the songwriters', performers', and composers' respective copyrights to the material. That means, in practice, that although you can get a mechanical license to a song, you still have to get the master use rights to the song recording from the recording company that owns them. It comes down to getting the rights to use the song at all (mechanical license), getting the right to perform it (performance license), and then getting the right to use that specific song recording off a CD (master use license).

Digital Performance Rights (right to stream or download)

Digital performance rights, created by new US legislation in 1995, created a new revenue stream for songwriters and performers by collecting royalties for the new digital radio-like services, such as satellite radio, digital radio cable, digital elevator music, and webcasting. In traditional radio, there was no royalty for the owners of the sound recordings, only for the composers and writers. With digital radio, the rights holder for the sound recording itself gets in on the action as well.

The RIAA formed and spun off a nonprofit organization called *SoundExchange*, which is authorized by the government to collect and distribute the royalty fees paid for sound recordings. Note that this does not apply to downloads, only "ephemeral," temporary, transitory, radio-like digital broadcasts.

Derivative Work Rights (right to create a work based on another work)
Derivative work rights apply to all kinds of copyright, not just music. They are held by the creator or subsequent rights holder of the work, and give them exclusive control over who can make additional works that build on the original work (by altering it, using its elements, etc.) Examples of derivative works are a movie based on a book, or sampling a song. Sampling, i.e., taking portions of a song and putting them into another song or audio recording, is particularly relevant to podcasting.

When musical sampling first became widespread in rap music in the 1980s, there were no set rules and many mainstream artists used samples from other music liberally. After some court rulings in the early 1990s, however, unauthorized sampling, like skateboarding, essentially became a crime. Now, all samples of music, even when altered beyond recognition, are painstakingly cleared with the rights holders and are negotiated and paid for. But the rates demanded by sampled artists often exceed the potential revenue of the song.

Fair Use Rights (right to ignore the above rights in special cases)
Fair use rights are specific rights held by the public, not the author of the work, to use it in specific ways. As the term implies, there are certain "fair uses" of a copyrighted work that are completely justified by law. The basic legal rationale behind fair use is to permit reasonable criticism, commentary, or parody of a copyrighted work. (For more information, see the section "Fair Use" under "Applying these Rights" later in this chapter.)

Inside the Industry
Applying These Rights
Let's take a hypothetical piece of music. The melody to the song is created by a musical composer. Some lyrics are then written for it by a songwriter. Now, an arranger comes into the puzzle and adds a variety of additional instrument parts to the song. Finally, the song is performed by a group of musicians, recorded by a professional sound engineer, and pressed to a CD or encoded in an MP3. And just to complicate matters, one company shares the lyric rights with the

(continued on next page)

lyricist, another company represents the composer, and a record label that commissioned the work and paid for the studio time owns the mechanical rights.

Now, you come along and want to use this song in your podcast. What can you do? Well, first, you'll need to pay a performance fee to the groups representing the composer and author of the songs, probably through organizations such as ASCAP or BMI. You'll also need to negotiate the right to include the song in your podcast. If you're not going to alter the song, and you're going to distribute it to less than a few thousand people, you might qualify for a simplified "download" license from the Harry Fox agency. But that will require you to carefully count your podcast audience, and just as that podcast is getting popular, you'll have to pull it down. So realistically, you'll have to get permission directly from the artist. Once you've got your performance, mechanical, and master use licenses in place, you're set to go—unless you want to mash up the song or mix it somehow. Then, you'll need a different type of permission—for a derivative work—that will require a different sort of negotiation with the song's author/rights holder, who can choose whether they want the song included at all.

If you're doing a video blog, things are even more complicated. You've basically put yourself in the category of a low budget or independent film, as far as existing rights and licensing structures go. In this case, you are still at the whim of the rights holder if they even want their music associated with your blog. And for a nonprofit or nonprofit-motivated weblog, the license fees will probably be out of range.

Although this sounds complicated, realize that video bloggers and podcasters are digital vanguards and that rights licensing structures have barely caught up with digital downloads, much less the low-profit, digitally sampled cut-and-paste free-for-all that podcasts represent to the uninitiated rights holder.

But all is not lost. The example above would be simpler if one singer/composer/songwriter/performer had created the whole song. And if that performer retained *all* the rights to their work, by not participating with BMI or getting signed to a record label that was a member of the RIAA, that rights owner could negotiate directly (and more affordably) with an independent podcaster, without requiring a minimum payment for every copy of a song. In essence, it's more like matching scale: A blockbuster movie can afford to license a major-label hit song, and an independent podcaster can afford to license music from an independent musician.

The less people and organizations are involved in the creation and licensing of a work, the less written permissions need to be sought. So the general rule is, to include music in a podcast or a video blog, get permission. If you find out the price is too high, then create it yourself or hire someone else to create it from scratch, or find an unsigned, independent artist who owns all their rights and license it from them.

Video Rights

The copyright laws and legal protections for video are just as protective as for audio. However, there are some major licensing differences due to the different business structures around television and film vs. music.

Musicians generally sign to a major label and are then under contract for a number of albums. So generally, their music rights are "locked up" as soon as they are signed. Because a cinematic film is much more involved to produce than a record album, multipicture deals are not the rule, especially for starting filmmakers. That means in many cases, the rights to a student or independent film are not assigned to a major studio.

However, films are much more complicated to make, sometimes involving large numbers of participants each with a financial stake in the final piece, and the legal language in the actor contracts probably don't cover video blogging the actual film, or using the film as a source of stock footage. If you've ever been involved as an extra to a film or on TV, you're probably how the producers painstakingly ensure that every single person has signed a rights assignment and permission form to allow their likeness (pictures of them) to be used in the production. For flat-fee extra work, most of these legal forms are sufficient. But for any professional writers, actors, and so on, the rights release forms need to explicitly describe possible online downloadable video use, or have very broad terms of release.

Often, independent or student films are shot with *step* licensing agreements, where artists get paid if the film profits. Generally, all of the creative inputs to the film, in the form of acting, writing, composing, performing, licensing existing music, and so on, are granted to the film only for the purposes of showing it in film festivals. The agreement is that if the film gets "picked up" and taken to higher levels of financial success: major studio release, straight to DVD, shown on cable, or otherwise profitably shown, each of the performers will get some specific cut of the profits. These agreements rarely have a clause allowing the original producers or directors to simply put the movie online, in a video blog or otherwise.

So the good news is that filmmakers, unlike signed artists, can freely create media for video blogging purposes. The bad news is that existing video works, including independent films, are probably not usable in video blogs, in part or in whole, without additional legal work.

If you are just getting into video blogging, there is another annoying aspect of copyright in video that you need to know. In some cases, you cannot legally include copyrighted or trademarked images in video without getting permission. Just as you have to get a synchronization license to include bits of music in a movie, mainstream filmmakers get rights clearance for every brand and copyrighted work they include, even incidentally, in their films. There are some notable exceptions (see the section on fair use), but just for fun, rent a movie and look for trademarks. Except for specific brand sponsorships, you'll find that even the posters over children's beds have been carefully modified, and that the children are playing "Pretendo" instead of a popular video game with a similar name.

The bottom line is, everyone involved in a video should be under a written agreement to ensure that they agree with the eventual use of the footage, and every copyrighted or trademarked "thing" visible in the video should be similarly rights-cleared.

Photo Rights

The World Wide Web has pushed the limits of what is comfortable for rights holders. Search engines have relied heavily on technologies of caching, keeping temporary copies of files from other sites. For instance, if you do an image search in Google, you will find thousands of pictures, and Google has technically made a copy of these images to show them to you. However, you generally still need to get permission from the copyright holder of that image to use it on your web page.

The hyperlinked nature of web pages has also made more flexible content mixing possible. For instance, even if you don't have permission to serve an image from your website, you can sometimes link to a copy of the image on another website. Then, although the image is on your site, it is technically being served from the content owner's site. Is your website a derivative work? Does it infringe on the copyrights of the original creator? Perhaps yes, but in practice, most websites get away with such linking without issue. For instance, fan websites for fiction works, Sci Fi, TV shows, and so forth have been granted, on a case by case basis, wide leniency by the content owners, who would rather permit a limited use of their copyrighted multimedia elements than alienate their most avid fan base.

But this simple expedient of linking over to the original image is not technically possible (currently) to an author of podcasts and video blogs. This is because, with current technology, source media (audio, video, pictures, text) has to be incorporated into the compressed audio or video file in order to be delivered to the audience as a packaged piece of media. The photographer or artist who created the picture generally has the right to control how it is integrated with other artistic works.

Just as with any other copyrights, the safest approach to inclusion of copyrighted materials is to get permission. Because of the myriad of laws surrounding privacy, copyrights, and art, even if you don't think you're pushing the boundaries with your work, you may inadvertently infringe on some law or another.

For the most part, most of the pictures you take yourself can be included in a blog. But if you're in doubt, it pays to read up on the policy issues involved.

> ## Author's Tip
>
> Even if you take the photo yourself, there are other permissions you may need to get. One common example is a picture of a sculpture. In certain cases, if the sculpture is a copyrighted work, a photograph of the sculpture will be considered a derivative work, and permission from the sculpture rights holder would be necessary to profit from the pictures. Similarly, any building is a work of architecture, and covered by copyright. So technically, a picture of just one building, without appropriate permission, cannot be published for profit. (Photos of a skyline showing a number of buildings, not just one, are more defensible.)

Trademarks

There is another part of intellectual property law that is different than copyright. *Trademarks* are distinctive designs, phrases, or marks used to identify goods or services. Unlike copyrights, in US law they do not expire if consistently used and renewed.

Trademarks are designed to uniquely identify a company within a certain area of trade.

You are probably familiar with a vast number of product trademarks, as billions of dollars are spent to hammer these images into your mind and associate them with the products they promote.

While a treatment of trademark law is outside the scope of this book, the bottom line is pretty simple: Trademark holders do not tolerate their brands used without their permission. One of the main problems with true trademark violation is that it creates confusion between the infringer's products or services and the true products and services of the mark holder.

Some examples will make this clear:

- Don't call your blog "Coca-Cola" radio
- Don't use the Disney "mouse ears" logo to start all your video blogs

But it gets more complicated than that. As mentioned in the Video Rights section, protected trademarks can sneak into an otherwise innocent video clip. If "The Simpsons" is playing on the television in the background, or if a Pepsi truck drives recognizably close to where you are filming, these powerful trademarks *could* give viewers the false impression that your video blog is sponsored by those brand owners. And heaven forbid you associate the brand with something they find objectionable.

Luckily, brands are designed to be recognizable, so it's pretty obvious when one sneaks into your video.

In general, you're going to want to remove brand names, unless those brands are actually sponsoring your podcast, or if your use of the brand is *protected speech*, covered under the *Fair Use* areas of the copyright law (see section on Fair Use).

Privacy and Publicity Rights

There's another pair of rights you should be aware of relating to video blogging. The *privacy rights* of individuals prevent you from using a telephoto lens to take pictures inside their house from a mile away. And *publicity rights* give people the right to control who uses their likeness to advertise products.

The actual form of these rights varies from state to state and country to country, but together the laws about privacy and publicity restrict, to some degree, the unauthorized use video or pictures of people's faces. These rights also apply to podcast interviews: just because someone grants an interview and allows it to be audiotaped, does not mean they've given up their privacy rights.

ALERT
!
If the subject of your recording has any "reasonable expectation of privacy" (and you should verify with your own attorney exactly what that means) then you're risking a lawsuit if you don't get a written agreement to use the material.

Podsafe Source Material

After looking at all the copyrights and other rights that creators have over their material, you may be asking yourself, "how can I work with all these rules?" Well, there are quite a few solutions, depending on what kind of blog you intend to create.

Podsafe content is any media (audio, video, etc.) that can be safely (i.e., legally) included in a podcast. The term *podsafe* was initially coined to describe music suitable for inclusions in podcasts and *mash-ups*, combinations of two different styles of music popular on Adam Curry's *Daily Source Code* show on PodShow.com.

Podsafe music is, broadly, any music that can be safely (i.e., legally) included in a podcast. Because of the large, complicated, and well-defended business structures that power the music industry, it is virtually impossible (today) to get permission to use RIAA-commercial music (i.e., major label music) in a podcast. Even if that permission were granted, each copy of a downloaded podcast would result in an additional royalty owed (assuming the podcast only used one song!) and unless tremendous advertising or sponsorship revenue was being generated, it would be hard to offset this cost.

Even if a podcast is reaching radio-scale audiences, the lack of digital rights management technology for podcasts and their open, MP3-based downloadability, will result in higher fees than any comparable radio station would. In fact, the only real way to get around these fees today would be to stream, not download, the shows, defeating the time- and space-shifting features of podcasting.

The Podsafe Music Network (music.podshow.com) was one of the first sites devoted to collecting podsafe music. Since then, a number of other sites for podsafe material have developed. A Google search of "podsafe" will bring an up-to-date listing of podsafe media sources.

There is still a lot of licensing ambiguity, even for so-called podsafe content. Just because a song, picture, or video clip is on a podsafe site does not mean you can simply incorporate it in your podcast without getting permission. Some of the sites are designed to implement a royalty system, collecting money for the authors of the creative works they host. Some simply host or point to material others have designated as "podsafe" but each of which has its own licensing terms. Some of the licensing terms still require you to contact the artist; in some cases, the site has cleared the work for incorporation in your podcast with no further rights clearance. It's up to you to verify the terms of a particular work before you incorporate it, to ensure you are getting proper permission and giving proper credit and payment (if applicable) to the creator of the work.

Another ambiguity comes from licensing terms that specify free "noncommercial" use. Currently, the definition of "commercial" as it applies to a podcast (and many websites for that matter) is difficult to determine. Does a podcast that has advertisements or sponsorships only to offset bandwidth costs count as for-profit? What if, as many podcasts do, the show slowly morphs into a commercial entity as it gets popular? Are royalties owed on the earlier shows, still available in archives, now that the show has gone commercial?

Fortunately, these questions, as well as a number of other ramifications of copyright licensing, have been anticipated and addressed by a helpful nonprofit group called the *Creative Commons*.

Creative Commons

There are many well-documented, but poorly publicized problems with the copyright system today. Basically, everything published since the 1920s is copyrighted in some way, even if the author has abandoned the work and the publishing company has gone out of business. Copyrights have extended several times—while they were originally 14 to 28 years, all newly created works are copyrighted for the life of the creator, plus another 70 or more years (possibly longer for corporations), making it next to impossible use the majority of noncommercial or commercial works that don't need such long copyrights.

Automatic, century-long copyrights create a situation where almost no part of the popular culture can be re-incorporated into new creative works without a complex and expensive recourse to numerous rights holders. And the reasonable actions of big-label content creators in establishing a licensing market for their material has worked almost too well. This has resulted in runaway inflation in content licensing, limiting artistic access to our culture to affluent commercial creators.

The Creative Commons (*http://www.creativecommons.org*) has created alternative licensing schemes for content creators. In their own words:

"We have built upon the 'all rights reserved' of traditional copyright to create a voluntary 'some rights reserved' copyright."

Creative Commons (creativecommons.org) developed the licensing structures used for most podsafe media. These standardized licenses assist content creators such as musicians to publish their material freely online, while explicitly spelling out the terms on which others may use their content. This helps podcast creators know whether they, for instance, can use a particular piece of music outright, or must contact the artist directly and get licensing terms and permission first.

Here's a description, taken directly from the Creative Commons website of their easily understandable content licenses (taken from *http://creativecommons.org/about/licenses/*):

Inside the Industry

 ### Choosing a License
Offering your work under a Creative Commons license does not mean giving up your copyright. It means offering some of your rights to any member of the public but only on certain conditions.

What conditions? *You can find an overview of the Creative Commons licenses here* [*http://creativecommons.org/about/licenses/meet-the-licenses*]. All of our licenses require that you give attribution in the manner specified by the author or licensor.

 Attribution. You let others copy, distribute, display, and perform your copyrighted work—and derivative works based upon it—but only if they give credit the way you request.

Example: Jane publishes her photograph with an Attribution license, because she wants the world to use her pictures provided they give her credit. Bob finds her photograph online and wants to display it on the front page of his website. Bob puts Jane's picture on his site, and clearly indicates Jane's authorship.

(continued on following page)

Our core licensing suite will also let you mix and match conditions from the list of options below. There are a total of six Creative Commons licenses to choose from our core licensing suite.

 Noncommercial. You let others copy, distribute, display, and perform your work—and derivative works based upon it—but for noncommercial purposes only

Example: Gus publishes his photograph on his website with a Noncommercial license. Camille prints Gus' photograph. Camille is not allowed to sell the print photograph without Gus's permission.

 No Derivative Works. You let others copy, distribute, display, and perform only verbatim copies of your work, not derivative works based upon it.

Example: Sara licenses a recording of her song with a No Derivative Works license. Joe would like to cut Sara's track and mix it with his own to produce an entirely new song. Joe cannot do this without Sara's permission (unless his song amounts to fair use).

 Share Alike. You allow others to distribute derivative works only under a license identical to the license that governs your work.

Note: A license cannot feature both the Share Alike and No Derivative Works options. The Share Alike requirement applies only to derivative works.

Example: Gus's online photo is licensed under the Noncommercial and Share Alike terms. Camille is an amateur collage artist, and she takes Gus's photo and puts it into one of her collages. This Share Alike language requires Camille to make her collage available on a Noncommercial plus Share Alike license. It makes her offer her work back to the world on the same terms Gus gave her.

More examples are available on *our examples page* [*http://creativecommons.org/about/licenses/examples*] . Also note that every license carries with it *a full set of other rights* [*http://creativecommons.org/about/licenses/fullrights*] in addition to the allowances specifically made here.

Taking a License

When you've made your choices, you'll get the appropriate license expressed in three ways:

1. Commons Deed. A simple, plain-language summary of the license, complete with the relevant icons.

2. Legal Code. The fine print that you need to be sure the license will stand up in court.

(continued on following page)

3. Digital Code. A machine-readable translation of the license that helps search engines and other applications identify your work by its terms of use.

Using a License

You should then include a Creative Commons "Some Rights Reserved" button on your site, near your work. *Help and tips on doing this are covered here* [*http://creativecommons.org/technology/usingmarkup*]. This button will link back to the Commons Deed, so that the world can be notified of the license terms. If you find that your license is being violated, you may have grounds to sue under copyright infringement.

It's worth noting that, in the writing of this book, I was able to lift this entire section from their website—without requesting permission—because the site itself was licensed under a Creative Commons Attribution license, which simply means I needed to credit the source of the material. Many blogs are already licensed under a Creative Commons license—wherever you see a logo such as the one shown in **Figure 14-1**.

Figure 14-1
Some Rights Reserved

When you see this icon or a similar text about "some rights reserved," you can click it quickly find out the terms under which it is licensed, such as in **Figure 14-2**.

Figure 14-2
Creative Commons Deed

If you are creating a new podcast or video blog, it's highly recommended that you publish it under a Creative Commons license. The benefit is that people can readily identify the rights you wish to retain to the work, and with the appropriate license you will not give up any ability to license your work in other media. Millions of pages of web, and printed material are now licensed this way, and a number of books have been published online with a Creative Commons license and in book (paper) format, without adversely affecting the sales of the printed copy.

A starting point for finding media under the flexible Creative Commons licensing is on their site, at *http://creativecommons.org/find/*.

Public Domain

So big-label content is prohibitively expensive, podsafe content is still in short supply, and fair use is too risky. Isn't there any free content with *no* restrictions?

Fortunately, yes. After the copyright on any work expires, the work goes into what is called the *public domain*, meaning that the public owns it.

Every 19th century novel you read in high school is free of copyright. You could write a sequel, put it in a movie (as many have done), take passages out of it, and derive from it creatively to your hearts content with no rights holder demanding a royalty. This is not so true of 20th century works created after 1922, as described in the section on copyrights.

One of the ironies of our hyperprotective copyright system it is harder to make your work public domain than to copyright it (copyright is automatic). If you wish to put your blog or podcast into the public domain, the Creative Commons website provides a "public domain dedication" that you can use to explicitly relinquish your rights to the work. (*http://creativecommons.org/licenses/publicdomain/*)

Fair Use

Despite all the detailed warnings given in earlier sections, there are many situations in which quoting a portion of another copyrighted work is completely permissible. These are called "*fair uses*"—instances in which copyrighted material can be incorporated into your own without getting permission, and without paying royalties.

Fair use is not just what you think is fair; it's a complex set of legal precedents and unknowns that has little to do with a fair-use ignorant "but VCRs are legal!" view of the world.

There are four basic criteria used by courts to determine if a use is fair use. Unfortunately for the average fair user, there are no clear lines or hard and fast rules to determine fair use. And it costs thousands to millions of dollars and years of lawsuits when the courts have to decide.

To determine whether your use of copyrighted material is "fair," you can begin by examining four factors:

1. How are you using the material: For journalism? Nonprofit use? Personal, unpublished use? Criticism? Parody of the work itself? Satire of society using the work? Commentary on the work? Commercial use, i.e., making money on a version of the work?

2. What is the source material: Published already? Currently being sold? Unpublished and/or personal? Is it mostly factual, like a phone book or a list of standard information available elsewhere? Or is it highly or uniquely creative?

3. How much are you using? The whole work? 50% of it? 1% of it? And even if you're taking a small part, is it the most important part, or the juiciest parts you're quoting?

4. What will your use do to the sales of the work? Will you make it harder for the original to be profitable? Is the original out of print and not even being sold? Is it work that is currently available for license and you're just trying to avoid paying? Will your work make people not even buy the original?

While even a cursory treatment of fair use is outside the scope of this book, the above questions show some of the major factors that are looked at when determining a fair use.

ALERT   **Figuring out Fair Use in Your Case**

!

Like extreme sports or investment, fair use should only be attempted if you understand the risks involved.

http://fairuse.stanford.edu/ A great thorough site on copyright. The subsection on Fair Use also contains a list of examples of fair and unfair use, as illustrated by specific court cases.

http://www.utsystem.edu/ogc/intellectualproperty/cprtindx.htm the University of Texas has a "crash course in copyright" with another excellent tutorial on fair use.

http://www.centerforsocialmedia.org/fairuse.htm has a *Best Practices in Fair Use* statement as well as many practical examples of fair use in documentary filmmaking.

Best Practices

Anyone in the business of integrating or copying copyrighted material has to set policies by which they will operate. By following these policies, and watching carefully every few years when someone pushes the envelope, they establish best practices. Each major industry or institution has developed best practices: journalism (radio, television, newspaper, newsmagazine, and gossip rag), documentary filmmaking, political filmmaking, political campaigning, photography, writing, educational publishing, music, entertainment film, law, science, and copy shops.

Staying within these best practices, when followed by everyone else in the industry, tends to reduce their liability in the case that they are ever found by a court to be infringing, which limits their exposure to high penalties and angry judges. "But everyone else was doing it" is actually a reasonably effective defense when it comes to copyright infringement. However,

"What did others get away with?" doesn't always work; sometimes judges decide against a seemingly fair use because they were offended by the use. This may be very ambiguous advice, but it is an ambiguous area of law.

Since podcasting is fairly new, it does not yet have its own "industry statement of best practices." However, your podcast or video blog may fit into an existing category for which there is an existing framework of practices. For instance, if your video blog is documentary in nature, you could follow the guidelines for documentary filmmaking at *http://www.centerforsocialmedia.org/rock/ backgrounddocs/bestpractices.pdf*. Similarly, if your podcast is focused on journalism, news, movie reviews, and so forth, there are countless online resources on how far you can go in quoting, using pictures, video, and so on.

Author's Tip

If you're feeling overwhelmed about the task of getting permission for all the copyrighted material you will be incorporating into your blog, this site has a list of resources for locating the owners and understanding the process.

http://www.utsystem.edu/ogc/ intellectualproperty/permissn.htm

If your blog is a fictional or creative satirical work, critiquing the culture in clever ways, you will need to be very careful in your study of fair use. A common misconception of fair use is that "parody" automatically makes a use fair. But parody in fair use is very narrowly defined as a mockery of the *source material*, not something else using the source material. And factors of how much material was copied, the commercial motive, and the actual creativity of the parody come into play if the use was ever tested in court. It may even surprise you that most commercial parodies (Austin Powers, Weird Al Yankovic) actually get permission from the content they parody.

The bottom line is, fair use takes judgement, and sometimes, guts. Before you decide not to get permission to use copyrighted material, make sure you know what you're doing.

Conclusion

By now, you've probably realized that sampling pieces of content here and there without getting permission is a risky activity. Fortunately, the rights holder for mainstream media culture is easy to find. Unfortunately, if your use requires licensing, it may be unaffordable for your podcasting project.

The good news is that the exponential growth of citizen journalists, bloggers, and media creators has triggered a new market for inexpensive audio and video. Thus, while mainstream media continues to price itself out of the blogosphere, Podsafe and Creative Commons-licensed content has risen to fill the demand.

The key to producing a legal podcast are to stick to the best practices for your area of content—be it journalism, education, or entertainment—and to study up thoroughly on fair use so you know how the laws apply to you.

And, if you can't get access to the content you need, create it yourself or hire someone to create it for you. Then you can contract them to ensure you get all the rights you need to use it in your podcasts and video blogs.

CHAPTER 15

Case Studies

This chapter presents three case studies. These case studies were primarily constructed from information provided on the bloggers' own websites and from interviews. They are designed to show a few perspectives and best practices on video blogging and podcasting for different kinds of blogs.

1. EricRice.com, a text blog/podcast/video blog
2. RyanEdit.com, a personal blog
3. Rocketboom.com, a daily 3-minute news video blog

For each blog we will cover

- Show format
- Development, growth
- Available statistics
- Success criteria or business model
- Plans for expansion
- Studio and tools
- Hosting

EricRice.com

Eric Rice has been blogging, podcasting, streaming, and creating online multimedia programming since before any of the current buzzwords were settled. His home page quotes one of his admirers calling him "the Prototype of the new Journalist" (**Figure 15-1**).

Figure 15-1
The Prototype of the New Journalist

As is the case with many prolific video/pod/bloggers, there Eric has a variety of shows and posts, all cross linked across a variety of URLs so that it's hard to take in at first glance all shows he's involved in.

Show Format

In their own words, "Somewhere between a sophomoric morning zoo and smart public radio, you'll find the Eric Rice Show. Musing on everything from entertainment, technology, and culture, this show from California is led by Silicon Valley's Eric Rice and joined by a cast of millions. The Eric Rice Show is a spinoff of Slackstreet Radio, which has been entertaining small, shady corners of the Internet since late 2001."

Eric blogs frequently, and adds podcasts and video blogs interspersed with the main content. Eric's primary podcast vehicle, The Eric Rice Show, is in his own words "a format inspired by every talk radio show in America." Eric moderates, and the show includes a handful of friends, most of whom have high-tech day jobs in the Silicon Valley.

Figure 15-2
Grog, Schlomo, Josh, Eric, Irina, tonyB, Eddie from *The Eric Rice Show*

The format is straightforward: short form variety and entertainment. The show is all over the place; topics range from video-blogged dogsledding to technology gadgets to Silicon Valley culture. Very California; very geek, but with sort of a hip-hop edge. The dynamic of the show comes from the guys (and girls) with totally different personalities interacting on the mic. The show also features lots of podsafe music. Eric contacts all the artists and gets permission for the material.

Development, Growth
The show actually has its roots in Slackstreet, an online audio show started in 2001. In 2002 the crew got serious and started to up the frequency of there postings. Growth continued through 2003 when audio blogging was finally catching on as its own form.

Eric recently added another element to the show, a video blog at backstaging.com. This blog covers various McGyver-esque improvisational methods of making a video blogging studio and getting the shot on-the-go.

Statistics
Technorati Rank: 9,320 (304 links from 154 sites) out of 28 million blogs (Early 2006).

Success Criteria/Business model
Operationally, the program "is a break even deal." Eric compares the efforts to that of a band, where the players keep their day job. The show has a great brand; they're well known; they get the celebrity feeling that comes with running into people frequently and having them know you.

In their day jobs, most of the gang has lucrative Silicon Valley jobs. Even if the show was doing fantastic by any standards, they wouldn't quit their day job.

The show has a bigger infrastructure than most out there, better equipment than some of the big guys out there.

Revenue comes from a variety of sources, including product placement, web advertisements, and sponsorship. Eric is very honest and tongue-in-cheek about the advertising, "keeping it real" for the audience.

To sell the "rate card" for the program, Eric emphasizes the powerful niche reach the program has—influential Silicon Valley and entertainment industry audience.

Success for the show really has to do with producing great content, getting it out to the masses, leveraging the brand to do more of the same.

Ultimately success is to be able to do what you love, and get paid for it. Getting both.

Plans for Expansion

Eric really considers the show to be a blend of Hollywood and the Silicon Valley attitude.

A variety of shows including the Eric Rice Show are aggregated under the kssx.com brand, and Eric is adding more. Recently, Eric started making special short forms of the programming for mobile listeners accessing the show via Mobilcast.

The show is starting to do more of the shows live, with an IRC chat back channel, and then immediately post it as a podcast. Also more "meatspace," in person interaction is planned, namely, more travel and on-site shows. This includes some worldwide live-venue blogging, focused on music and entertainment. Oh, and the show is not opposed to Hollywood; they're making an aggressive push into traditional media outlets.

Finally, the plan is to stay ahead of curve. Because the show is content, it can go anywhere that content goes in the future.

Philosophy

Eric strongly advocates the use of understandable terms so that the uninitiated web audience who aren't part of the digirati can still comprehend and participate in blogging. Terms like RSS or even feed can be more easily explained as "episodes" or just "a show" on the Internet. Don't explain what a blog/podcast/vlogcast/vodcast is; ask what they're interested in; send them to a podcaster/blogger/vlogger that covers that section. Be it soap opera discussion or movie reviews or cooking, it's at that point they'll be engaged in the media.

Eric, being a radio personality, waxes philosophical and at great length about the tensions between purely personal blogging and for-pay blogging. A frequent speaker at the various blog and podcast conferences, he has put together a conceptual framework encompassing the various reasons people create media, shown in **Figure 15-3**.

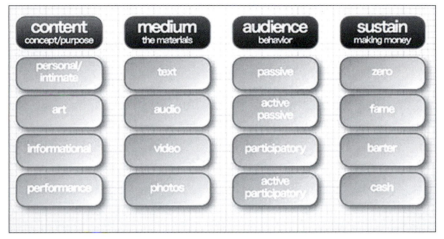

Figure 15-3
The Epsilon Construct

The theory that everything can be grouped into fours. The four top elements result in your 'thing' whether it's a product or performance or software. This example, for new media, illustrates the four elements with four sub-elements. You must have at least one, although many times you have more than one. There are no right or wrong answers. You can make money or not, you can be passive or participatory. No medium is better than another. Do whatcha like.

- **Content: Concept/Purpose**: Content falls into these four categories. Pick one. You might fit two or all of these categories. What's the purpose of your content... what's the concept? Is it for personal/friends/family? Is it to make art? Is it for information/journalism/propaganda? Is it performance/entertainment?

- **Medium/The Materials**: In the context of media, how are you going to deliver this? What works best? Text, Audio, Video, Photos. I tend to like video as it transcends language barriers easier than audio. Yet I can't write code in video. Pick the best medium—or best tool or best service. For me personally, I use all of them. Text is handled by wordpress/blogware; audio and video by audioblog. com; photos by flickr/buzznet.

- **Audience Behavior**: To use flickr as an example to see the different behaviors of people, let's see what these mean. Passive might mean, you just look at photos here. Nothing more. Nothing less. Active Passive might mean that you seek out specific photos to look at. Participatory is what we do when we post photos here. Active Participatory is when we post photos, engage in conversation, post to groups, make sets, blog them, etc. The food metaphor? Sometimes we make dinner together, active participatory, like a potluck or BBQ. Sometimes we just hit the drive through... Passive.

- **Sustaining/Making Money**: Do we hear the question, "Hey how do you make money with that XBOX 360 and collection of games you got?" Not likely. Our sustainability is our happiness. Yet if for some reason, we get really good at a video game, we might be able to get a job there or become an expert on a certain genre of game. Fame/Awareness/Notoriety is a sustainable model also. Don't do advertising, but blog about important stuff. If it's important, people take notice. You become an expert, perhaps, and make more potential money by speaking vs. AdSense. You can do what you do for barter. You can do what you do for direct compensation. There's no right or wrong way.

Studio and Tools
Aside from a periodically used TASCAM USB-122 and the pocket sized iRiver 899 (never use external mic) the primary gear we use to do a show (most of which is what we've been using for four years now) is:

- Mackie 1402 VLZ Pro
- DBX 166a dual compressor
- dbx166xl dual compressor (hardware compression)
- Gentner GT700 (phone interface)
- (there's a random headphone amp in there someplace)
- Dual AudioTechnica AT2025 on swing arms
- And yes the rockstar mic is the Shure 55s
- Sony Headphones are used, as are various Audio Technica vocal mics

Software used:

- Garageband
- Audioblog.com
- iTunes
- Nicecast
- Shoutcast (we are starting to do our show live now, concurrent with recording it)

Hosting
Eric actually runs a leading podcasting/video blogging services company (*http://www.audioblog.com*), so naturally that's what powers the blogs. As of this writing, Audioblog was getting its hosting and bandwidth from ThePlanet (*http://theplanet.com/*).

RyanEdit.com

Show format

Ryanne Hodson, however, the name of her blog is ryanEdit, is one of the pioneering video bloggers. She has worked as a video editor on a kid's TV show for WGBH in Boston for years, but her passion is video blogging.

In late 2004 the media started taking an interest in this new "vlogging" phenomenon and Ryanne, along with Steve Garfield and Jay Dedman were profiled in an very accurate *Newsweek* article on online video.

Things took off around that time.

If you're familiar with the format of a personal diary blog, Ryanne's vlog is almost a direct translation to the digital film medium. The mundane, the intimate, the ranting, the moods— are all captured on her blog. And just as the cleverness and personality of a blogger some-how makes us care what they had for breakfast that day, so does Ryanne's video skills and dry wit keep viewers coming back for more (**Figure 15-4**).

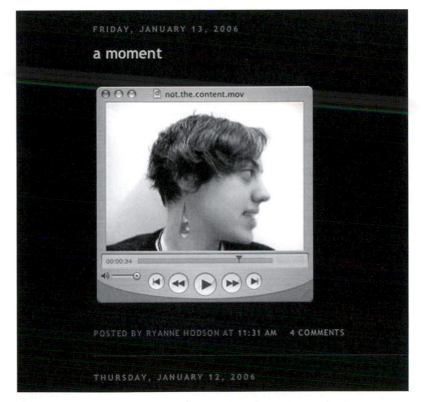

Figure 15-4
A snapshot of Ryanne's vlog *http://ryanedit.blogspot.com/*

Development, Growth

In early 2005 she started meeting the various people who would play a bigger role in her master plans for video blog domination. Through video blogging conversations (where each party posted their response on video), participation in the video blogging Yahoo! group started by Jay Dedman, Ryanne meets Michael Verdi who had put up *http://www.freevlog.org*, a tutorial to help anyone put up a video blog (**Figure 15-5**).

Figure 15-5
FreeVlog!

Ryanne, Jay, and Michael all began planning what would become Node101. Ryanne and Verdi enhanced the Freevlog tutorial. A quote from the site probably sums up how Ryanne occupied her free time during all this:

> Don't forget to take the video bloggers' oath:
>
> I _____ do solemnly promise to post video regularly. I promise to post video even if I don't really have time to or even if I really need to get some sleep. Also, I promise to teach others to video blog or at the very least, point them over here when they get inspired from watching my videos.

Video blogging was gaining more and more steam throughout 2005. By mid year Node101 was formed with the mission to activate more video bloggers by providing the necessary tools and training, at little to no cost to the participants. The plan of creating sustainable nodes, people and locations in each city to teach more people to vlog, began taking hold.

One of the first teaching events was a series of presentations called Meet the Vloggers, often held at Apple Stores. Ryanne had flown to the West coast over and over as demand her to teach at vlogging conferences increased:

> "If you had told me last summer that I would, within one year, travel to California three times, I would think you were crazy. Who, me? Traveling all over the country to tell people about video blogging? Yes me. They asked me! And I'm so honored to be here at BlogHer."

Nodes popped up in New York, San Antonio, Ojai, and the Bay Area to as part of the growing Node101 movement (**Figure 15-6**).

Figure 15-6
node101.org

By the end of '05, Ryanne was co-authoring a book with Michael Verdi on the Secrets of Video Blogging.

Available Statistics
Technorati Rank: 7,281 (350 links from 186 sites) out of 28 million blogs (Early 2006).

Success Criteria Business model
"Make a living through video blogging, I'm on my way."

Plans for Expansion
Ryanne just relocated from the East Coast to San Francisco. She's taking on more video blogging and advocacy-related projects.

Philosophy

According to her Bio on Node101:

"Ryanne Hodson *http://ryanedit.blogspot.com* Ryanne Hodson started her career as a video editor at WGBH PBS Boston and in Boston public access. Another disillusioned television producer struggling to get distribution for artists, video blogging has become her medium of choice for uncensored, unmediated communication. She envisions a huge population who have transformed themselves from media consumers to media creators."

Ryanne had this to say in response to the self-conscious:

People keep talking about video blogging as being narcissistic. I ask you, is that such a bad thing? This is a document of my life that I wish to share with you. And I hope you do the same. This is how we get to know each other and I think it's pretty damn important.

This quote from Ryanne's blog in early 2005 displays some of her passion:

"The LOVE

it's sunday 10am.

vloggercon is over and it was perfect.

we couldnt have asked for a better day.

a lot of us were in town early and are staying late

to be with each other in person.

make connections.

jakob held an after party at his loft (there is like 25 hours of footage, which i'll be linking to, i'm sure)

and when i was saying good bye to people

i found myself saying "see you on the web"

which is sad and also not sad at the same time.

we will create and be with each other in the second world.

i am getting tears in my eyes as i write this.

why so sappy all of a sudden?

i feel elated that i know all these passionate people

who traveled in a snow storm across the country

and, some, across the world to be here.

i'll link to the videos that people are posting

as well as my own, when i get it up here.

but i just wanted to roll out of bed this morning

and say that i miss you all already.

like i said in an earlier video

there are people and places that when you have to say goodbye

you just break down and cry because they have such an effect on you.

this is that moment.

my cheeks are wet with tears of joy.

video video video.

yes

i heart video bloggers.

–ryanne

Studio and Tools

On Freevlog.org, Ryanne and Michael list all the easily accessible tools that people can use to make vlogs. Their list includes:

Hardware:

- Any DV camera
- A web camera
- A digital still camera w/video capabilities
- Any camera that can get video into your computer!

Software:

- iMovie
- Final Cut Pro
- Windows Movie Maker
- QuickTime Pro (Mac/PC)
- Avid FreeDV (*http://avid.com/freedv/index.asp*)

Hosting

- Blogger (it's free!)
- Internet Archive (archive.org)
- Ourmedia.org
- Blip.tv
- FeedBurner.com

Rocketboom.com

If you recognize any of the blogs in this case study chapter you'll recognize Rocketboom (**Figure 15-7**).

Figure 15-7
rocketboom.com

Rocketboom, created by Andrew Baron and co-written and hosted by Amanda Congdon, has been a media darling because it of several vital statistics and close resemblance to mainstream media. It has grown in a little over a year to a daily audience upwards of 150,000 viewers (Q1 2006) and is growing quickly. You can view the three-minute show five days a week on rocketboom.com, via an RSS feed, in iTunes, or on your TiVo over a broadband connection. It's available, well, everywhere that TV is now trying to be. And it has a viewership rivaling cable network shows.

Show format

Rocketboom is a 3 minute daily video blog based in New York City. We cover and create a wide range of information and commentary from top news stories to quirky Internet culture. Agenda includes releasing each new clip at 9:00 A.M. EST, Monday through Friday. With a heavy emphasis on international arts, technology and weblog drama, Rocketboom is presented via online video and widely distributed through RSS.

Development, Growth

Andrew Baron:

> "I basically just saved up a bunch of money, put out a call for a blogger actress and just did it.
>
> I realized the time for video was now. I figured that the weblog medium, which was heavily text based, would eventually evolve to a presentation style that was video heavy. So that's what I set out to do in the spring of 2004 and it took me until October to get it all together and launch it.
>
> We already had the laptop and camera but these cheap tools are not a part of the daily production costs. We started on my University server account, then moved to a $15/month server and costs only grew once the audience got to be REALLY big (over 10,000 regular people, every day). Meanwhile, over the past year, bandwidth costs have fallen dramatically, from $1/gig to .25/gig. Just because of our numbers, once we moved out of the $15/mo category, we already had opportunities to run ads, take sponsorships, sell merchandise, licensing, subscription, consulting, book writing, show opportunities and dozens of venture capital pursuits, none of which we sought—all found us (thus we are holding out to do things exactly the way we would like)."[1]

Statistics

*   Technorati Rank: 124 (4,661 links from 2,044 sites) (Early 2006).
*   Over 200,000 downloads a day
*   Over 1,000,000 viewings each week
*   Available on TiVo

---

[1] From a blog post by C.K. Sample III on The Unofficial Apple Weblog
    http://www.tuaw com/2005/11/03/interview-with-andrew-baron-from-rocketboom/

Rocketboom is currently one of the most popular video blogs on the Internet with more daily subscribers for original syndicated multimedia content than nearly any other site, including podcasts.

Success criteria/Business model

Rocketboom is distributed online, all around the world and on demand, and thus has a much larger potential audience than any TV broadcast. However, we spend $0 on promotion, relying entirely on word-of-mouth, and close to $0 on distribution because bandwidth costs and space are so inexpensive. While TV programs have traditionally been uni-directional, Rocketboom engages its international audience in a wide range of topical discussions.

Andrew Baron:

> "We decided from the start to not worry about a business model and wait until we were actually able to create a value before trying to extract a value. That time has passed now as we have a nice market value and our growing expenses are becoming quite a burden.
>
> The beauty of this all of course is that it can be done for so cheap. Aside from the minimal consumer equipment, a laptop and camera, the only substantial cost besides salary is bandwidth. Yet bandwidth is so cheap and getting cheaper. The most obvious form of revenue, especially on a large scale, is through video advertising.
>
> But, we will never play invasive, pre-roll advertising in short form, video file content. And we don't believe in product placement and will not use this technique.
>
> We find that people come back to Rocketboom mostly because they enjoy the interesting stories we cover or exhibit from around the world. When we choose and create our stories, we opt for the most interesting and timely material to make up each show.
>
> It's the audience and their comments that is absolutely amongst the most important things to us, and for better or for worse, we take their advice. We all work this out together I feel. That has happened since the beginning."[2]

Rocketboom has taken the completely innovative approach of auctioning off advertising inventory for its blog on eBay. The first auction brought in a final price of $40,000, which for their viewership translates to a healthy $40 CPM (**Figure 15-8**).

---

[2] From a blog post by C.K. Sample III on The Unofficial Apple Weblog
http://www.tuaw.com/2005/11/03/interview-with-andrew-baron-from-rocketboom/

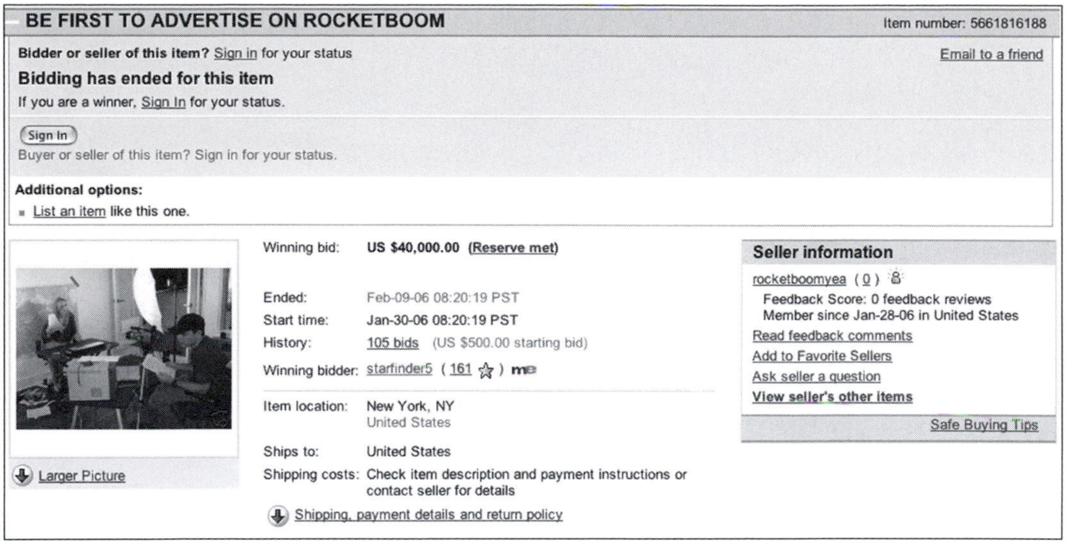

Figure 15-8
Rocketboom ad space on eBay

But the really innovative part of the advertising is that Rocketboom retains complete creative control. For their first client, Rocketboom created a series of unique, original advertisements for the company. In other cases, Rocketboom incorporates the company's own advertisements. In all cases, Rocketboom works with the advertiser to ensure commercials will satisfy the dual goals of delivering effective value for the advertiser, while resonating with Rocketboom's unique audience.

The eBay auction simply kickstarted their advertising sales. Immediately after the auction, Earthlink bought a week of spots. Now, advertisers are approaching them directly.

Plans for expansion
Rocketboom has been taking on additional domestic and international correspondents, as well as production staff. The dream is to have a network of citizen journalists all over the world, submitting stories.

In conjunction with launching an ad-based service, Rocketboom also announced their intent to launch a subscription service. For a reasonably small fee ($3–4 per month), viewers will have access to an HD version of the blog, outtakes, extra footage, and a full-screen experience.

Rocketboom's long-term goals include creating new video blogs. These blogs would be hosted, and would focus on new areas, such as events and documentaries.

Philosophy

Andrew Baron says:

"I am saying that you can jump in here—it's not too late at all—without an investment beyond your time, and shoot for the stars—you can get there on your own if you really want to. This is the awesome headline: "If you've got twenty-five bucks, you can build it up into something really, really big." $25 IS the actual production cost to create an episode, usually less.

In short, people that are truly motivated and resourceful, would simply not need to invest any money. If you can find or borrow a camera, a computer and an Internet connection, you can very easily create work that will support itself at any size. The news story behind Rocketboom right now, and the story for any other dreamers out there is the daunting magnitude in which our humongous monetary value has outpaced our tiny costs.

I would recommend getting into the process and creating several posts that you are happy with before going live with it. But I would say definitely just dive in, even without a theme or an idea, just to get the juices flowing and get the technical stuff down, because there is a lot to it, at the end of the day.

Consider how the content fits in with this medium. You can't just take old news and throw it up online. Right now new formats are being created due to technology, interactivity, human desires, etc. It's different to sit at a computer, compared to a couch. It's also different traveling around with it in your hand. But the most exciting thing for these people who already have content is that it's so cheap and easy to get it up and out there to an audience, all you need is a college kid to handle the tech end.

It's very easy to get started technically. All you need is a video camera and a computer and an idea. As for the idea, I would like to see more people who are interested in a particular field use the medium to show off that expertise.

For instance, what do you do for a living? Are you a musician? Create a video blog telling us about gear, about method, about experience on the road, record deal problems, things along that thread. If you write software, let's see some interviews with people in your field; let's get some tips on how you do it. Just as blogging has helped us get a "real" or "personal" perspective on important information, video blogging can do that too. The intention of keeping a thread is important to gain authority and build depth to your presentation. It will be good for people with that interest, because they will want to keep coming back because it will be related to them. Otherwise, like a personal diary, you may only like one post and not be interested in the rest. The other great thing is that, if you are revealing information of interest, no one will care if you can't get the production quality right or if you don't look like Tom Cruise or Katie Holmes: it's about the content."[3]

---

[3] From a blog post on *http://www.dembot.com*, Andrew Barron's personal blog

---

Amanda Congden:

"I kinda got submerged into this Internet culture crazyness, and I'm loving it, loving blogs, and video blogs and podcasts because of their potential to really create a global community and to connect people that would never normally be connected. One of the most exciting things is how a kid in the middle of Arkansas can connect with a kid in the middle of China—two 12 year old kids talking about the same things and seeing the similarities that everyone really shares."[4]

Studio and Tools

Rocketboom differs from a regular TV program in many important ways. Instead of costing millions of dollars to produce, Rocketboom is created with a consumer-level video camera, a laptop, two lights and a map with no additional overhead or costs (**Figure 15-9**).

Figure 15-9
The Rocketboom studio

---

[4]   From *http://www.rocketboom.com/vlog/archives/2006/03/rb_06_mar_16.html*

These are the software and publishing tools used to make Rocketboom:

Software:
- QuickTime Pro
- Flip4Mac
- Snapz Pro with Movie Capture
- 3ivX codec

Editing:
- Audacity
- i-Movie
- Final Cut Pro

Publishing:
- Weblog Software: Moveable Type
- RSS with Enclosure DIY in Moveable Type
- Brandon Fuller's Pearl MT Plug-in
- FeedBurner.com
- Prodigem
- Creative Commons Publishing Licenses

Rocketboom uses QuickTime as its primary format.

The major technical considerations for producing video online are determined by user experience. From the perspective of Rocketboom, QuickTime is indisputably the most advanced and attuned technology to accommodate the best human experience, where broadband speeds currently lie en masse:

- **Fast Start technology**. Without the need to use streaming, progressive Quick-Time .mov files begin playing after a certain amount of the file is loaded into RAM. Because the video plays back from RAM, and not the online connection stream, a video of comparable size and quality can play back much faster, on demand and not get clogged up by future speed variables.
- **Playback Controls**. In addition to starting up quicker, and maintaining a constant playback speed, the .mov file, when played back in QuickTime, allows the user to scroll, scrub and jump around through the file with the least amount of latency and the finest amount of resolution between frames. As a result, the user is able to consume the content in a more customizable way by scanning the entire

piece visually at various speeds, jumping back and forth between points along with frame advance which provides more detailed information about the dynamics of the content.

- **Interactivity**. QuickTime has the ability to handle hyper-linking of space within a video, chapter reference points, SMIL which is useful for stringing multiple videos together and text tracks, to name a few. A QuickTime file can also send pings when certain points are viewed in the file.

- **Cross platform playback**. While .mov files do not reach every operating system, QuickTime is available for Windows and is capable of exporting to wrapper-independent files that will work on various operating systems.

- **Importing/Exporting**. This is an end-solution for importing and exporting to and from any file format. I have never seen another player that can handle as much video so well.

Why the 3ivX codec is used:

- 3IVX is a compression compatible with MPEG-4 and it's Rocketboom's choice for the CODEC to use when creating .mov files. Instead of exporting a final video to an MPEG-4 compression, 3iVX allows you to export to an MPEG-4 compatible compression that is WAY better in terms of quality/file size ratio.

According to the 3IVX website:

- 3ivx is up to twice as efficient as Apple MPEG-4. It produces the same quality video in half the size.

- 3ivx is up to five times faster at encoding.

- 3ivx is completely compatible with the Apple MPEG-4 Decoder built into and shipped with every copy of QuickTime 6.

- 3ivx is a faster and better decoder, but you don't need 3ivx to decode.

- When making .MOV files, because MPEG-4 is perhaps the most pervasive, cross platform CODEC, using 3IVX is the best option for creating quality files at the best file sizes, while not requiring your audience to install additional plug-ins or obscure 3rd party players.

Hosting

Originally, Rocketboom used one dedicated 100 mbs server on Dreamhost.com to handle the database and webpages alone. Gradually they added two dedicated 100 mbs servers on Datagram (*http://www.datagram.com*) to host the videos and the images, for a total of a 300 mbit/sec pipe size. This increased to three and then four servers. The Datagram servers are mirror images (they all hold the same video and image files) and every single request for a video or image is alternated like a switch back and forth to each of the servers.

Late last year, Rocketboom used perhaps 12 terabytes of data transfer on the two Datagram servers and not more than a terabyte on the Dreamhost server (mostly html and xml pages). That was when they were getting about 100,000 viewers. As of March 2006, they've far exceeded these numbers and are moving all of their hosting to Datagram (for a total of five 100 Mbps pipes) to accomodate their bandwidth, customer service, and uptime requirements. Rocketboom's audience has grown to about 250,000 users a day , spiking over 300,000. Every video also gets hundreds of thousands of additional downloads after the first day.

Each weekday morning, after uploading the show at 9AM, Rocketboom use the Ping-o-matic service (*http://www.pingomatic.com*) to inform the world of a new episode.

About five minutes later, the aggregators take automatic action all at once, and the servers get swarmed with requests. Last year, with two Datagram servers and one Dreamhost server, Rocketboom would get completely maxed out (300 Kbps full on) for about 30 minutes while things ran slow. After adding additional servers and expanded their service with Datagram, they no longer max out when pings go out.

Rocketboom has been though some pretty heavy days where a lot of major sites have linked to them all at once, and having 300 mbps has worked fine (as long as it was not around the release hour where the aggregators were all at work).

Rocketboom recommends that any video blog anticipating growth and wishing to provide a solid user experience so that everyone gets their file quickly and easily (a strategy they have demanded from the start which used to put almost all of the major news video sites to shame with their famous "buffering" messages) should:

1. get a bigger pipe (and/or more servers)
2. don't stream! (i.e., allow files to be downloaded)

On the contrary, an individual video blogger doing their own thing, or a commercial video blogger that does not anticipate fast growth and can deal with being affected from time to time, could effectively use a small $10-a-month hosting plan.

APPENDIX

Administration

File and directory administration is no fun. It's also no fun to have to go back into a large file archive and figure out what goes with what. Blogging programs make it easy to fire and forget, leaving directories filled with oddly named files and temporary directories that ended up not being temporary.

A few simple steps can be taken to be sure that you know what you've got and that no one else is using your files and bandwidth. Google, MSN, Yahoo! and other search engines have great results because they go out and scour the Internet for every last file it can find and put them in a search result. Sometimes, particularly with image files, a descriptive file name can end up being a liability.

Unscrupulous or lazy people use Google Image Search and other similar engines to find a photo they want for their site. Instead of simply stealing the file which is illegal to begin with, they link to your file. If their page or posting is popular, the file is loaded over and over, hundreds or thousands of time. Each time the file is loaded, you pay for it, not them.

Often the only way you can know who is linking to you is to look through your refer logs (see **Figure A-1**). In all likelihood, they found your photo through a search engine. You have a few choices; you could try to contact the offender or you could change the file name and the link to that file in your post. You could go one step further and create a new image with the original file name but the new file is a graphic with text saying "I am a thoughtless bandwidth thief" or simply use it as a venue to advertise your own site by replacing the original image with your own banner. Check your stats to see how much bandwidth is devoted to graphic files (see **Figure A-2**).

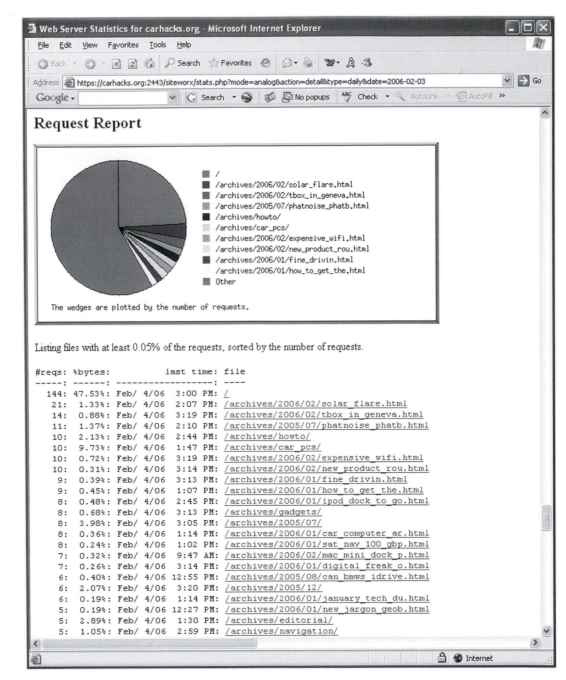

Figure A-1
Movable Type refer log

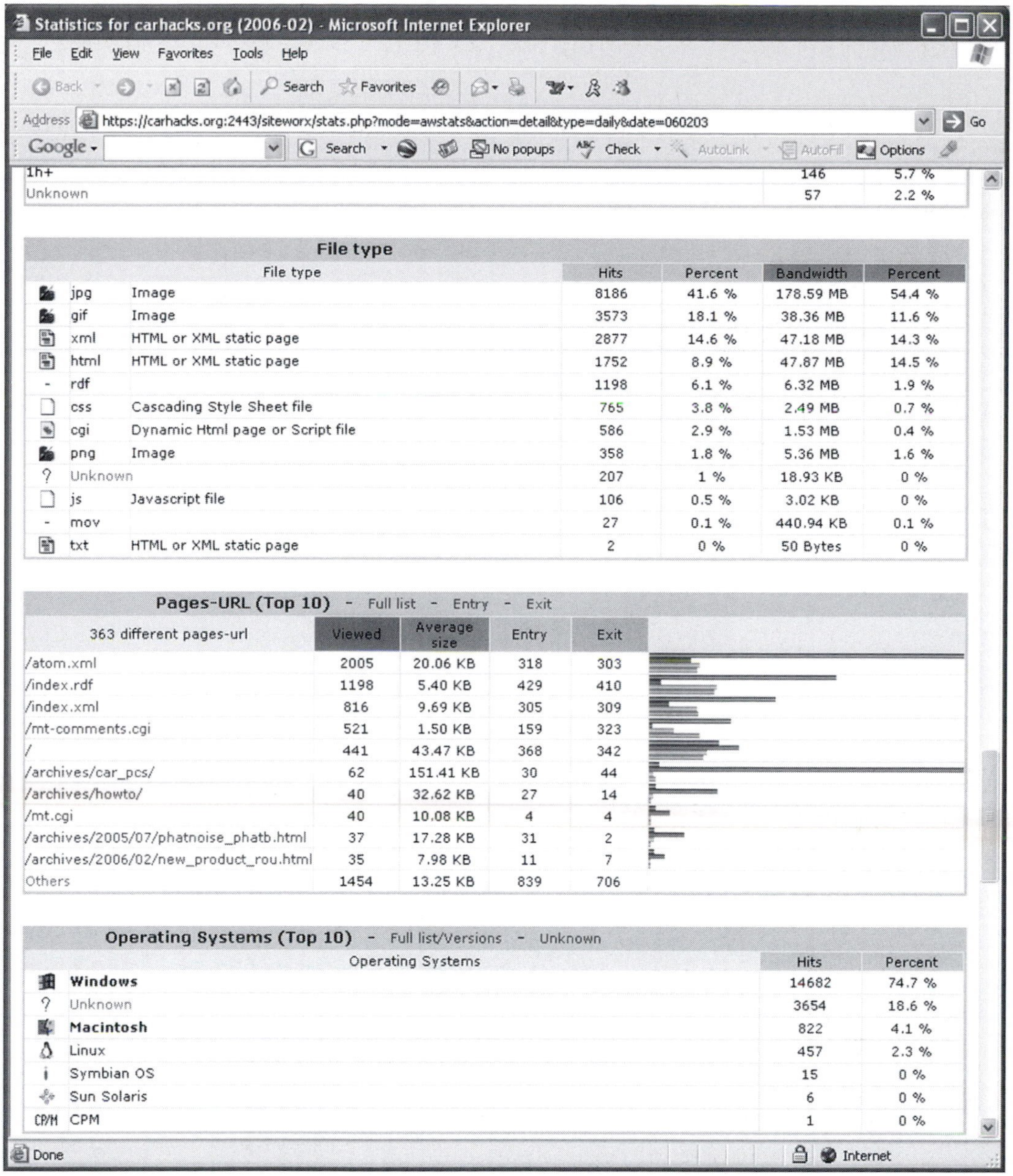

1h+		146	5.7 %
Unknown		57	2.2 %

File type

	File type		Hits	Percent	Bandwidth	Percent
	jpg	Image	8186	41.6 %	178.59 MB	54.4 %
	gif	Image	3573	18.1 %	38.36 MB	11.6 %
	xml	HTML or XML static page	2877	14.6 %	47.18 MB	14.3 %
	html	HTML or XML static page	1752	8.9 %	47.87 MB	14.5 %
-	rdf		1198	6.1 %	6.32 MB	1.9 %
	css	Cascading Style Sheet file	765	3.8 %	2.49 MB	0.7 %
	cgi	Dynamic Html page or Script file	586	2.9 %	1.53 MB	0.4 %
	png	Image	358	1.8 %	5.36 MB	1.6 %
?	Unknown		207	1 %	18.93 KB	0 %
	js	Javascript file	106	0.5 %	3.02 KB	0 %
-	mov		27	0.1 %	440.94 KB	0.1 %
	txt	HTML or XML static page	2	0 %	50 Bytes	0 %

Pages-URL (Top 10)   -   Full list   -   Entry   -   Exit

363 different pages-url	Viewed	Average size	Entry	Exit	
/atom.xml	2005	20.06 KB	318	303	
/index.rdf	1198	5.40 KB	429	410	
/index.xml	816	9.69 KB	305	309	
/mt-comments.cgi	521	1.50 KB	159	323	
/	441	43.47 KB	368	342	
/archives/car_pcs/	62	151.41 KB	30	44	
/archives/howto/	40	32.62 KB	27	14	
/mt.cgi	40	10.08 KB	4	4	
/archives/2005/07/phatnoise_phatb.html	37	17.28 KB	31	2	
/archives/2006/02/new_product_rou.html	35	7.98 KB	11	7	
Others	1454	13.25 KB	839	706	

Operating Systems (Top 10)   -   Full list/Versions   -   Unknown

Operating Systems	Hits	Percent
Windows	14682	74.7 %
Unknown	3654	18.6 %
Macintosh	822	4.1 %
Linux	457	2.3 %
Symbian OS	15	0 %
Sun Solaris	6	0 %
CPM	1	0 %

Done   Internet

Figure A-2
Movable Type file type statistics

The Robots Will Save Us

Keeping people out of your images can be done two ways. The first method is to use non-descriptive file names that search engines will likely pass over. Sometimes this will not work since search engines can associate an image with the context of the text surrounding it or referring to it. The more effective way to get your files out of the hands of search engines is to simply tell them no. Search engines respect only one thing, Robots.txt. They will not go out of their way to make it easy to opt out of their searches but at the end of the day, they do need to have a way to honor those who just want out.

There are a number of very good resources on the Internet detailing the ins and outs of using robots.txt but it's worth mentioning the main points of it. Search engines look for a ro-bots.txt file when they spider a site. They parse the basic rules in the file to know what they are not allowed to index. It's based on a disallow rule set rather than an allow set. They will just assume that if no robot file is present, it's a free for all.

The first entry in the file is the agent. The spider will only respect a perfectly coded file so syntax must be perfect. User agent is entered as "`User-agent: `". Meaning, User-agent has to have the dash "`-`" as well as the colon "`:`" and then a space after the colon. The next part of that command is the specific agent to be disallowed.

Each robot has its own name, making this process very specific but potentially arduous. Google's image bot is called Googlebot-Image. Not googlebot image, not image-googlebot or googlebot_image. If the robot does not see its very specific name it will walk right on in and index your files. With the last two bits of information the first line of the text file will be "`User-agent: Goolebot-Image`". The quotes are only for illustration purposes and are not used in the text of the file.

The next line of text defines what Googlebot-Image is not allowed to see. The most common command is to limit directories. The disallow command is straight forward, "`Disallow: `" with a space after the colon and before the thing to be disallowed. If you add a front-slash "/" after the space, you've disallowed the Googlebot-image from indexing anything in the root directory. If you keep your files in /blogstuff/images/ as well then add a second disallow line and include that directory and so on. What we have so far:

```
User-agent: Googlebot-Image
Disallow: /
Disallow: /blogstuff/images/
```

One thing to notice is the final "/" after images. Without it the bot will assume it's not sup-posed to index a file called images. The backslash at the end tells the bot it's a directory.

Most podcasters will want people to be able to find them in the most places possible. By replacing the Googlebot-image user agent with an asterisk "*" you're telling all robots to ignore the directories specified. It could be useful if all of your media files are located in a few directories that are separate from where your posts are stored. That way, no robots will go near your images and other media. If everything is mashed together in one place, telling every robot to get lost will wipe your blog off the face of all search engines.

The last thing to do is put the file where it belongs. Once you save the file you'll need to put the file in the root of your blog. That will require having file access through FTP or a web-based file manager. Once the file is in place it's a good idea to have a robots.txt syntax checker look at your file to make sure it will deliver the results you want. *http://www.searchengineworld.com/cgi-bin/robotcheck.cgi* will parse your file and tell you if it thinks the file needs editing. Don't get discouraged, most of these files have to be tweaked a few times before they work right. *http://www.searchtools.com/robots/ robots-txt.html* is a good reference for creating robots.txt files that protect your sites assets. It may take a week or so before your site is re-checked by the spiders so have a little patience. If there are a particular few files that are being abused it's better to just rename them so your bandwidth bill doesn't skyrocket.

Backing Up
Local backup
Podcasts and video blogs are a culmination of a great deal of effort. Effort to write the posts, shoot and edit the video, record the audio, it's all work. If for some reason something happens and you need to re-post everything or want to have a local copy it's good to regularly backup your posts.

Blogger
Blogger does not have any built-in function to back up an entire blog to file, making it available for download. There is, however, a work-around that creates the archive file. It's quite manual but does work. The process requires changing out your blog template and replacing it with one that creates the archive. If you want to keep using your Blogger.com blog, you'll need to make a copy of your working template and reinstate it after the backup process is complete.

1. Sign in to your Blogger.com account and select the "Template" tab. This dialog allows you to edit your template directly.

2. Copy your entire current template and paste it into a text document on your own computer. Save the file with a name that makes sense. You'll need this later.

3. Copy the text below into your template exactly as its written (see **Figure A-3**):

```
<Blogger>
AUTHOR: <$BlogItemAuthor$>
DATE: <$BlogItemDateTime$>
-----
BODY:
<$BlogItemBody$>
--------
</Blogger>
```

Note: If you want to keep the comments as well, copy the text below above the </Blogger>
tag:

```
<BlogItemCommentsEnabled>
<BlogItemComments>
COMMENT-AUTHOR:<$BlogCommentAuthor$>
COMMENT-DATE:<$BlogCommentDateTime$>
COMMENT-BODY:<$BlogCommentBody$>
--------
</BlogItemComments>
</BlogItemCommentsEnabled>
```

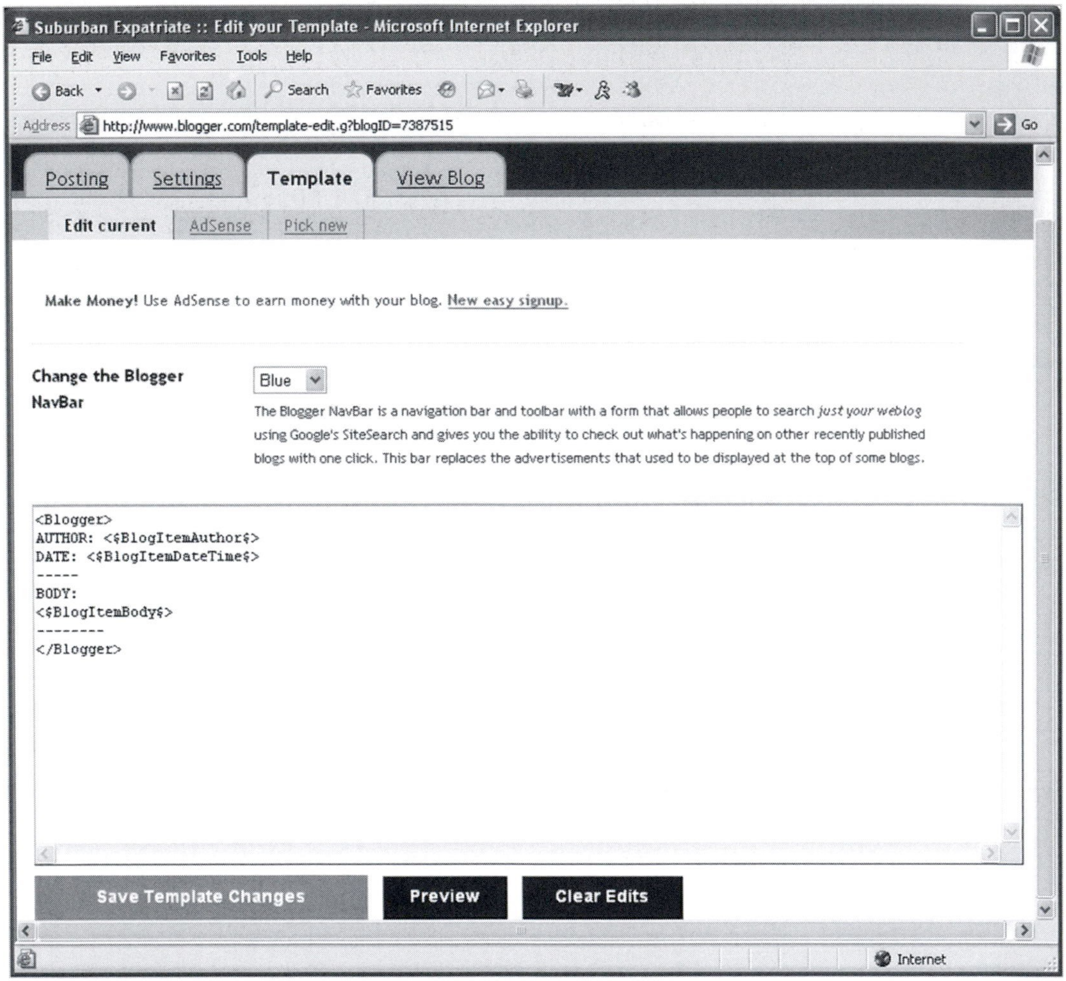

Figure 16.3
Blogger template editor

4.   In the Settings | Publishing tab, rename the Blog Filename to something other
      than the current one, something descriptive would be best. If you don't rename

it you'll overwrite the main index file. Write down the current file name so you can restore it properly later.

[**Note:** This is only required by bloggers using FTP. Free BlogSpot must over-write their existing blog page. It will be overwritten when the blog is republished with your original template.]

5. In Settings | Formatting, set your blog to display all of your posts on the main index page. There is no specific command to do this so you should change the number of days displayed on your front page (Show X days posts on main page) to a number higher than the total number of days since you've been blogging. It will force all days to be published (see **Figure A-4**).

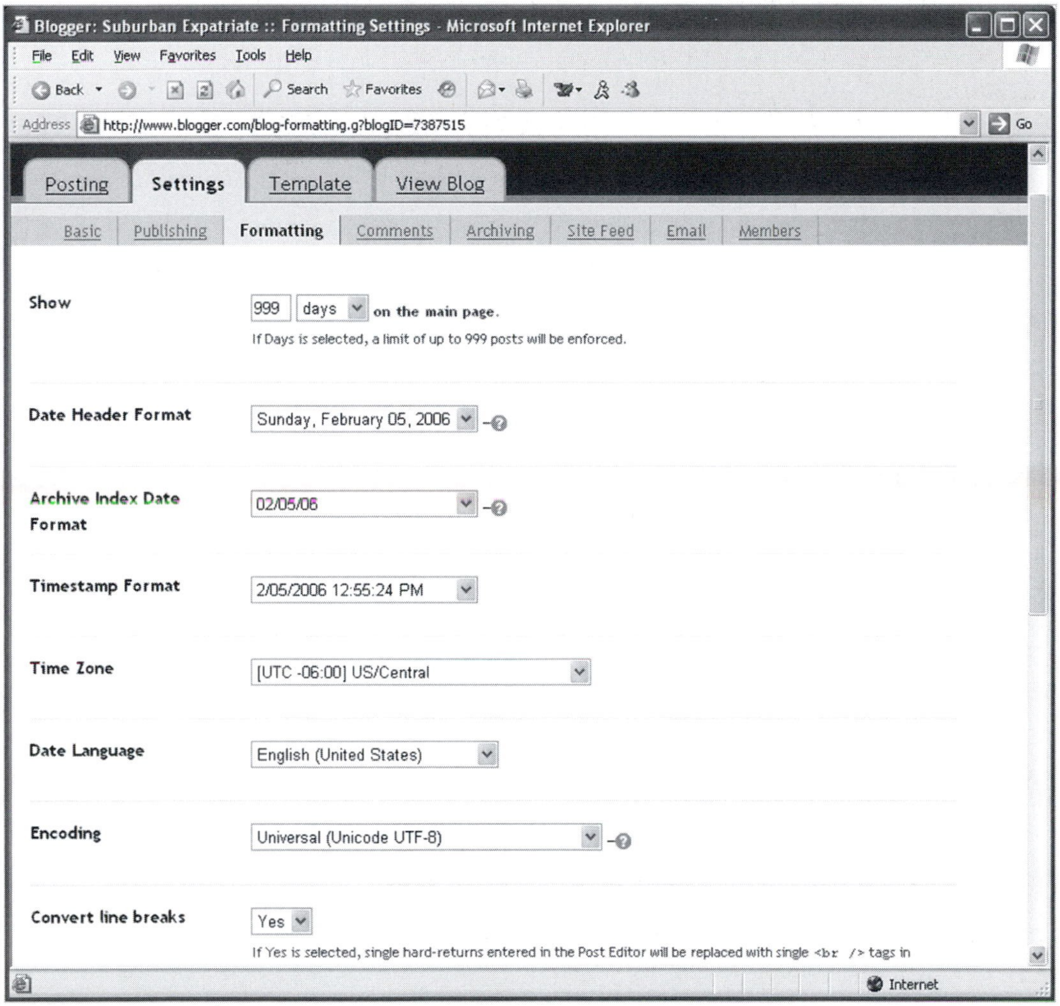

Figure A-4
Displaying all posts In Blogger

6.   In Settings | Formatting set Date/Time Format to the format `MM/DD/YYYY HH:MM:SS AM|PM`. (**Note**: the format will not look like this in the menu; instead it will be the current time, formatted.) Write down your current setting so you can set it back later.

7.   Also in Settings | Formatting set Convert Line Breaks to No.

8.   In Settings | Archiving, set Archive Frequency to No Archive. This will prevent your archives from being overwritten with the new template.

9.   Republish your blog; you will end up with a single file with all of your posts, formatted using the above template, at the location specified in your Settings. Open this file in your web browser and save the file to your local hard drive.

10.   Restore the previous settings (Blog filename, archive frequency, timestamp, etc.) in your blog and replace the temporary template with your saved copy. Publish the blog and view the page to check that everything is correct.

WordPress

Like Blogger, WordPress does not have a built-in export or backup function so it requires manual scripting. There are a number of user-created scripts on the Internet that were developed by WordPress so they are to be found and used knowing there is a risk involved. The directions provided by PapaScott *http://www.papascott.de/archives/2004/09/01/export-from-wordpress/* have received a number of positive comments from users.

> **ALERT**
>
> !
>
> Any code downloaded from the web should be tested in a safe place first. Applications can change and older versions of scripts might not work correctly and could very easily wipe out a great deal of work which would be somewhat ironic if it occurred while trying to back it up for safety.
>
> Treat all code you did not write yourself as suspect. If you don't test it first you could be setting yourself up for disappointment.

TypePad

The process for exporting posts in TypePad is much simpler as they have a tool built directly into the application allowing a direct export (see **Figure A-5**). Under the tab Weblogs there is a link to "List Posts." Click on that to get to a full listing of all of your blog posts. Within that page there is an "Import/Export" tab. Inside that dialog, at the bottom of the page is a function to create a post export file. It's not fancy nor will it export media files but it will offer a good backup of all text you've created for that blog.

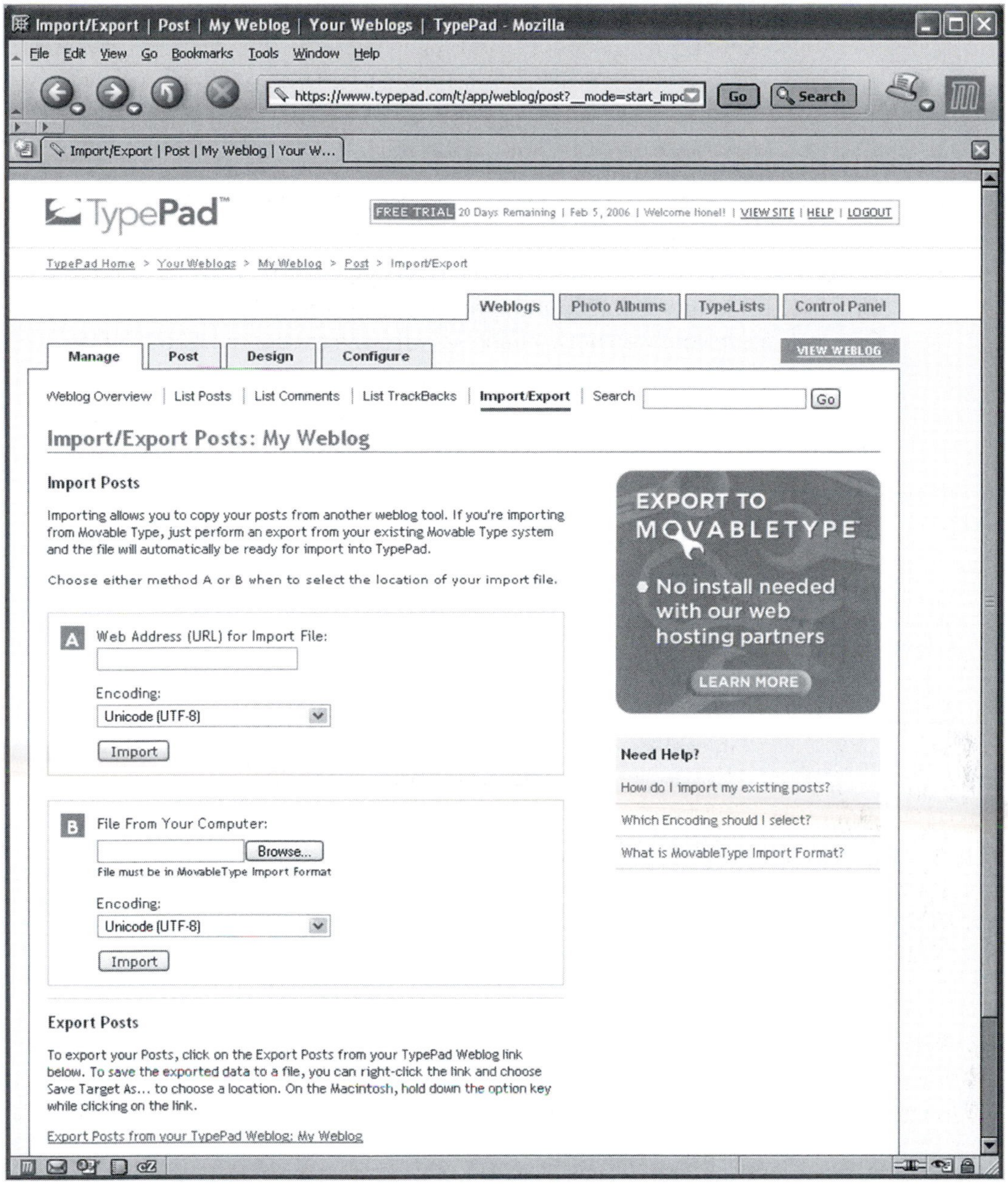

Figure A-5
TypePad blog export dialogue

Movable Type

Also under SixApart, Movable Type offers an automated export function. From the main menu select your weblog. In the main page for your weblog there is a link to "Import / Export" in the left hand navigation bar. Simply select the "Export" tab and click on "Export

Entries From YourBlog" (see **Figure A-6**). Movable Type will download a text file to your computer that you should keep in a safe place. If you have to restore your blog the import function is in the same place and will take the exported file.

Figure A-6
Movable Type blog export dialogue

Another way to get your posts from the host to your local system is to simply FTP into the site and download the files. By mirroring the directories from the host to your local computer, you'll have the posts, media, and templates broken out into their directories and individual files.

Re-assembling a blog that has been wiped out will not be a simple process only taking a few minutes. Take care to download everything you can and in the event of a major catastrophe, call their tech support people and have them help you restore the site. Without support you might end up uploading something that caused it to fall apart in the first place.

Spring Cleaning

With every blog post there is growth. Hosting your own content will certainly add to that growth much faster than having the rich media hosted with a service like archive.org. Even so, images and other locally stored content adds to your storage footprint. Each blog host will have a limitation on how much room you get with your blog. It's a good idea to go into the directories and see which files can be re-edited, re-compressed or deleted.

If you're hosting videos and audio files on your blog host, you may set a 6-month limit on full size files. After a certain amount of time those files may have very few accesses and will do little more than take up space. If a 15 MB MOV file can be re-compressed into a smaller video using higher compression, you can still have it up but not have it account for nearly as much storage space. Some compression applications can batch compress which makes scheduled archives as simple as dragging a pile of files into a dialog box and hitting "encode". Once it's done you can upload and overwrite the original files.

The same can be done with large image files. Check your directories to make sure you've not been uploading the uncompressed layered Photoshop PSD files. It's not uncommon to sync an entire directory over FTP and forget to remove the source originals. A multi-layered PSD can be 50X the size of the final JPG.

Take a tour of the blog though your FTP application. Browse the directories and make sure files in directories are supposed to be there. Temporary directories you created to share a large file can be easily forgotten or worse forgotten and found. People might be curious about a 500MB MOV file sitting in a public place. If a few people download it you might get hit with a big bill. Once every 6 months make sure you've emptied out temp directories and scoured for files not related to the blog that might have ended up there by accident.

Naming Conventions

One simple way to make regular maintenance and backup simpler is to use a naming convention for files and directories as well as breaking out media types into their own directories. Here are a few common conventions for file system management

- Images that are used in the page templates or as part of the site design should be separated from images for posts. Creating a new directory called "site-img" will make a discrete spot for site assets without risking having an uploaded image with the same name overwrite and cause havoc.

- Images that are used in posts should have their own place. Making a directory called "post-img" will simplify differentiating site images from post images

- A separate place for video and audio files also provides some order to the site. "post-audio" and "post-video" will not only make individual and descriptive space, the way "post-" directories are named keeps them next to each other in directory listings.

- If you're going to need a directory that you'll use as a space to put large files for download but on a temporary basis, give it a descriptive and easy to remember name. "temp-dist" can remain a permanent directory but you can add test notes to the directory about when a file should be deleted so you don't end up with a huge space filled with random stuff. The good thing about the temporary directory is that it's used from non-site critical files and can be completely wiped out without having an effect on site operations.

- Image, audio and video files benefit from having a standardized naming convention applied to them. Some people prefer the date prefix format: "2006-01-31-t650.jpg". The format is "YYYY-MM-DD-name.filetype" Although the image is of a Treo 650, giving it that name might cause the image to show up in image searches by robots and spiders that don't respect your robots.txt file. Don't use descriptive names in files unless you want spiders and robots to find the files. Using the date format that has year, month, day makes sorting the files by name sort by date. You could use a type convention such as "rant-001-politics.mp3" which creates groups for each type of audio post, assigning it a number that can grow without throwing off the sort and subject. Being able to find the file you need to by file name only is a trick but it can be done, it all depends on your subject matter and what makes sense to you.

Conclusion

No one likes to be told to keep their room clean but it's something that has to be done if things are to happen in an efficient and effective manner. Cleaning out old files, giving some thought to the naming and structure will pay off when you need it to. The day to day operations of a vlog or podcast make it easy to ignore the administrative aspects. When something does need to be found, renamed, re-encoded or restored, having done the legwork will be the difference between a 2-hour restore and having to rebuild it from scratch.

Glossary

Ad Inventory: Term used to describe all the time slots or blank pages or banner space available for ad insertion. As a general rule, there are more advertising dollars available than there is good advertising inventory available to supply that demand.

Aggregator: An application or website that subscribes to multiple blog feeds and automatically pulls down, combines, and presents all the information culled for the viewer. Some aggregators can automatically download large multimedia attachments enclosed in blogs, and are called *podcatchers* or *vlogcatchers*.

Apache: UNIX-based web server software.

Application Service Provider: A completely turn-key solution for online applications ranging from HR functions to storefronts and blogs. These require no customer-side systems administration.

ASP: See *Application Service Provider*.

Atom: A flexible and improved standard competitive with RSS that achieves similar goals. One of the three main formats used in blog syndication. See also *RSS 1.0* and *RSS 2.0*.

Audio Blog: Digital audio recording, most often as an MP3, posted to a blog and available for download as an enclosure.

Auto-render: A program that automatically creates the correct XML code.

AVI: A *container* file format, not a codec, used to hold codecs. It can contain MP3, MPEG-4, DivX, XviD, and other audio and video codecs.

Balanced Audio: Used for low-voltage audio equipment where long runs of cable can cause RF interference and line-noise.

Bargain: Something that at first seems like a good deal and ends up not being one.

BitTorrent: A peer-to-peer (P2P) distribution network developed to share the load of hosting and downloading very large files by leveraging people's personal and under utilized DSL and cable modem connections.

Blog Service: Hosted service that manages and owns the back-end process of blogs that may or may not charge a fee.

Blogosphere: A coined term for the sum of all blogs, the people who write blogs, and the information found in these blogs.

Blogroll: List of associated or favorite blogs. Typically located in a sidebar.

Bluescreen: See *Chroma Keying*.

BSOD: This stands for Blue Screen of Death. When Windows has the digital equivalent of a stroke, the screen turns blue and offers up a cryptic error message.

Cache: Content that is kept in the RAM or very close storage of servers in a CDN. Caching reduces delays in serving data.

Capture Device: External or internal hardware that converts audio and video into a digital format.

Capture: Recording media into a digital format from an external device. Also known as *Importing* or *Acquiring*.

Cardioid: Pickup pattern shaped like a heart. Very popular for recording studios.

CDN: See *Content Delivery Network*.

Chroma Keying: Technique for superimposing one video source over another still or moving image, by filming the first source in front of a blue or greenscreen. This is a common technique of newscasters and weather people. Done by replacing a color in the frame, either a specific blue or green and replacing what has been removed with the alternate video.

Clearing: The process of getting written permission from each of the necessary rights holders so that a new artistic work containing these elements can be legally distributed.

Clip: Segment of video or audio.

Codec: Stands for compressor-decompressor. Examples include MPEG-2 video or MP3 audio. Each codec has advantages and disadvantages, that is, MP3 is the most widely-known and compatible format, but it is not indistinguishable from CD. Video codecs can look blocky, discolored, etc.

Colo: See *Colocation Facility*.

Colocation Facility: A facility that specializes in providing the space, racks, air conditioning, power and network connectivity for companies needing a place for their servers outside of their own offices. Colocation facilities manage the infrastructure for the hardware and often offer administration for the customer servers and network equipment as an added cost.

Compressed Video: Completed edits are rendered to a final, lossy format like MOV, which significantly reduces the file size and makes them more efficient for Internet downloading while preserving a high quality picture.

Condenser Microphone: Audio signal is created through a diaphragm that vibrates two plates within a capacitor. More sensitive, but more fragile.

Content Delivery Network: Distributed infrastructure of servers and networks that distribute content elements such as video, images and audio from strategically selected points on the Internet providing fast and consistent downloads.

Copyright: A set of laws and policies intended to allow the creator of an intellectual work to control how it is copied.

CPM: Cost Per Mil, where Mil means thousands.

Crawl: To automatically search through blogs or websites to check for updates and index them, usually done by search engines.

De Facto: Latin for "In fact." A de facto standard is a standard just because everybody uses it, as opposed to being selected by a duly-authorized and convened committee.

Derivative Work Rights: Applies to all kinds of copyright, not just music. They are held by the creator or subsequent rights' holder of the work, and gives them exclusive control over who can make additional works that build on the original work by altering it, using its elements, etc.

Digital Performance Rights: Created by new US legislation in 1995, created a new revenue stream for songwriters and performers by collecting royalties for the new digital radio-like services, such as satellite radio, digital radio cable, digital elevator music, and webcasting.

Digital Video Recorder: A consumer electronics device that records TV for later viewing.

DivX: High quality video compression codec, based on MPEG-4 part 2, used mainly for long format video distribution over the Internet. See also MPEG-4.

DVD Ripping: Turning a DVD into a digital video file.

DVR: See *Digital Video Recorder*.

DVR-MS: File type created by Microsoft Windows Media Center PC DVRs. Proprietary but is simply an MPEG-2 file with a special wrapper.

Dynamic Microphone: Microphone that uses a wire coil over a magnet with a diaphragm attached to the coil. When sound waves hit the diaphragm the coil moves, that creates an electrical current by moving across the magnet.

Earballs: Listeners.

Elements: In HTML and XML, elements are the specific-purpose labels stored between angle brackets, such as <title>My Blog</title>. From older terminology they are also sometimes called *tags*.

Embedded Media: Similar to enclosures but not as widely supported by RSS readers, embedded media shows up in the blog post only when it is viewed as a web page. Feed readers require media to be included as an enclosure.

Enclosure: A multimedia file that is specially referenced by the blog post for retrieval along with the blog's feed. Depending on the feed standard used by the publishing system, the enclosure can be seen by readers and automatically downloaded. Enclosures allow blogs to become automatic multimedia delivery systems.

Encoder: Software or hardware that takes a video or audio signal and turns it into a digital file that can be edited or viewed.

Extensions: proposed standards that build upon an existing standard. For instance, both Yahoo! and Apple have created *extensions* that add additional information to media stored in RSS 2.0 feeds.

Eyeballs: A PR/marketing term for viewers.

FAT32: Older disk formatting technique before Windows NT/XP. Compare NTFS.

Feed: The file that a reader or aggregator links to as a URL to get blog updates, usually an XML file in RSS or Atom formats.

Flash: A compression method and player wherein vector graphics (made of shapes) are put on screen and then animation commands are sent as opposed to having the whole picture change every frame.

FLV: A file extension denoting a video made in Macromedia Flash.

Folksonomy: a coined term to describe categorization by groups of people, as in viewers assigning their own keywords to photos, movies, etc.

FPS: See *Frames Per Second*.

Frames Per Second: Standard video in the US (NTSC) is recorded and broadcast at 30 frames per second. Digital video FPS are sometimes decreased to reduce video file size for downloads and streaming.

FTP: File Transfer Protocol, a predecessor of HTTP. It is used frequently for uploading files to servers and updating web pages.

Gated Community: A portal, website, media-player application, or other digital "experi-ence" where visitors are provided with filtered, well produced content choices, usually for an added fee or subscription. Examples include AOL's enhanced ISP service, or ad-free subscription access to premium areas of a website.

Greenscreen: See *Chroma Keying*.

HFS: Apple Computer's disk drive format.

Hosted Service: A company that provides all of the hardware, applications, network and support for an array of services that can include websites, merchant services, email, etc.

HTML: See *Hypertext Markup Language*.

HTTP: See *Hypertext Transfer Protocol*.

Hypercardioid: Pickup pattern with a focused sweet spot, also known as a *shotgun microphone*.

Hypertext Markup Language: The language used to "mark up" or compose "hyper," or interlinked, text. The code used to write web pages and understood by web browsers.

Hypertext Transfer Protocol: The protocol used to transfer files from web servers to web browsers or other programs. Language web servers speak and understand.

ID3 Tag: Metadata tag associated with MP3 files.

IIS: See *Internet Information Server*.

Impressions: In advertising/marketing, an impression is a single instance of an audience member reading, viewing, hearing, or otherwise.

Internet Information Server: Windows-based web server software.

iPod: An extremely popular, small, portable/mobile audio and video player manufactured by Apple Computer.

Lens Flare: A bright spot in the frame cased by the sun or a very bight light.

Licensing: A license is a temporary or limited permission to use copyrighted works, often in a very specific and narrow way.

Loop: Audio or video file that has a beginning and end that when stacked one after the other become seamless; used in music and backgrounds in video.

Marker: Used for trimming and selecting within an editor.

Master: Final high quality render of audio or video in a lossless format.

Mechanical Rights: Royalties on sales of a CD, tape, record, or digital download of a piece of music (i.e., a copy of the song that is played back through some mechanical device).

Media RSS: Yahoo!'s extensions to RSS 2.0 to add metadata to multimedia blogs.

Metadata: Data about data. In multimedia, metadata refers to everything about the audio or video, such as title, author, composer, date released, copyright holder, track number, whether it is part of a compilation, etc.

Metafile: Small XML-based file that tells a web browser to activate a media player to connect to a link.

Microformat: A new standard being advocated by some companies for enhancing HTML without adding new elements to the existing standard. Technorati.com (a blog search engine) created a way of adding tags to any blog using a microformat.

MMS: See *Multimedia Messaging Service*.

Moblog: A blog based on mobile blog posts.

Moblogging: Posting to a blog from a mobile device such as a cell phone or PDA.

Monetize: MBA speak for making money (with), making a product generate revenue.

MOV: A *container* file format, not a codec, popularized by Apple's QuickTime. It holds codecs, such as MP3, MPEG-2, MPEG-4, inside it, like AVI.

MP3: Overwhelmingly popular digital audio file format, and the de-facto standard for audio blogs/podcasts. MP3 delivers near-CD quality audio.

MPEG-1: The compression technique used in video CDs, on some game CDs in the mid-1990s (i.e., Playstation), CD-Interactive, and commonly seen in .mpg files.

MPEG-2: The most widely deployed digital video standard. It is the standard used by digital satellite systems (DSS), DVD players, and digital cable systems, TiVos, and Media Center PCs.

MPEG-4: Encompasses a large group of standards for digital video delivery, of which audio/video compression is only a part. When describing a video codec, MPEG-4 has multiple layers from mobile phone video (part of 3gp), to digital camera video clips, all the way up to HD on Blu-Ray and HD DVDs. It is the basis of the familiar video formats DivX, XviD, and all of Apple's newer video codecs. MPEG-4 part 2 is the original codec that forms the basis of DivX. A newer version, MPEG-4 part 10, is also known as AVC and H.264, and is a state-of-the-art video codec competitive with Windows Media Video 9. MPEG-4 Audio is a successor of MP3 (which was part of MPEG-1 in fact) and includes the AAC video codec as well as the codec used by XM Radio.

Multimedia Messaging Service: Technology that allows you to create, send, and receive text messages that also include an image, audio, and/or video clip. MMS messages are sent from one mobile phone to another, or to an email address.

Music Bed: See *Sound Bed*.

Narrowcasting: Creating and distributing media to a narrow "niche" audience.

Noise Canceling: A process that sends out the same signal as the one received, canceling out background noise.

Normalize: Processing a sound clip so the overall volume is consistent and at the optimal level.

NTFS: Current disk drive formatting technique used by Windows operating systems.

Omnidirectional: Microphone pickup pattern that accepts sound from every direction.

OS X: Apple's current computer operating system based on UNIX.

Payola: A system where music labels illegally pay radio station execs to play singles from their artists.

Performance Rights: Licensing fees for public performances of live or pre-recorded music almost anywhere.

Phantom Power: Power supplied by a pre-amp or mixer to condenser microphones that do not have on-board power.

Photoblog: Blog consisting mainly of photos.

Podcast: A term for audio (and sometimes, video) attached to a blog. The term was popularized outside of Apple, but Apple quickly put its marketing support behind the name. See also audio blog and video blog.

Podcaster: Someone who posts podcasts.

Podcatcher: See *Aggregator*.

Podsafe Content: Any media (audio, video, etc.) that can be safely (i.e., legally) included in a podcast.

Preview: What the video and or audio looks and sounds like in its current state in the editing process.

Privacy Rights: Rights of individuals prevent you from using a telephoto lens to take pictures inside their house from a mile away.

Professional: A word used in marketing-speak to justify a higher product cost. Often unrelated to the actual quality of the product.

Progressive Download: Watching wile still downloading. Saves time so you don't have to wait until the entire media file has been received to start viewing.

Project File: Set of commands contained in a file that dictate what edits will be made, the settings used and the location of the project elements.

Prosumer: High end consumer products that have professional options without the professional price tags.

Publicity Rights: Gives people the right to control who uses their likeness to advertise products.

Publishing Rights: The right to publish sheet music and lyrics to songs.

Push Technology: Any of a variety of Internet technologies that automatically update recipients with updated information instead of requiring a proactive request.

Real-Time Streaming Protocol: The language spoken by the Real suite of client products and streaming servers.

Render Farm: Group of computers whose sole task is to share their processing power to render media faster.

Render Wander: Wandering around the office bothering people while your computer is completely occupied with a lengthy render process.

Render: In processing process digital media, rendering is where some or all of a video file goes through a change such as compression, normalizing audio or adding a visual effect. This is sometimes known as exporting. Rendering is often a long process.

Rights Holder: The owner or user of a particular right to a creative work. There are a wide variety of rights held by both the creators and the public audience of creative works.

Royalties: Payments made to a rights holder by a party that has a legal contract to distribute the work and remunerate the rights holder.

RSS 1.0: One of the three main blog syndication protocol standards. See also *Atom* and *RSS 2.0.*

RSS 2.0: The simplest of the blogging standards and the one embraced by Yahoo! One of the three main blog syndication protocol standards. Also see *Atom* and *RSS 1.0.*

RSS: A protocol for computers to automatically update each other about changes to information, such as on a website. RSS *feeds* describe a list of time-stamped updates to an information source. RSS is the enabling technology behind blogs. It stands for Really Simple Syndication, Rich Site Summary, and several other things depending on who's explaining it.

RTSP: See *Real-Time Streaming Protocol*.

Service Level Agreement: A contract that dictates what level of service the provider is obligated to provide and what credits/remuneration is required, if any, when the SLA is not met.

Session Description Protocol File: Small file that is automatically created by the Quick-Time broadcasting application.

Shotgun Microphone: See *Hypercardioid*.

Shuttle: A circular spring-loaded knob used in video editing to move through the timeline from a slow crawl to an excited fast-forward.

SLA: See *Service Level Agreement*.

Soundbed: Ambient music or sound added to media to create a soundtrack or general ambience.

Streaming: Technically, the consumption of audio or video data from the Internet without downloading it. Streaming media is viewed without being stored on the hard disk. Also used generically to describe any audio and video on the Internet.

Subscribe: To cause a blog *feed* into an *aggregator* to download blog content at regular intervals.

SWF: The file extension for Flash movies.

Synchronization Rights: Necessary for any use of music synchronized with other multimedia elements as in movies, television, video games, and so on.

Tags: Single-word categories assigned by people to add useful *metadata* on multimedia content. See also *Folksonomy*.

TBC: See *Time Base Corrector*.

Time Base Corrector: A device used to sync different video sources such as multiple cameras connected together at once so their frame timing occurs simultaneously. Also used to fix shaky video signal from a source such as Macrovision encoded DVDs or old video tape stock.

Timeline: Visual representation of the length of a clip in an editing program.

Torrents: See *Bittorrent*.

Track: Element of video or audio within the editor. Video renders to a single track and audio renders into two tracks for stereo, one for mono.

Trademarks: Distinctive designs, phrases, or marks used to identify goods or services. Unlike copyrights, in US law they do not expire if consistently used and renewed.

Transcode: Convert audio or video by changing it from one compression technique to another.

Trim: To cut unneeded ends of a video clip.

Uncompressed: Captured video from a high-end camera can be uncompressed, meaning no codecs were used to try to squeeze down the raw video data. Uncompressed video consumes upwards of 1 GB per minute. This is the highest quality and is preferred for broadcast-quality editing but consumes hard disk and processor resources.

Video Blog: A media format where video clips are attached to a blog and serially updated.

Vlog: Another term for *Video Blog*.

Vlogger: Someone who posts vlogs.

Voice over Internet Protocol: Phone service that works through the Internet, often bypassing Telcos entirely.

VoIP: See *Voice over Internet Protocol*.

Walled Garden: See *Gated Community*.

Web Server: Server that acts as the front end for a website, serving up HTML pages, images and scripts.

White Balance: Setting on a camera to define what in the frame is white so the camera can re-calculate the differences between images in the frame and what is defined as white.

WMV: *Windows Media Video*.

Work: Creations such as: music, art, writing, speech, designs, drawings, etc.

Workflow: Defined process that takes a task from inception to completion.

XML Feed: See *Feed*.

XML: eXtensible markup language, a general-purpose, human-readable, text-based file format. To those familiar with web pages, XML looks like HTML, but new elements can be created so that an XML document can describe anything, from an address book to a web page to a music database to a blog. XML is the basis of the various blog *feed* languages such as RSS and Atom.

XviD: An open-source implementation of the MPEG-4 codec compatible with DivX.

Index

Symbols

.Mac hosting service 14
3-point lighting 145
3G2 167
3GP 125, 137, 167, 200

A

AAC 80, 118, 321
acoustic foam 143
acoustics 139–140
ad inventory 69, 315
administration 303
  backing up 307
    Blogger 9, 27, 112, 129, 136,
        232, 235, 249–250, 252, 254,
        257, 294, 307–310
    local backup 307
    Movable Type 311
    TypePad 310
    WordPress 310
Adobe Audition 164, 194–195
Adobe Premiere 4–5, 152, 163
advertisers 68–72, 77–80, 83
advertising 28, 38–41, 65, 68–71,
        77–79, 83–85, 87, 90, 110,
        185, 273, 286, 288, 296–297,
        315, 320
advertising revenues 68
aggregator program 18
aggregators 7, 10–11, 14, 18, 27,
        43–45, 48, 50, 64, 74, 78, 81,
        85, 87, 98–100, 113, 120,
        122, 129, 228, 257, 302, 315,
        319, 324
Amadeus 163
Apache 227, 315

Apple xvi, xvii, 7, 10, 14, 20, 22, 47,
        66, 68, 74, 80, 90, 110–111,
        113–114, 117, 120, 151, 161–
        162, 165, 168, 206, 219–220,
        239, 291, 301, 318–322
Application Service Providers (ASPs)
        229, 240, 315
archive 12, 17, 35, 38–39, 90, 166,
        195, 199, 201, 234, 258, 294,
        303, 307, 310, 313
Archive.org 199, 257
ASF 168
Ask Jeeves 103
ASP 229, 240, 315
ATI All-In-Wonder 3
atom 45, 98, 112–113, 120, 315, 319,
        323
Attensa 60
Audible 74, 80–81
audio/video capture board 3
audio blog 315
audioblog 129, 136–137, 237,
        250–251, 288
audioblog.com 129, 137, 237, 288
audio blogging xvii, 20–23, 66, 285
audio capture 4, 135, 170
audio compressor 190
audio editing
    A/V format converters and trans-
        coders 157
    audio capture 157
    Mac editing 157, 161
    PC editing 157, 163
Audio Hijack 170
audiovisual media xviii, 89
auto-render 317
AVC 166, 168–169, 226, 321
AVI 7, 125, 168, 200, 317, 321

B

backing up 307
  local backup 307
  Movable Type 311
  WordPress 310
balanced audio 316
bandwidth xvi, 8, 19–20, 43, 86–87,
        90, 110, 157, 214, 221–223,
        225–226, 228, 232–233,
        236–238, 240–245, 274,
        295–296, 303, 307
  pricing 222
    bucket 222–223
    instability 225
    percentile 222–223
    pipe 222–223
    storage 222–223
bargain 316
base URL 12
BitTorrent 232, 316
BitTorrent sharing 232
blip.tv 12, 235
blog 9, 16–17, 19, 91–93, 95, 97, 99,
        103–104, 108, 136–137, 233,
        235, 245, 249, 257, 308, 310,
        312, 315–316, 318, 322
  anatomy of a blog 15–16
  basic layout of a blog 16
  blogroll 17
  corporate uses 36–37, 39
  entries 17
    archive 12, 17, 90, 166, 195, 199,
        201, 234, 258, 294, 303, 307,
        310, 313
    permalink 17
    ping 17, 102, 103–104
    trackback 17, 102
  history 19

posts xvii, 10–11, 14, 17–19, 52, 102, 128–129, 135, 237, 250, 284, 298, 307, 309–310, 312–313, 321–322
  tags 9–10, 12, 17–18, 105–106, 110, 114, 120, 128–129, 137, 318, 321, 323
  syndicated 18, 69, 228, 296
  tagging 17, 89, 105–106
blog directories 103
blog feed 10, 45, 85, 95, 113, 126, 232, 324
blogger 9, 27, 112, 129, 136, 232, 235, 249–250, 252, 254, 257, 294, 307–310
Blogger.com 9, 112, 232, 257, 307
blogging applications 245, 247, 249, 251
  audioblog 129, 136–137, 237, 250–251, 288
  Blogger 9, 27, 112, 129, 136, 232, 235, 249–250, 252, 254, 257, 294, 307–310
  Movable Type 92, 112, 114–115, 129, 136, 229, 231, 235, 249–250, 252, 254, 304–305, 311–312
  TypePad 245–250, 254
  WordPress 129, 229, 249–250, 252, 254
bloglines 46, 50, 53, 61
blogosphere xvi, 15, 18, 105, 108, 166, 281, 316
  definition 18
blogroll 17, 316
blog search engines 91, 103, 120
blog service 316
blogware 129
bluescreen 316
blue screening 152
Bluetooth 129, 131
boom microphone 149, 172
BSOD 316
built-in microphone 153, 158, 171, 177

C

cache 316
CafePress 84
Canopus ProCoder 2 7
Canopus ProCoder Express 7
capture 170, 173, 204, 207–208, 300, 316
capture card 3–4
  ATI All-In-Wonder card 3
  dedicated 4
  Osprey 4

  Winnov 4
capture device 316
capture utility 207
Cardioid 316
case studies 283
  EricRice.com 283, 285, 287
  rocketboom.com 283, 294–295, 297, 299, 301
  RyanEdit.com 283, 289, 291, 293
Castpodder 58
CDBaby 77
CDN 239–240, 261, 316
chroma keying 152, 316
clearing 316
clip 317
clipping 183, 189, 190
colocation facility 317
codecs 47, 168–169, 315, 317, 321
  3ivX 168, 300–301
  AVC 166, 168–169, 226, 321
  DivX 166, 168–169, 176, 257, 315, 318, 321, 326
  FLV 168, 319
  MPEG-1 168, 321
  MPEG-2 168, 317–318, 321
  MPEG-4 20, 165–166, 168–169, 176, 301, 315, 318, 321
  Sorenson 168
  SWF 168, 324
  WMA 168
  WMV 125, 137, 168–169, 215
Cogent 86, 238, 239
comments 17, 102, 120, 298, 308, 310
comments link 17
commercials 39–40, 79
compressed video 317
compressing 7, 195
compression 6–8, 47, 177, 191, 288, 301, 313, 318–319, 321, 323
  FFMpeg 8, 166
  QuickTime Pro 7–8, 134, 295, 300
compression program 7
compressor 168, 190, 288, 317
condenser microphone 178, 180, 317
connection speeds 222
content delivery networks (CDNs) 86, 239
content hosting 225
  bandwidth amount 226
  scalability 226
content hosting 14, 76, 225, 226, 227
  free 233
  high volume 238
content management systems (CMS) 92
conversion 7, 163, 166–167, 176, 200, 202–203, 217

conversion tools 7, 166
  Canopus ProCoder 2 7
  Canopus ProCoder Express 7
  QuickTime Pro 7, 8, 134, 165, 200, 216, 217, 219, 293, 300
copyright 114, 144, 234, 263–267, 269–275, 277, 279–280, 317, 320
copyrighted material 199, 279–281
CPM 70, 296, 317
Crawl 317
Creative Commons license 90, 234, 236, 274–279, 281, 300

D

de facto 317
derivative work rights 269, 317
digital audio recorder 188
digital performance rights 268, 318
digital rights management 74, 90, 265, 274
digital video (DV) camera 2
digital video recorder 318
DivX 166, 168–169, 176, 257, 315, 318, 321, 326
DNS server 92
domain name service (DNS) 92
domain registrar 92
double ending 150
DV cam 2, 5, 133
  non-DV cameras 2, 132
DVD ripping 318
DVR 318
DVR-MS 318
dynamic microphone 178, 318

E

earballs 318
EDGE 130–131
edit/trim function 218
edit decision list (EDL) 6
Egress 62
elements 318
embedded media 318
enclosure 318
enclosure element 20
enclosure tags 9–10, 128
encoder 318
EVDO 130–131
eXtensible markup language (XML) 95, 98, 326
extensions 318
eyeballs 319

F

fair use rights 267
FAT32 319
FeedBurner 10–12, 112, 232, 245,
 249–250, 252–256, 259, 261,
 294, 300
feed converters 232
FeederReader 61
feed flags 45
FeedForAll 112
feeds xvii, 1, 10–14, 18, 21, 33,
 40, 44–46, 48, 65, 85, 91,
 93, 95–98, 101–103, 110,
 112–115, 119, 126, 129,
 136–137, 153, 228, 232, 245,
 249, 252–254, 256, 286, 295,
 318–319, 324
 Atom 10, 45, 47–48, 55, 60, 62, 99,
  112–115, 120, 231–232, 315,
  318, 320, 323
 RSS 1.0 10, 45, 47–48, 55, 60, 62,
  99, 112–115, 120, 231–232,
  315, 318, 320, 323
 RSS 2.0 10, 45, 47–48, 55, 60, 62,
  99, 112–115, 120, 231–232,
  315, 318, 320, 323
file conversion 199
file format 133, 166, 168, 187, 301,
 315, 321
 AIFF 187, 196
 AVI 7, 125, 168, 200, 315, 321
 lossless format 187, 320
 MOV 7, 125, 133, 136–137, 168,
  190, 199, 203, 214, 219–220,
  257, 301, 313, 317, 321
 RM 168
 SWF 168, 324
 WAV 168, 187, 189, 196
 WMF 168
file transfer protocol (FTP) 319
Final Cut Express 162
Final Cut Pro 6, 152, 162, 293, 300
FireAnt 10, 21, 30, 52, 67, 74, 101,
 109, 128, 137, 168–169, 249,
 256
Firefox 53, 95, 97–98, 169
FireWire 132–133, 174–175
FireWire port 2, 133
Flash 18, 78, 93, 119, 129, 137,
 168–169, 175–176, 236–237,
 319, 324
flat-fee hosting providers 86
 Cogent 86
folksonomy 105, 319
Frames Per Second (FPS) 319
Fruitcast.com 80
FTP 319

G

GarageBand 14, 151, 161–162, 194,
 220
gated communities 108, 319
Google 8, 21, 50–51, 67–68, 75–76,
 90, 92, 98, 103, 119, 199,
 236, 271, 274, 303, 306
GPRS 130–131
greenscreen 2, 319
greenscreen 152, 316
GSM 32, 131

H

H.264 8, 168–169, 321
headline 62
headphones 158, 172, 288
HFS 319
High8 2, 5
hosted service 319
hosting xviii, xix, 9, 14, 18–20,
 75–76, 82, 85–88, 92, 119,
 128–129, 136–137, 221–223,
 225–229, 232–233, 235–236,
 238, 240–242, 244–245, 250,
 314, 316
 free 6, 9–10, 12, 17, 28, 47, 66–67,
  75, 77, 86–87, 90, 108, 110,
  112, 121, 123, 128–129, 132,
  137, 154, 163, 166, 170,
  199–200, 203, 215–216, 229,
  232–237, 244–245, 252, 257,
  261, 268, 274, 279, 290, 294,
  306, 319
HTML 9–10, 12, 46, 91–92, 95, 98,
 105–106, 135, 228, 238, 240,
 247, 318–319, 321
HTML mode 9
HTML tags 12
HTTP 319
hyperlinking 92
hypertext markup language 320
hypertext transfer protocol 320

I

iChat 151
ID3 Tag 320
IEEE1394 2
IIS 320
iLife 14, 151, 161–162, 220
iLink 2, 133, 174–175
iMovie 6, 14, 161–162, 204, 208–
 209, 212, 219–220, 293
impressions 320
in-house IT 240
Internet-based TV xviii
Internet Archive 12, 234, 294

Internet Explorer 7 95
Internet Explorer Mobile Edition 136
Internet Information Server 320
Internet TV xviii
interview kits 158, 173
IP address 92
iPod xvii, 1, 8, 20–22, 47, 55, 64,
 80, 88, 100, 126, 129, 137,
 165–166, 168–169, 219, 226,
 236–237, 320
iTunes 1, 7, 10–14, 18, 20–21, 45,
 52–55, 66, 74, 80, 86, 101,
 109–111, 113–114, 117–118,
 120, 122, 128–129, 136–137,
 165–166, 168–169, 176
iWeb 161, 220

J

JPG 8, 125, 313
jPodder 54, 55

L

lavalier 5, 134, 149, 153, 171–172,
 179
lens flare 320
licensing xix, 20, 87, 89–90,
 263–265, 268–269, 274–276,
 278, 281, 295, 320
licensing and copyrights xix
 best practices 280
 Creative Commons Attribution
  license 277
  Some Rights Reserved 277
 fair use 144, 200, 267, 270, 276,
  279–282
 public domain 90, 279
Lifera 57
lighting 144–148, 153, 197
Linux 8, 44, 54, 57–59
 Castpodder 58
 Lifera 57
 RSSOwl 58–59
LiveJournal 129
loop 320
lossless format 187, 320

M

M4V 7, 168–169
Mac editing 161
Macrovision 201, 325
marker 320
marketing 36, 65–66, 69, 77, 85, 90,
 240, 265, 319–320, 322
master 320
master use rights 266
mechanical rights 265, 320

media card 217
media file storage utility 257
  Archive.org 199, 257
  Ourmedia.com 257
metadata 14, 105, 115, 120, 258–259, 320, 324
metafile 320
microformat 106, 120, 321
microphone pre-amp 181
microphones 85, 144, 153, 158, 161, 171–172, 176–183, 188, 196, 322
  bidirectional 178
  cardioid 178–179
  condenser microphone 178, 180
    phantom power 181–182, 188–189
  dynamic microphone 178
  hypercardioid 178–179, 319, 324
  omnidirectional 178–179, 322
  pop filter 183
mixdown 177, 195
mixers 177, 179, 181, 183
  software-based mixer 182
  stand-alone mixer 182
MMS 321
mobilblogg.net 128
Mobilcast 74–75, 286
mobile data access 131
mobile phones 43, 64, 74, 77, 121
mobile video blogging 121
mobile video players 64
moblog 19, 121–123, 126–129, 136, 321
moblogging 121, 122, 123, 125, 126, 127, 128, 136–137, 321
monetization xix, 73, 82, 240
monetize 65, 76, 321
MOV 7, 125, 133, 136–137, 168, 190, 199, 203, 214, 219–220, 257, 301, 313, 317, 321
Movable Type 92, 112, 114–115, 129, 136, 229, 231, 235, 249–250, 252, 254, 304–305, 311–312
MOV format 7
MP3 1, 10, 20–21, 27, 43–44, 77, 85, 93, 100, 118, 136–137, 153, 168, 170, 177, 182, 186–190, 194–196, 213, 225–226, 257, 267, 274, 315, 317, 320–321
MP3 player and recorder 188
MP4 8, 125, 129, 165–166, 168–169, 237
MPEG-1 168
MPEG-2 168
MPEG-4 20, 165–166, 168–169, 176, 301, 315, 318, 321

MPG 125, 168
MSN 21, 98, 303
multimedia blog xvii, xix, 15, 21, 44, 91, 137, 221, 229
multimedia blog hosting 221
multimedia enclosure element 20
multimedia messaging service 321
multitrack editor 194
music bed 190, 321
music rights 264
MyYahoo! 10, 46, 49, 53

N

naming convention 203, 313–314
Napster 20, 72
narrowcasting 31, 71, 78, 321
NewsGator 46, 48, 256
noise canceling 322
normalize 322
NTFS 322

O

Osprey 4, 158, 160
OS X 322
Our Media 12
Ourmedia.com 257

P

P2P 27, 77, 82, 87, 232, 316
Palm devices 60, 63, 135–136, 167
Palm OS 60, 135–136
payola 322
PayPal 84
PayPal tip jars 84
PC editing 163
PCMCIA cardbus data cards 131
PDAs 43, 121, 129, 135, 136, 137
performance rights 265, 322
permalink 17
permissions 263, 268, 271
phantom power 322
photoblog 19, 322
photo rights 271
ping 17, 102–104, 120, 301
Pinnacle 3
Playstation Portable 8, 129, 165, 169
Pluck 53–54
pMachine 129
Pocket PC 61
  FeedReader 61
podcast xix, 1, 10, 12, 20–21, 25, 44–45, 52, 58, 64–66, 68, 72–74, 77–80, 83, 85–90, 93–94, 99, 106, 109–110, 112–114, 116, 129, 134, 139, 147, 161, 163,

173, 176, 178, 190, 193–194, 221, 225, 236–238, 250, 261, 263, 268, 271, 273–274, 282, 284, 296, 321–322
podcast (definition) 322
podcaster (definition) 322
podcast feed in Firefox 97
podcatcher 43, 317, 322
podcatching 66, 86, 100
PodNova 46
podsafe 89, 263, 273–275, 277, 279, 281, 322
  definition 273
podsafe music 273
podsafe source material 273, 275, 277, 279
Podtrac 79
PointCast 98
pop filter 183
Premiere Elements 5, 163, 204, 212, 215
preview (definition) 322
privacy rights 273
  definition 322
Pro Coder 2 167
professional (definition) 322
progressive download xvi
  definition 322
project file (definition) 323
prosumer (definition) 323
ProTools 162
public domain 90, 279
publicity rights 273
  definition 323
publicly accessible server 8
publishing rights 266
  definition 323
push technology (definition) 323

Q

Quick Start 1
QuickTime 7–8, 47, 93, 118–119, 134, 137, 165, 167–169, 200, 214–220, 293, 300–301, 321, 324
QuickTime Pro 7–8, 134, 293, 300

R

RAID 159,–161
  RAID 0 159–160
  RAID 1 160
  RAID 5 160
RAM 158–161, 175, 300, 316
real-time streaming protocol 323
really simple syndication (RSS) 25, 98

real simple syndication 18, 43
RealVideo 43, 169
render (definition) 323
render farm (definition) 323
rendering 6, 8, 11, 132, 177, 179,
        202, 207, 214, 219, 220, 250
    definition 323
render wander (definition) 323
Revver 82
RGB signals 2
RIAA restrictions 89
rich-media blogging 20, 28
rich site summary (RSS) 18, 98
rights
    clearing 316
rights holder 323
rocketboom.com 24, 31, 48, 53, 74,
        283, 294–302
royalties (definition) 323
RSS xvii, 1, 10, 12, 18, 21, 25, 27,
        37, 43–48, 50–52, 55, 57–58,
        60, 62–64, 85–86, 98–99,
        110, 112–115, 120, 126,
        128–129, 136–137, 220, 228,
        231–232, 240, 245, 248–250,
        252–254, 256, 286, 295, 300,
        315, 318–320, 323–324
RSS feed 1, 10, 12, 18, 44–45, 48,
        110, 113–114, 129, 253, 295
RSS feed formats 45
    Atom 45
    RSS 1.0 45
    RSS 2.0 45
RSSOwl 58–59
RTSP 324

S

Safari 95, 98
SATA hard drive 159–160
SCSI drives 159
SD card 189
search engine 18, 88, 106, 109, 303,
        321
search engine optimization 88
search engines 88
SEO 88
Service Level Agreements (SLA)
        227, 240
    definition 324
session description protocol file 324
set 144
    3-point lighting 145
    backdrops 144
    lighting 144–148, 153, 197
    props 144
    tools 147–148
shotgun microphone 324

shuttle 324
Skype 150–151
Skypecasting 150, 151, 170, 173
SLA 227, 240, 324
Solaris 58
Sony 5–6, 62, 131, 163–164, 168,
        172–173
Sony Acid Music Studio 164
Sony Sound Forge 164, 192
Sony Sound Forge Audio Studio 164
Soundbed 213
    definition 324
sound levels 189, 212, 220
speakers 158, 173
sponsorship 78–79, 83, 273, 286
stock footage 90, 190, 198–199, 204,
        269
streaming (definition) 324
streaming media 28, 65–66, 85–86,
        89, 221, 238
streaming server 8, 221
subscribe (definition) 324
subscription 18, 52, 68, 77, 84, 99,
        112–113, 240, 249, 254, 295,
        297, 319
SVHS 2
Symbian 60, 62
synchronization rights 266
    definition 324
syndicated 18, 69, 228, 296
syndication 18, 25, 31, 33, 35, 43,
        91, 98, 113, 120, 231–232,
        315, 323

T

T-Mobile 130–132
tagging 17, 89, 105–106
tags 17, 91, 105–106, 324
TBC 201, 324
Technorati 10, 103, 105–106, 120,
        285, 292, 295, 321
Textamerica 122–125, 136–137
text editor mode 9
Time Base Corrector 201, 324–325
timeline 325
TiVo xv, 28, 37, 64, 74, 99, 101,201,
        295, 321
Torrents 221, 232, 325
track 325
trackback 17, 102
trademarks 263, 272, 325
transcode (definition) 325
transcoding 133, 137, 165, 200–201,
        237
transcoding applications 200
transfer speeds 222

Transistr 55–56
trim 325
trimming 194, 212, 216, 220, 320
tripods 158, 175
two-track editor 191–193
TypePad 9, 11–12, 128–129,
        136–137, 245–250, 254,
        310–311
typepad.com 9, 19

U

uncompressed (definition) 325
uniform resource locator (URL) 92
Unix 57

V

Vegas Movie Studio + DVD 5
Vegas Movie Studio Platinum 163,
        207, 211
Vegas Video 4–5
Vegas Video Pro 6 5
VHS-C 2, 175
video blog 1, 7, 10, 19–21, 24–25, 28,
        30–35, 41, 45, 47, 52, 64–67,
        72–74, 78–79, 82, 86–91,
        93–94, 99, 108–110, 112–
        113, 118–121, 126, 129, 132,
        137, 139, 144, 147, 150, 152,
        155, 162, 164–166, 168–169,
        171, 173–174, 176, 180–181,
        187, 190, 194, 197–198, 214,
        220–221, 225–226, 229,
        235–238, 241–242, 244–246,
        250, 261, 263–264, 268–272,
        278, 281–285, 290, 295–297,
        298, 307, 322
video blogging 1, 3, 7, 14–16, 20–21,
        23–24, 64, 66–67, 71–74,
        77, 84–85, 88–90, 101, 106,
        110, 120, 128, 133, 136–137,
        144, 150–151, 155, 157, 161,
        169, 171, 179, 184–185, 192,
        220, 233, 237, 241, 244, 249,
        269–270, 273, 283, 285,
        288–292, 298
video capture 2–4, 132–133,
        158–161, 205, 207, 209, 215,
        217, 220
video capture device 2–3
video conversion 7, 166–167
video conversion tools 7, 166
video editing 5–7, 88, 152, 157, 159,
        161, 163, 206–209, 211, 213,
        219–220, 324
    A/V format converters and trans-
        coders 157

Mac editing 157, 161
PC editing 157, 163
transcoding 133, 137, 165,
    200–201, 237
video editing keyboard 210
video editing programs 204
videoegg.com 88
video podcast 21, 29, 176
video podcasting xvii
video rights 271, 274
Vlog 21, 129, 176, 207, 209, 216, 293
    definition 325
Vlogger (definition) 325
vlogging 7, 23, 67, 91, 134, 209, 214,
    216, 219, 233, 289, 291
VODcasting xvii
vodlogs 21
Voice over Internet Protocol 150
    definition 325
VoIP 150
    definition 325

W

walled gardens 108
    definition 325
web-based streaming 15
webcam 5, 133–134, 150
web hosting 221, 223, 225, 227, 236,
    238
weblog 15, 103, 310
web server 325
white balance 2, 133, 153, 174, 175
    definition 325
WiFi 132
Windows Media 47, 54, 93, 119,
    168–169, 200–201, 318, 321
    definition 324
Windows Mobile 60, 125, 135, 136
Windows Movie Maker 4, 163,
    204–205, 208, 210, 215–216,
    293
Winnov 4, 158, 160
wireless microphones 158, 171
WMV 125, 137, 168–169, 215, 324

WordPress 6, 92, 112, 129, 229, 231,
    249, 250, 252, 254, 310
workflow (definition) 324
World Wide Web 92

X

XLR connection 182
XML 10–12, 14, 46, 48, 53, 91,
    95–96, 98, 105, 136–137,
    228, 238, 245, 248–250, 254,
    259, 261, 315, 318–320, 324
XML-based podcast feed 96
XML feed URL 14, 254
XviD 166, 169, 315, 321, 324

Y

Yahoo! 18, 21, 45, 49, 90, 98, 103,
    109–110, 113–114, 120, 229,
    290, 303, 318, 320, 323
YouTube 119